NATIONS OF THE MODERN WORLD

ARGENTINA   H. S. Ferns
Professor of Political Science,
University of Birmingham

AUSTRALIA   O. H. K. Spate
Director, Research School of Pacific Studies,
Australian National University, Canberra

BELGIUM   Vernon Mallinson
Professor of Comparative Education,
University of Reading

BURMA   F. S. V. Donnison
Formerly Chief Secretary to the Government of Burma
Historian, Cabinet Office, Historical Section 1949–66

CEYLON   S. A. Pakeman
Formerly Professor of Modern History,
Ceylon University College; Appointed
Member, House of Representatives,
Ceylon, 1947-52

CYPRUS   H. D. Purcell
Lecturer in English Literature, the Queen's
University, Belfast

DENMARK   W. Glyn Jones
Reader in Danish, University College London

EAST   David Childs
  GERMANY   *Lecturer in Politics, University of Nottingham*

MODERN EGYPT   Tom Little
Managing Director and General Manager of
Regional News Services (Middle East), Ltd, London

ENGLAND   John Bowle
Professor of Political Theory, Collège d'Europe,
Bruges

FINLAND	**W. R. Mead** *Professor of Geography, University College, London*
MODERN GREECE	**John Campbell** *Fellow of St Antony's College, Oxford* **Philip Sherrard** *Assistant Director, British School of Archaeology,* *Athens, 1958–62*
MODERN INDIA	**Sir Percival Griffiths** *President India, Pakistan and Burma Association*
MODERN IRAN	**Peter Avery** *Lecturer in Persian and Fellow of King's College,* *Cambridge*
ITALY	**Muriel Grindrod** *Formerly Editor of* International Affairs *and* The World Today *Assistant Editor* The Annual Register
KENYA	**A. Marshall MacPhee** *Formerly Managing Editor with* *the* East African Standard *Group*
LIBYA	**John Wright** *Formerly of the* Sunday Ghibli, *Tripoli*
MALAYSIA	**J. M. Gullick** *Formerly of the Malayan Civil Service*
MOROCCO	**Mark I. Cohen** *Director of Taxation, American Express* **Lorna Hahn** *Professor of African Studies, American University*
NEW ZEALAND	**James W. Rowe** *Director of New Zealand Institute of Economic* *Research* **Margaret A. Rowe** *Tutor in English at Victoria University, Wellington*
NIGERIA	**Sir Rex Niven** *Administrative Service of Nigeria, 1921–54* *Member, President and Speaker of Northern House* *of Assembly, 1947–59*

PAKISTAN	Ian Stephens *Formerly Editor of* The Statesman *Calcutta and Delhi, 1942–51* *Fellow of King's College, Cambridge, 1952–58*
PERU	Sir Robert Marett *H.M. Ambassador in Lima, 1963–67*
SOUTH AFRICA	John Cope *Formerly Editor-in-Chief of* The Forum *and South African Correspondent of* The Guardian
SPAIN	George Hills *Formerly Correspondent and Spanish Programme Organizer, British Broadcasting Corporation*
SUDAN REPUBLIC	K. D. D. Henderson *Formerly of the Sudan Political Service and Governor of Darfur Province, 1949–53*
TURKEY	Geoffrey Lewis *Senior Lecturer in Islamic Studies, Oxford*
WEST GERMANY	Michael Balfour *Reader in European History, University of East Anglia*
YUGOSLAVIA	Muriel Heppell and F. B. Singleton

NATIONS OF THE MODERN WORLD

DENMARK

DENMARK

By

W. GLYN JONES

PRAEGER PUBLISHERS

New York · Washington

Published in the United States of America in 1970
by Praeger Publishers, Inc., 111 Fourth Avenue,
New York, N.Y. 10003

Library of Congress Catalog Card Number: 77-109476

Printed in Great Britain

Preface

In their book *Theory of Literature* René Wellek and Austin Warren touch on the question of literary historians who move into fields which are not their own. They observe that 'the literary historian is not automatically transformed into a proper historian of these disciplines. He becomes simply a compiler, a self-conscious intruder'. There may well be a grain of truth in this assertion – which it was slightly embarrassing to discover soon after writing this book – but I nevertheless hope that even as a literary historian I have been able to put modern Denmark into its historical perspective and to make it intelligible to a non-Scandinavian public. More especially I have concentrated on showing how the highly developed society of today has emerged over the last 150 years. In so doing, I have inevitably been forced to intrude more deeply into the political history of the nineteenth and twentieth centuries than I would have liked, but this has by no means been entirely at the expense of social and cultural history. The interplay of politics, society, and 'culture' is a fact, and party splits and constitutional crises are as fundamentally important as the transition from serf to independent farmer, from peninsular self-absorption to a direct and conscious concern with affairs far from the Danish borders, or, for that matter, from the music of the medieval ballad to that of Carl Nielsen.

All selection and arrangement of fact naturally implies a personal choice. One such has to do with the spelling of place names in Schleswig and Holstein. That I have decided on the German rather than the Danish spellings indicates no desire to take sides in the politics of the area, but is simply an acceptance of the fact that these are the forms normally used in English. To talk of *Slesvig* and *Holsten* would, to my mind, be an affectation, a consequence of which would surely be that I should refer to the Danish capital as *København*.

As an intruder I have naturally not ventured far beyond the confines of printed and readily available Danish sources, translations from which are my own. Any Englishman writing of Danish history would be shortsighted to ignore the excellent and volumin-

9

ous histories published by Schultz and Politiken, and these have obviously played a large part in the preparation of this book. It is right that they should stand at the beginning of the bibliography.

The bibliography is selective. I have made no real attempt to list works on which my observations on things cultural are based. Surely, here, where I am not intruding, it was better to suggest further reading than to try to discover for myself the origins of my information and opinions. The few English works to which I make reference are in the main suggestions for further reading rather than books to which I myself have had recourse.

It might help the reader to know that in January 1970 the rates of exchange were 7.49 *kroner* to the US dollar and 18.01 *kroner* to the pound sterling.

For help in finding suitable illustrations for my book, I am much indebted to the Photographic Department of the Royal Library, Copenhagen, Messrs Gyldendal, the publishers, the National Historical Museum in Frederiksborg, and the Royal Danish Embassy in London. For help in producing the map my thanks go to the Department of Geography, University College London.

London   w.g.j.
February 1970

Contents

List of Illustrations

Map

facing page 248

Map of Denmark showing the former Danish
provinces in Sweden and the North German
duchies. The dotted line going south of Ribe
across Jutland shows the 1864–1920 frontier.
The line south of Tønder to Flensburg shows the
present frontier.

Acknowledgements

ACKNOWLEDGEMENT for kind permission to reproduce illustrations is made to the following, to whom the copyright of the illustrations belongs:

Messrs Gyldendal, Copenhagen: 3, 4, 5, 6, 7, 8, 9, 10, 12, 13, 15, 16, 17, 18

Den Hirschsprungske Samling, Copenhagen: 25, 26

Det Kongelige Bibliotek, Copenhagen: 19, 20, 21, 22

Press Department, Royal Danish Ministry for Foreign Affairs: 14, 23, 24

Chapter 1

c. 850–1814

Rise and Fall–A Bird's Eye View

THE STORY OF DENMARK is one of a territorially small country which, once it was organised as a unity, came to play a dominant role in north European history. Placed at the crossroads of trade north and south and east and west, and always at least partly in control of the entrance to the Baltic, it is a country which has had an importance far in excess of its size. For a period it led the Kalmar Union, that union of the northern countries which was in fact the largest unified kingdom in Europe, taking in not merely Denmark, Norway, and Sweden, but Swedish Finland to the east and Iceland and Greenland to the west and north. Even when the Union was dissolved, Denmark retained the whole of Norway and the Swedish Sound provinces, the southernmost of which, Scania, remained loyal to Denmark for centuries. To the south Denmark has for centuries been in at least partial control of what is now northern Germany as far south as Hamburg, and the north German coast has also known Danish rule. Yet her undoubted expansionist dreams in the early period brought their reactions, and Denmark had to relinquish her Baltic domains to Sweden and subsequently her southern duchies to Germany, becoming for a period at the end of the nineteenth century even smaller than she is today.

Socially the changes have also been enormous, from the Viking Age when there was a certain equality among the people to the rise of the nobility and aristocracy culminating in the seventeenth century. From being chieftains elected by common consent, the kings became absolute monarchs whose power was virtually unlimited and whose desire for glory rivalled that of Louis XIV himself. Subsequently the desire for equality reasserted itself, and the king's power diminished, until the advanced democratic system of today gradually evolved, a system in which there is still place for a king. The claim made by Rollo's Vikings on the Seine that they were all equal could perhaps be made again today, with about the same degree of accuracy.

The Viking Age and Early Denmark

In the twentieth century Denmark has little significance as a focal point of trade routes, though the widespread use of the free harbour in Copenhagen still helps to maintain something of its former importance. A thousand years ago, however, it was a different matter, and Denmark's importance as a trading centre was to have more than passing significance.

The Viking conquests were certainly partly occasioned by the need for trade and the discovery that wealth could perhaps be acquired by other means than peaceful trading. Conditions in both England and Normandy were such that the Viking marauders were able to plunder and subsequently to colonise or conquer.

In 878 the Danelaw was established, and by 1033 all England was under the Vikings. The year 911 saw Rollo in possession of Normandy as the first duke after his warriors had laid waste the land around the Seine. How many of these Vikings came from Denmark it is difficult to say, as the English tended to call them all Danes, whether they were from Denmark or Norway, while the French tended to call them Norsemen. There was little to distinguish them by, and even the languages were close to each other at the time. The Swedes went eastwards and traded and established colonies in Russia, of which Novgorod is the most famous. According to the Arab diplomat Ibn Fadlan, the Swedes were well established on the Volga in the early part of the tenth century, and it is largely thanks to his lengthy account that we have first-hand evidence of the customs and manners of the Vikings. Still farther afield the Vikings went to Byzantium, which they called Miklagard, and whence they brought fresh wealth.

With the increased wealth came an increasing population and this was doubtless partly responsible for the establishment of colonies in places of less immediate attraction, the islands of the north of Scotland, the Faroes, and Iceland, which were colonised largely by Norwegians and only came into Danish ownership with the Nordic Union under Margrethe.

Yet these Vikings, with all their warlikeness and strength, were strikingly receptive to foreign cultures wherever they established themselves. Celtic influence can be traced in early Norse literature and in the carvings and metalwork of the Viking Age. In England, where they found a people with whom they were distantly related, and with whom they could communicate in their own language, they were gradually assimilated into the population, and the same thing happened even in the Russian colonies. In Normandy the same assimilation took place, and the military skills of the Vikings were duly responsible for the superiority of the Norman warriors who invaded England in 1066. In religious matters, too, the Vikings were tolerant of a different culture and receptive to it, and all the evidence points to an easy assimilation to a religion superior to their own – even if the ancient Norse religion left its mark on popular superstition for centuries tfter the conversion of the North.

While the Vikings were thus ravaging far and wide, the population at home was gradually fashioning Denmark in the shape she was to have for centuries. The southern frontier with Germany was still vague, but it stretched roughly to the Ejder – a fact which was to have repercussions in the nineteenth century – while the sea formed a natural boundary between Denmark and the other Nordic lands. The people were farmers, and by about 1250 they had settled the entire country and founded the villages which to this day are the basis of Danish rural society. The land around the villages was divided up and run on the strip system, and in some parts of the country a sort of co-operative system was in existence, by which a farmer, though owning his own land, worked in conjunction with others and received his share of the produce. In making decisions, each farmer had his say and his vote, and it is reasonable to talk of a primitive sense of equality among them. Equality was not to last, and the more prosperous farmers gradually bought up land and leased it out, thus starting the system of leasehold which was to exist into the nineteenth century.

Independent farmers had either to pay taxes to the king or to provide him with military forces. While the small ones chose to pay tax, the wealthier and more powerful preferred to provide the military assistance. Consequently, a new class emerged who expected and received privileges from the king, and on whose support the king could rely to strengthen his own position in the country. This brought about a close relationship between the king and an incipient nobility at a time when the king was trying to centralise power. In time, however, as the nobles themselves sought to consolidate their rights, the resultant split between them and their monarchs was to have far-reaching consequences. It must be remembered in this connection that the kings of Denmark were elective monarchs, and although it was customary to choose the new king from among the sons of the previous one, it was by no means an unbreakable rule.

Another source of increasing power in the eleventh century was the Church. The first attempt at converting Denmark to Christianity was made by the Anglo-Saxon bishop Willibrordus around the year 700. He went to Denmark and was received by an early king, Angenthjor, whom, however, he did not succeed in converting,

finding him 'more cruel than any animal and harder than any
stone'. Nevertheless, Angenthjor received Willibrordus well and
allowed him to take thirty young Danes to Holland, where he was
resident, so that they should be converted to Christianity. One
suspects that it was Willibrordus' plan to send them back to Denmark as missionaries, but there are no records of this ever having
been done. It was in fact another hundred years before a concerted effort was made to overcome paganism in Denmark. The
first step was taken by the Emperor Louis the Pious who sent the
archbishop of Reims, Ebo, to Denmark with the aim of converting
the people. Ebo knew King Harald, and in the year 823 he and a
following of priests went to Denmark where they were allowed to
preach and make converts. In 826 King Harald himself, together
with a following of about 400, was baptised, and it looked as though
Christianity was about to assert itself over the country of which
Harald was king, despite the fact that in the three years since
Ebo's arrival the Church had failed to establish any sort of organisation.

The baptism of Harald took place near Mainz, and instead of
returning with him, Ebo sent with him a monk by the name of
Ansgar. Although the year 826, with the baptism of Harald, is
recognised as the year in which Denmark became Christian, Ansgar
found it difficult to make progress, and when Harald was forced
into exile, Ansgar had to go with him, and in fact spent very little
time in Denmark. Instead he settled in northern Germany, where
he could be in contact with developments in Denmark, and in 838
was made bishop of Bremen. Ten years later he was also made
archbishop of Hamburg. He still hoped to convert Denmark and
made fresh contacts with the Danish king, Haarek, who developed
a great confidence in him, and finally, though a pagan himself,
acceded to Ansgar's request that Christians in Denmark should be
allowed to practise their faith and build a church. Hitherto they
had not been in any way persecuted by the pagan majority, and
they had freely been allowed to be baptised; but they were not
permitted to have public worship or to build churches. Haarek
sanctioned the building of a church in Hedeby, the Viking trade
centre in Schleswig, and Christianity now established a firmer footing within Denmark than it had had so far. Haarek's death meant
a temporary reaction, as his successor was more under the influence
of pagan advisers, but he, too, allowed the church in Hedeby to be
reopened, after which Ansgar was given permission to build a new
church in Ribe. It was not, however, until the baptism of Harald
Bluetooth in 960 that the Church can really be said to have thoroughly established itself on Danish territory, and only then did the

pagans begin to lose ground rapidly. The conquest of England in the following century even further strengthened the influence of the Church in Denmark, for it must be remembered that England had long been Christian, and although politically dominated by Denmark, was herself able to exert a cultural influence.

Even so, the Church was by no means an established Church. It fell to King Knud II (St Knud) and his next successor but one Kink Erik the Kind-Hearted, *Erik Ejegod*, finally to establish it in all its power and independence. Knud, under the influence of Cluniac Christianity and Pope Gregory VII, did much to liberate the Church from the legal authority of the state, and he also sought to introduce tithes and to enforce celibacy, but he succeeded in neither of these efforts. His piety stood in some contrast to his treatment of his subjects, and finally, after an attempt to launch a new Viking expedition to England in 1086, the peasantry of Jutland rebelled. He fled, but was caught and murdered in Odense. Nine years later Erik was chosen as king, and he succeeded in freeing the Church in the North from the archbishopric of Hamburg. A new archbishopric was created in Lund, which at that time was Danish territory, and in 1104 Archbishop Asser was made archbishop of Lund and therefore primate of the North. With this appointment went, for the temporal authorities, the hope of greater political independence from the German states. As a further gesture of the close relationship between Church and Crown, the king now managed to introduce a system of tithes, which made the Church financially independent and enabled it to increase its influence. A further result of this new and regular influx of wealth to the Church was that it was now possible to build churches in stone instead of wood as hitherto, and so permanent buildings were erected, not least among which were the great cathedrals.

The Age of the Valdemars and Danish Expansion

King Erik had been a strong and determined monarch. He was succeeded by a weaker man, and for a generation the country was plunged into a series of civil wars, as kings fought against pretenders, and the throne became an object of dispute. It was not until 1157 that true stability was brought to the country with the acceptance as king of Valdemar I, and the period of growth and power known as the Age of the Valdemars was thus introduced. It lasted from the accession of Valdemar I, Valdemar the Great, to the death of Valdemar II, Valdemar the Victorious, in 1241, and alongside the kings the central figures in this age of glory were the three archbishops of Lund – Eskil, Absalon, and Anders Sunesøn.

When Valdemar I came to the throne, Denmark was weak, ravaged by the civil wars of the past decades, and overshadowed by Germany. Like his predecessors, Valdemar had to acknowledge the Holy Roman Emperor as his overlord, but he began to turn this dependence to his own advantage. During the period of weakness the Wends, the Slav peoples of the Baltic, had taken the opportunity of ravaging the Danish coasts and plundering the villages, in much the same way as the Vikings had plundered others in earlier centuries. Valdemar set about putting an end to this. To do so he needed the help of the Saxons, who were also enemies of the Wends. His armies supported theirs and took a small share of the booty, until they were powerful enough to conquer the Wendic stronghold of Rügen on their own.

Denmark was gradually fortified and began to assert herself as a power to be reckoned with both in Scandinavia and in the Baltic as a whole. Yet Valdemar had other plans which were equally ambitious and equally important to the country's internal affairs. So far the monarchy had been elective, and the main voice in choosing the new king had been that of the people, expressing themselves in *things* – the ancient Nordic gatherings of the people where laws were formulated and recited, and lawsuits heard. Valdemar wanted to strengthen the monarchy and make it independent, and between 1165 and 1170 he succeeded in his aim. In this he had the full support of Archbishop Eskil. No longer was kingship to be the gift of the people; it was to be bestowed by the Church instead. Although in theory the *things* continued to influence the choice of king, in practice hereditary monarchy was instituted. It was still not absolute monarchy, and until the seventeenth century it became the practice for each elected king to sign a charter limiting his powers. But in effect the system was in full flower, the monarchy strong internally and externally.

It enjoyed, moreover, the powerful support of the Church. When as an old man Eskil was forced to resign his archbishopric, the obvious choice as his successor was Absalon, who had so far been bishop of Roskilde and Valdemar's right-hand man. Absalon was not merely a zealous churchman, but a first-class organiser and military mind, a mixture not unknown elsewhere in the medieval Church, and he was bent on centralising power in Denmark and breaking down the influence of the various regions. When Valdemar died in 1182 and was succeeded by his son Knud, Absalon was able to continue the policies of Valdemar for the next two decades. It is Absalon who fuses the reigns of the two Valdemars into one glorious age.

His policy was one of expansion, and whereas Valdemar, coming to the throne at a time of weakness, was forced to acknowledge the emperor, Knud refused to do so. This refusal led to war, but Denmark was now strong, and gradually took possession of Mecklenburg and Pomerania as well as the territory as far south as the Elbe, including Lübeck. The most important trade centres in the north of Europe were thus under Danish rule. Only one year after Absalon's death, Knud was succeeded in 1202 by Valdemar II. The expansionist policy continued, and by 1219 Denmark owned the whole Baltic coast as far as the eastern boundary of Estonia. But Valdemar had gone too far. In 1223 he was taken prisoner by Count Henrik of Schwerin, and before he was released Denmark had to give up most of her Baltic possessions, while the southern boundary was drawn at the Ejder. Even here the seeds of future trouble were already sown, as the population in the area was no longer purely Danish. It contained many Saxons who had moved in from Holstein when Denmark was in possession there, and their presence was to be felt again in the nineteenth century with the Schleswig-Holstein problem.

Instead of external expansion, Valdemar II now worked for internal growth, and his reign saw profound internal changes in the country's administration. The legislative power, which hitherto had been with the *things*, passed more and more into the king's hands, as was made plain by his giving the people the Jutish Law of 1241. It was a law of good government, and it codified what in fact had been traditional law before this time. It is perfectly plain that the country was now unified both administratively and legally, and that a change was taking place from a primitive society to one which was sophisticated for the Middle Ages. There was no longer a general equality among the people, but neither were there any slaves (*thralls*), as there had been under earlier rule. Instead a community based on the three estates was emerging, and as a whole it was a community which could equal those of other European countries, with a literature, the ballads, and a culture of its own, a country with the ability to build and to fashion an architecture distinct from that of other countries.

After the Valdemars

The following sixty years, until about 1300, were a period of economic growth, and especially urban growth, in Denmark. Scania became a great trade centre, with merchants from the East and West meeting there, exchanging goods or purchasing Danish products. The merchants benefited directly from this trade, and the class which they represented, the *borger* class, grew very rapidly as a result. At the same time the increased prosperity in the towns led to the development of new crafts, and the emergence of craft and trade guilds.

In the country districts, however, times were not so good, and the number of independent farmers fell from about 50 per cent of the total about 1250 to between 10 and 15 per cent around 1400. This was partly the result of political conditions which made life unsafe unless a farmer enjoyed protection – *vornedskab* – from some noble lord. And if it was enjoyed, it was at the price of giving up the ownership of land and adopting a system of leasehold. A different legal relationship developed when a farmer who was crippled by tax handed over his land to a noble or to the Church, both of whom were untaxed, and leased it back from them for less than his tax would have been. But he sacrificed his freedom by doing so. When times were bad, he had to pay his dues in labour instead of money, and thus developed the system of villeinage – *hoveri* – whereby a small farmer was forced to work for his land-lord when required. By 1350 the system which was to last until the eighteenth century was beginning to take shape.

Politically these were troubled times. Valdemar II made his sons dukes in various parts of the country, and they quarrelled as to the succession and their rights under the new king, Erik Plough-penny. Under these conditions Schleswig acquired a degree of in-dependence not enjoyed by any other part of the country. Duke Abel of Schleswig, one of Erik Ploughpenny's brothers, fought for the independence of his duchy, and finally, with the support of the counts of Holstein – still completely independent of Denmark – murdered his brother and was made King of Denmark. Two years later he fell in battle, and although he left two sons, the Danes chose another of Valdemar's sons as Christoffer I. Abel's sons could do little in face of this, as they had no legal claim to the Danish throne, but they did manage to secure the semi-independence of Schleswig. Schleswig drifted closer to Holstein, and when in 1460 King Christian I of Denmark was elected duke of Schleswig and of Holstein against a promise never to divide the duchies, the seeds of the nineteenth-century conflict were planted deep.

Meanwhile, with the weakness of the kings after Valdemar the Victorious, the Danish nobles saw their chance of increasing their power, and a struggle developed between them and the Crown. It was a contest in which the nobility won, but which brought untold trouble to the country as a whole. In order to maintain his power and in an attempt to put down a rebellion which had been set in motion in Jutland and Funen by Count Gerhard of Holstein in 1326, King Christoffer II had to pawn large parts of Denmark. Holstein was in virtual control of Jutland, having taken it as a pledge for a sum of money which Christoffer had no hope of raising. Another Holstein count, Johan, was in control of Zealand and Scania. For a time it even seemed possible that Denmark might cease to be a unified state, and for eight years after the death of Christoffer II, the country was without a king.

Yet his son, almost symbolically named Valdemar, was to succeed in reuniting the country. In 1340 Count Gerhard was murdered in Jutland. The nobility of Denmark, disunited as they were, were tired of strife, so was the Church, and so were the ordinary people. The only hope was seen in the re-establishment of the monarchy, and negotiations led to the election of the son of the former king. It was to be his duty to free the country from foreign domination by paying off the money which was being extorted from it.

No one was better suited to the task. Valdemar IV was strong of character and determined, and these qualities he combined with shrewdness and ruthlessness. Within twenty years he had reunited the country. He had had to sell Denmark's one remaining Baltic possession, Estonia, but otherwise had restored the kingdom to its former status. At the same time he strengthened the Crown by seizing much of the land which his predecessors had given up to the nobles. As had happened before, however, a king went too far. In 1361 Valdemar attacked the Swedish island of Gotland and won it, but this move was to lead to his virtual downfall. Sweden, Holstein, Schleswig, and, most important, the Hansa, whose fleet Valdemar had defeated in 1362, joined forces against him. Peace was bought, but only at a price. The Peace of Stralsund (1370) gave the Hansa a number of outposts in Scania and the right to trade there for fifteen years.

The Kalmar Union

In 1375 Valdemar died without leaving a male heir, and as the other line with claims to the throne had also died out, a king had to be chosen. The choice fell on Oluf, the five-year-old son of Valdemar's daughter, Margrethe, and King Haakon VI of Norway. King Haakon himself was the son of the King of Sweden. In 1380 Haakon died, and Oluf succeeded to the Norwegian throne, thus uniting the two kingdoms in a union which was to last until 1814.

During Oluf's infancy, his mother ruled in his place, and when Oluf died in 1387, she was chosen as queen in her own right. Yet Margrethe had other ambitions, and their fulfilment turned out to be easier than anticipated. Sweden was also torn by internal strife between the Crown and nobility, and the nobles invited Margrethe to become Queen of Sweden. In the civil war which followed, she and her supporters were victorious and by 1389 the whole of Scandinavia, including that part of Finland which belonged to Sweden as well as the Norwegian possession, was united. To ensure the continuance of the union, Margrethe had her nephew, Erik of Pomerania, crowned King of the North in 1397, at which time she also executed a formal document of union, known as the Kalmar Union. The idea was that Scandinavia should be a form of federation, with each country enjoying its own internal legislation, but united under one monarch, and with a single foreign policy. The trouble was that Margrethe, herself a Dane, went too far in favouring her own countrymen, giving them high offices in Norway and Sweden, but not showing similar favours to the Norwegians and Swedes by giving them similar privileges in Denmark. Small as she was, Denmark was the most powerful and highly developed member of the Union, and the possibility of Danish domination was already obvious.

Margrethe herself succeeded in keeping the Union in being, but Erik of Pomerania was less successful, and finally lost his throne in 1439. This was not, however, before he had carried out important and far-reaching economic reforms within Denmark. In order to increase the wealth of the towns, he insisted that much foreign trade should go through Danish merchants instead of direct from Hanseatic merchants to his subjects. He also required that certain trades should only be carried out in the towns. Another way in which he sought to strengthen his country's finances was to introduce a toll on ships passing Elsinore; thus 1429 saw the start of the Sound Dues which were to be such a bone of contention in later centuries.

The Union did not come to an end with the overthrow of Erik, and his successors tried, with varying success, to keep it in being. Christian II, however, was a more purposeful king than those who had gone immediately before him, and he intended to maintain his proper authority in Sweden by any means at his disposal. When a rebellion broke out under Sten Sture, he fought hard against what was a true national uprising, and he won. But Christian had seen this sort of situation before, and determined that it should not be repeated. After his acknowledgement as King of Sweden, he arranged for his coronation to take place in Stockholm in 1520. To celebrate the occasion he had called together the flower of the Swedish nobility and the most powerful burghers and clerics. Some of them had been opposed to Christian in the uprising, but he had granted them an amnesty. Now, at the height of the celebrations, he closed the gates of the castle of Stockholm and arrested his guests. A show trial for heresy was engineered, and once the accused were found guilty of the charges, there was only one sentence possible: death. No fewer than eighty-two of the king's 'guests' were executed, by which action Christian hoped so to cow the Swedes that they would refrain from further revolt. To make his policy even more impressive, he carried out a series of bloody reprisals against those who had opposed him as he subsequently made his way back to Copenhagen.

Yet his actions had the opposite effect to what he had intended. In 1518, at the height of the rebellion, Christian had managed to secure six Swedish hostages, whom he had taken to Denmark. One of them, Gustav Eriksson, a member of the powerful Vasa family, was lodged with a relative in Jutland, but managed to escape, and by way of Lübeck made his way back to Sweden. He was chosen as leader in a revolt which drove Christian II out of Sweden and finally put an end to the Kalmar Union. All that now remained to Denmark were her ancient provinces along the Sound.

Christian's policies had made him unpopular not only in Sweden. He had created enemies elsewhere, both at home and abroad. Lübeck was worried about his intentions, and so was Holstein. Holland's indignation with Denmark had been aroused by an increase in Sound Dues, and because Dutch skippers who refused to pay the extra charges had been arrested and their men in some cases conscripted. At the same time the Danish nobles were unhappy with Christian's brutal methods and felt themselves threatened.

The ordinary people were, however, less dissatisfied, and many of the internal reforms which Christian introduced were in their favour. He continued the policy, started by Erik of Pomerania, of increasing the wealth of the towns, giving them wider trading rights; he sought to reform the currency; he introduced new laws which were to be valid for the whole country and replace the old medieval regional laws; he sought to limit both the power and the wealth of the nobles and the Church.

Sensing that Christian's object was to make Copenhagen the centre of Baltic trade in place of Lübeck, that city decided to support the Swedes in their struggle against Denmark. At first the Lübeck authorities merely gave help to the Swedish rebels, but it became apparent that war with Denmark was unavoidable. In August 1522 a Lübeck fleet sailed against Denmark, to be joined later by ships from Danzig and other Hanseatic cities. Together they wrought havoc around the coasts.

This action coincided with unrest in Jutland, where one of the king's sheriffs, who was probably typical of the rest, had been murdered for his brutality. The king repaid in kind, burning the city of Ålborg where the murder had taken place. By the end of the year a group of Jutlandic noblemen came together in a

conspiracy aimed at bringing down Christian, and they made contact with Duke Frederik of Gottorp, who also distrusted him. In
January 1523 they renounced their oaths of allegiance to the king,
and the province of Jutland came out in open rebellion. After
bloody battles the Jutlanders and Holsteiners got possession of Jutland and Funen, and Christian was left with only Zealand. There
news came to him of an impending invasion, and the plans were
so well thought out and the opposing forces so overwhelming that
Christian had to flee. On 13 April he sailed from Copenhagen for
Holland, whence he hoped to return with a new army. In his
place Duke Frederik of Gottorp was proclaimed King Frederik I.

He was made king by the grace of Lübeck and the Danish
nobility, and as such he was in many ways bound by what they
wanted of him. In particular, he was forced to give the nobles
greater privileges than they had had before, and the individual
noblemen came to enjoy greater power than they had ever known.
The chief sufferers were the ordinary people, and whereas they
had previously been at the mercy of the king's demands, now they
were at the mercy of those made by the nobility. It was not long
before those who only a few years earlier had been rebelling against
Christian II, were wishing for his return, a desire committed to
writing in what is considered to be the last of the Danish ballads,
the *Ballad of Christian the Second and the Nobles*. It is an allegory
portraying Christian as the eagle who is forced to leave the forest
by the hawk – the nobility. The ordinary people, portrayed as the
smaller birds, complain bitterly of the oppressive hawk, and long
for the return of the eagle : 'May God help the poor eagle flying
over the wild heath; he knows neither shelter nor refuge where he
dare build a nest. But the eagle is building in the mountains.' In
Jutland the peasants showed signs of rising against the new oppression, while in Scania a large-scale rebellion got under way and
showed signs of succeeding until it was finally crushed.

The Reformation

There was more, however, to the discontent in the country than
mere political oppression. Already in the final years of Christian
II's reign, the first signs of the Reformation had appeared in Denmark. Christian himself had shown some sympathy for the Lutheran cause, and had had discussions with the leading Catholic
spokesman – the monk Paulus Helie – on the new teaching. Both
were in basic agreement as to the need for introducing reforms
within the Catholic Church, and at first both agreed that the
reform should be from within, and not aimed at any break with
Rome. In time, however, Christian changed his views on this.

There were two main causes of discontent in Denmark. First, there was the manner in which bishops and high-ranking prelates were chosen and rewarded. Although the Church in Denmark was under the authority of Rome, it was customary for the archbishop of Lund and all bishops to be chosen by the king, and the choice confirmed by the Pope. This had given rise to abuses, not least because it was in the Crown's interest to choose its prelates from among its own supporters, irrespective of whether they were spiritually suited. The bishops were a political and military power in the country, and this side of their activities was of interest to the kind. In addition, being entitled to a third part of the Church's income from tithes, the bishops were exceedingly wealthy men, and lived in a high style. At the other end of the clerical scale there were the mendicant friars, who in recent years had become a veritable plague in Denmark; and although they and their orders were pledged to poverty, the vows were not kept. The sale of indulgences was, of course, a thorn in the flesh in Denmark as elsewhere.

When Frederik came to the throne in 1523, he was determined to consolidate his kingdom, and thus he sought to avoid taking sides in the religious dispute which was growing in intensity. A Catholic himself, he made it his aim to be neutral and to allow the Lutherans a certain freedom. In practice, as the new faith gradually began to gain support from the lower classes, he began to lean more and more towards them. He gave protection to the leading Danish reformer, Hans Tavsen, when he was preaching in Viborg, and in time he allowed most of the Catholic churches there to be pulled down, despite protests. Tavsen was called to Copenhagen, where he was also allowed to preach, and there, too, he enjoyed royal protection, despite the fact that Frederik was not and never became a Lutheran. Even had he wished to do so, he could scarcely have become a Protestant for fear of upsetting the German emperor. On the other hand, he did not wish to make too great a stand against the Lutherans for fear of losing popular support.

And popular support was just what he needed. Christian II was trying to make a comeback. After an abortive attempt to make an early return, he had settled in the Netherlands for a time, when he had in practice become a Lutheran. Now the Emperor Charles V, who was Christian's brother-in-law, offered to help him, provided that he returned to the Catholic faith and promised to fight for its restoration in Denmark if he succeeded in re-establishing himself. The promise was made, though whether it would have gone the way of so many of Christian's other promises, it is not easy to say.

At all events, he gathered an army and attacked Norway, where he dug himself in, though without achieving any notable victory. Under pressure from Lübeck, who wanted him out of the way, Christian was offered a safe conduct to Copenhagen to negotiate. He went and was enticed to Sønderborg Castle, where he was imprisoned many years before being removed to Kalundborg for the remainder of his life. Another promise broken, though its breaking meant the end of, instead of the beginning of more, bloodshed.

Christian was taken prisoner in 1532. The following year Frederik I died, and the fate of the Reformation was seen to depend on the choice of his successor. He had two sons, and the elder, Christian, was more likely to succeed him. However, Christian made no secret of his Lutheran leanings, and thus his younger half-brother, Hans, who was only twelve years old and a Catholic, was favoured by most of the nobles and all the bishops. When the choice was finally made, it was for Christian. And by 1536 the Reformation in Denmark was a fact.

The main reason for the establishment of the Lutheran Church in Denmark was not exclusively, perhaps not even mainly, a religious one. Frederik I had made an alliance with Holland, the ancient rival of Lübeck, despite the fact that he had depended on Lübeck for his throne. Upon his death, therefore, a Lübeck army landed in Zealand and occupied it, the object being to reinstate Lübeck's old opponent Christian II. With the same object in view the leaders of the lower aristocracy in Jutland started a fresh rebellion in northern Jutland. The nobles had to make a quick choice for their new king, and they chose Christian, already acclaimed as duke of Schleswig. As Christian III, he sent an army into Jutland and amidst great bloodshed recaptured the insurgent areas, after which he turned his attention to Funen and retook it from the Lübeck army. Finally he succeeded in crossing to Zealand and encircled Copenhagen. All this activity had plunged Christian deeper and deeper into debt. It was only human that he, a zealous Lutheran, should decide that the wealth of the Catholic Church in Denmark should be the means of his temporal salvation. In August 1536 he imprisoned all the bishops, and only released them when they agreed to support his new Church. There was very little trouble, and all the old bishops but one embraced Lutheranism, while Christian took their wealth, using some of it to pay his debts and some to train pastors for the new Church.

A new church constitution was worked out with the help of Johan Bugenhagen. There was to be a state Church, with the king as its head, and its teaching was to be in accordance with that of

Luther. There were to be no bishops and the main administrators were to be called superintendents. (With the passage of time they have again taken the title of bishop, but they pretend to be nothing but titular bishops, and the idea of hierarchy is no longer present in the Church of Denmark.) The superintendents were consecrated by Bugenhagen – himself not a bishop – at a ceremony in Copenhagen, whereby the Danish Church demonstratively lost its claim to Apostolic Succession – in contrast to the Swedish Church, which claims to have kept it. The new constitution provided the close link between the established Lutheran Church and the Crown, which was to be the basis of the absolute monarchy some hundred years later. And so eager were the leaders of the new Church to maintain this position that they made vigorous efforts to keep out any other doctrine. They were vigilant not only against Catholicism – though without the excesses which were found in Britain under similar circumstances – but also, and zealously, against any other form of Protestantism. The new Lutheran Church soon showed itself to be intolerant in the extreme.

Rivalry between Denmark and Sweden

During the following century, however, Denmark became preoccupied with more worldly matters. Trade prospered, and thanks to rising prices and plentiful supplies of money in southern Europe, Denmark succeeded in exporting more corn than ever before. Later, under Christian IV, there was to be a period of veritable mercantilism with the establishment of an East Indies Company based on a small colony which Denmark managed to found in Tranquebar.

As prices in northern Europe did not rise at the same rate as those in the south, trade flourished in the Baltic, and the number of ships, especially Dutch, making for the Baltic ports increased rapidly. During this period Denmark was master in this part of the world, and although she did not interfere with trade, she controlled the approaches through the Sound, being at that time still in possession of both coasts. Sweden, on the other hand, was badly furnished with ports. The only part of the present west coast which she owned was a small enclave at the mouth of the Göta river (where Gothenburg now stands). To the east Denmark owned the island of Gotland, and thus commanded the east coast of Sweden as well.

Sweden determined to try to free herself from this Danish domination; but Denmark had no intention of being reduced in stature, and, on the contrary, at one time cherished the ambition of re-establishing the Kalmar Union. The result was a series of wars between the two countries, spread over the greater part of a

century : first the Nordic Seven Years War (1563–70), the result of
King Frederik II's attempts to re-establish the Union. In fact, little
was achieved by this war, except a vast new devastation, and at
the end of it things were much as before.

Sweden next turned her attention to Russia, and managed
gradually to acquire mastery of the entire eastern Baltic, as far as
Estonia. In time this domination was extended right round the
Baltic, until Sweden bordered on Denmark to the south as well as
to the north. Such Swedish power was not to Denmark's taste, and
Christian IV decided to try to stop it by bringing Denmark into
the Thirty Years War and securing the north coast of Germany.
This episode, which lasted from 1625 until 1629, led to a resounding defeat and the occupation of Jutland by Wallenstein's forces,
until the Danes made a promise not to take any further part in the
war.

It was then Sweden's turn, and Swedish soldiers under Gustav II
Adolf joined the Protestant north Germans, and helped to decide
the outcome of the war in the North. From the Swedish point of
view, however, mastery of the Baltic was of paramount importance.
And having established themselves there, the Swedes, infuriated
by continued Danish opposition, followed Wallenstein's example
and occupied Jutland. By the resultant Treaty of Brømsebro in
1645, Sweden acquired some of the Danish provinces in the north
of the Sound, and also ensured freedom from Sound Dues both
for the Swedish mainland and for all Swedish possessions in the
Baltic. The Dutch, for their part, were delighted to see the Danish
monopoly of power broken, and they managed to have the Sound
Dues reduced at the same time.

The next stage in the struggle between Denmark and Sweden
came in 1657 when Sweden was fighting a nationalist uprising in
Poland. Denmark, now under Frederik III, saw the chance of
revenge and declared war on Sweden. Again the Swedes immediately occupied Jutland, while the Danes withdrew to Funen, where
they appeared to be safe. Then the unforeseeable happened. In the
extremely harsh winter of that year the water between Jutland
and Funen, and between Funen and Zealand, froze over to enable
the Swedish army to cross the ice on foot and thus make for Copenhagen. By the terms of the Treaty of Roskilde, Denmark had to
give up her possessions north of the Sound, and Sweden acquired
the entire coastline south of the Norwegian border. Some parts of
central Norway also went to Sweden. Peace seemed to be restored,
and Denmark humiliated, but Sweden did not trust her southern
neighbour to keep out of the war she was still waging in north
Germany, and consequently broke the treaty within months by

invading Zealand without warning, the object being to take over
the whole of the country. This was too much for the Dutch. Little
as they had liked the Danish mastery of the Sound, they did not
relish the prospect of Swedish domination either, and they sent a
fleet to the relief of Copenhagen, which had withstood a lengthy
siege. There was also an uprising in the occupied parts of Denmark, and this, together with an attack by Polish and Brandenburg
forces on Sweden, forced her to sue for peace. In 1660 the Treaty
of Copenhagen acknowledged that Sweden had been defeated, but
did not give back to Denmark all the provinces that Sweden had
taken after the Treaty of Roskilde. It was in the interests of all
parties to the treaty that neither Sweden nor Denmark should be
in sole control of the Sound, and consequently Sweden was allowed
to keep the Sound provinces – whereby that country took on something like its present shape. A position of some stability had now
been reached, and the wars between Denmark and Sweden were
over. But they had left a legacy of intense hatred between the two
peoples who had suffered so much at each other's hands.

*Internal Developments and the Establishment of the Absolute
Monarchy*

Despite the many wars and the expenditure connected with
them, this period, and especially the years up to about 1600, was
one of economic growth, symbolised perhaps by the architectural
glories of the age of Christian IV.[1] Yet the benefits were not evenly
distributed. Exactly what advantage came to the farming community is not clear, but it is certain that as a whole this period
saw a further loss to the farmer of freedom and independence.
He became less an independent farmer, whether an owner or a
lessee, and more and more a man in the employment of the
local landowner. The king was the first to set the trend towards
increasing the size of his estates, which he did both by exchanging outlying farms which he owned for others closer to
the royal domain, and also by refusing to renew land leases
when the lessee died. The example was quickly followed by
the nobility, and the sixteenth and seventeenth centuries thus
saw the emergence of the really large estate in Denmark, together with the resultant building of the impressive mansions in
which the aristocracy took such pride. The farmers, meanwhile,
could never be sure of continuing their leases, nor indeed be cer-

[1] Christian's sister Anne was married to James I of England. For a
hilarious account of the revels at the English court during his state visit in
1606, see Sir John Harrington, *Nugae Antiquae* (2 vols., London, 1804), I,
348–51. See also G. P. V. Akrigg, *Jacobean Pageant* (London, 1962), pp.
79–84.

3—D * *

tain that they would not be forced to move from one farm to another. And at the same time they were compelled to put in more time working for their landlords. With the increasing size of the estates came a need for more help, and it was quite natural that the landlord should require it of those who had worked for him in the past, with the difference that what had once been a limited duty now became unlimited and dependent on the landowner's needs and whims. In another sense, too, the landowners tended to exploit their lessees to a greater extent: it had been customary that dues should be paid in kind rather than money, and the amounts payable were fixed. Yet with the generally rising prices, it was the landowner, not the lessee, who benefited.

The economic changes also benefited the towns, and the period was thus characterised by the emergence of a limited middle class. Denmark, freed from the domination of Lübeck merchants and not yet under the thumb of the Dutch merchants who finally took their place, started overseas trading on her own account. The trade was organised from the towns, and townspeople derived the main benefit from it. Furthermore, it became the policy of Christian IV to give some form of state support to trade, both by partially financing overseas companies, such as the East Indies Company, which colonised Tranquebar but did not last for long, and also by encouraging home industry. For this latter purpose clothing industries and a silk industry were started, but in the long run they lacked both the capital and the skill necessary to keep them going. These and other attempts, however, did benefit the emerging middle class, and the end of the sixteenth century saw the establishment of a Copenhagen bourgeoisie which was to play an important part in establishing the absolute monarchy when the final struggle between the Crown and the aristocracy got under way in the second half of the following century.

Since the rise of the aristocracy as a political power with the privilege of forcing a charter upon each king before allowing him to take the throne, and indeed with the theoretical right to depose a king if the occasion arose, there had been an obvious source of strain between the nobility and the king. In practice the nobles had not been as strong as the theory might suggest, but no king was happy at the thought of having his power thus limited. Nevertheless, each king had been to a great extent militarily dependent on the nobility. In times of war he looked to the nobles to provide his armed forces, and in return they were given widespread privileges, especially with regard to taxation. In the first half of the seventeenth century, however, things began to change. The wider use of firearm's made the king less dependent on the foot-soldiers whom the nobles could provide, and at the same time the nobles were less wealthy than they had been, partly because of a fall in prices which hit those whose income ultimately depended on trade. Indeed, many of the ancient noble families were impoverished by the seventeenth century, and others had died out. The king's power, on the other hand, was obviously in the ascendant, especially when Frederik III had the nobility's leaders exiled.

His chance to break the power of the nobility once and for all came immediately after the siege of Copenhagen was raised. In order to encourage the citizens to hold out, he had promised Copenhagen special privileges, including that of deciding how much tax they should pay. Accordingly, a meeting of the estates was called in September 1660 to decide the question, and the citizens and clergy insisted that all, including the nobility, should be liable to pay taxes. Despite attempts to avoid the issue, the nobles had to give in. Sensing their new influence and realising that they as well as the king would have advantages from seeing the power of the nobles reduced, the Copenhagen citizens then went on to suggest that the king should be declared a hereditary monarch, which would, of course, put an end to the system of charters. The king made at least a pretence of hesitating, but he made sure that the gates of the city were closed so that no noble could slip out and avoid the issue. Then he decided to accept the offer, and was acclaimed hereditary king amidst great ceremony, during which he made a show of friendship towards the leaders of the Copenhagen citizens, some of whom he then appointed to posts which would hitherto have been reserved for the nobility.

A new constitution of some sort to cope with the changed circumstances was clearly necessary, but here agreement proved difficult and looked like being impossible. The delegates preferred to leave this question to the king himself. The result was not quite what they had foreseen. In 1661 the king whom they had invited to become a hereditary monarch sent out a document for signature in which he called himself the *absolute* hereditary monarch, and on its progress round the country from one noble to another, no one dared to withhold his name. When in 1665 the constitution was finally published, it was seen that Frederik III had indeed taken absolute power. Whether this had been his intention in 1660, it is not possible to say with any certainty, and it may be well to remember that in 1661 Louis XIV of France was proclaimed absolute king. Once his absolutism had been recognised, however, Frederik III set about consolidating as arbitrary a system as was to be found anywhere else in Europe.

The only limitations placed on him were that he should support

the Lutheran Church and ensure that the kingdom remained un-
divided. Otherwise he was supreme in the country. And yet none
of the Danish absolute kings made any attempt to act as a true
despot. Although final decisions were left to the king, he was
usually content to accept the recommendations of his closest advisers, who formed a Privy Council. The members of this Privy
Council were themselves mainly drawn from the top ranks of the
various departments of the administration, known as colleges. Basically the same as the modern concept of Ministries, these colleges
were run not by one responsible Minister, but by committees
drawn from the senior officials in them. Where the king did make
greater use of his prerogative was in the choice of civil servants
and advisers, and in the way he bestowed the favours which were
eagerly sought.

Now that the leading positions were no longer reserved for the
aristocracy, there was competition to gain them, and, when a commoner had gained them, to secure distinctions and possibly ennoblement. Christian V's[2] leading Minister and adviser, Peder
Schumacher, by his career showed the possibilities and dangers to
which the new system gave rise. He was a commoner, the son of a
rich wine merchant, who worked his way to the very top by means
of his own capabilities, but then, thanks to a rather too subtle
foreign policy, was brought down by the enemies and rivals he had
created. The king, however, changed his sentence at the very last
minute to one of lifelong imprisonment after he had been pardoned
on the scaffold. The significant aspect of Peder Schumacher's career
is not to be seen in his fall, but in his rise to power and influence –
and ennoblement under the name of Griffenfeld. Under the old
dispensation a commoner such as he would never have had such
chances, and the country would have lacked the benefits which his
brilliant mind brought to its problems. The dangers – favouritism
and sycophancy – were common under the system as under any
other absolute rule.

The kings trusted such people as Schumacher because of their
total dependence on the goodwill of the Crown. On the other hand,
the old noble houses could scarcely be relied on, having been
ousted from their position of power; and the absolute kings began
systematically to bring in new upstart aristocrats either from outside Denmark or from the Danish Third Estate. These new men
took over much of the land which the impoverished Danish nobility
had owned, and they began a period of more intensive abuse of
the peasantry than had been seen before. Harsh as the old nobility

[2] Christian's brother George married Princess Anne of York, later Queen
Anne of England, in 1683.

had been, they had had something of a patriarchal attitude towards the farmers, an attitude not shared by the new aristocrats. These men merely wanted as large a profit as possible, and they forced the farmers even more into subservience, insisting on three or four days' labour from them each week. The farmers' own land was consequently neglected and a humiliated peasantry reached the nadir of its fortunes. Its legal status was ill-defined, and even when the king in 1702 ended *vornedskab*, its lot scarcely improved; for to prevent peasants from fleeing and leaving the new aristocracy short of labour, a new rule was introduced whereby no man between the ages of fourteen and thirty-six could leave the estate on which he had been born. In effect, the farmers were reduced to a form of serfdom.

The rather exaggerated love of grandeur which has often gone with absolutism also had its effect on late seventeenth-century Denmark. It persuaded the kings to build magnificent squares and palaces – Kongens Nytorv in Copenhagen is one example – and it gave rise to the baroque style in architecture and poetry. But the one field in which glory could be won by the absolute kings would be in the recovery of the Swedish provinces, the loss of which had been an enormous blow to national pride. Denmark was allied to Holland, but Sweden with France, and it was obviously impossible for Denmark to wage war on Sweden while she had such an ally. However, in 1675 the pretext and the opportunity came. France, herself at war with Holland, persuaded Sweden to attack Brandenburg, where a defeat was inflicted on the Swedes. Denmark could wait no longer, and after occupying Sweden's small ally to the south, Gottorp, which included parts of Schleswig, the Danes landed an army in Scania, where it was well received by the local population. It was still a dangerous move, to which Griffenfeld was opposed, and it was because he played a double game with France in order to keep her from interfering that he was finally brought down. France did, however, refrain from interfering, and Denmark won the Scanian War. Yet once more the wishes of a major power, France, prevented the return of the old Danish territories. Despite terrible losses, Denmark was allowed to keep nothing of what she had conquered.

But Denmark was still not prepared to give up the attempt, and a *rapprochement* with France took place just at the same time as Sweden made a move to improve relations with England and Holland, who had previously supported Denmark. This new constellation was in existence at the beginning of the Great Nordic War, which lasted from 1700 to 1720, the war in which the Swedish king, Charles XII, fought against Russia only to be beaten by

the Russian winter when he marched on Moscow. The final outcome of the war was that Sweden once and for all lost most of her
Baltic possessions, while Russia for the first time played a dominant
role in the Baltic. Denmark failed to regain the Swedish provinces,
however, and merely achieved an end to the Swedish freedom from
Sound Dues and the cessation of Swedish support for Gottorp. As
a result of this Frederik IV was able to strengthen his own position
in Schleswig, while allowing the duke of Gottorp to keep Holstein.
It was hoped thereby to remove the frontier problem to the south
and north. Peace between Denmark and Sweden seemed likely.

The Eighteenth Century: Pietism and Enlightenment

It has already been remarked that the Lutheranism which came
to Denmark with the Reformation in 1536 led quickly to a new
orthodoxy and intolerance. Nevertheless, the close connection
which existed between the Lutheran state Church and the Crown
meant little could be done to overcome this or to allow new ideas
to penetrate into Denmark. It was not until the beginning of the
eighteenth century that any new development took place with the
arrival from Germany of the pietist movement and the desire actually to live in a true Christian fashion and not merely maintain a
Christian façade. There was no obvious desire to stray from the
strictly Lutheran teaching, but merely to intensify the manner of
life, and so it was difficult for the state Church to prevent the
spread of pietism. By 1720 Frederik IV himself was sympathetic
towards the new movement, and his successor Christian VI was
himself a convinced pietist. Under his rule there was a period of
intensification of the religious life in Denmark. This was accompanied by a new form of intolerance which led the pietists, once
they occupied positions of authority, to frown on secular amuse-
ments. As a result, all entertainments were forbidden on Sundays;
but pietist influence also brought about the closing of Copenhagen's Royal Theatre for a period, just when Ludwig Holberg,
the greatest dramatist in the North, was at the height of his creative
powers, thereby doubtless changing the pattern of Holberg's productive effort. On the other hand, the pietists laid great stress on
charitable acts and help for those in need. Among those in need
were children in want of education, and under the pietists an
attempt was made to provide a minimum of schooling for all, an
attempt which only met with limited success because of opposition
from the landowners who had to finance it, and the farmers who
would rather have their sons in the fields than in the classroom.

Under the pietists, too, Sunday church attendance became compulsory, and masters were responsible for seeing to it that their

servants complied. Punishments were laid down for those refusing to attend. Then in 1736, to celebrate the two hundredth anniversary of the Reformation, a new law was introduced, making Confirmation compulsory, only after which did a citizen acquire full civil rights, such as the right to a passport and access to certain official positions. It was impossible to marry without having been confirmed. This explains the peculiar status of Confirmation in Denmark to this day, when it still retains vestiges of its old importance and symbolises the attainment of adulthood.

Nevertheless, the pietists' interest in education can be seen not only as a special aspect of their creed, but as the forerunner of the eighteenth-century Enlightenment which replaced pietism later in the century and led to an increased interest in education generally. At the end of the century schools such as the School for Civic Virtue were founded. This was a private, liberal, experimental school, inspired by German ideas, and aiming to give as wide an education as possible – as it turned out, far too wide. In effect it was a reaction against the established grammar schools, mainly medieval establishments often attached to the cathedrals, after which they were named – Cathedral Schools. Here learning was by rote, entirely devoid of inspiration, and the interminable learning by heart was aided by the liberal application of corporal punishment. N. F. S. Grundtvig, the nineteenth-century pioneer of the Folk High-School movement in Denmark, called them 'the black schools'. Establishments such as the School for Civic Virtue went to the other extreme, but they inculcated in the pupils a true and lasting love of their schools, and of learning in general.

Yet experimental as they were, they were symptomatic of an age which was realising the need for educational reform. Despite the fact that education was in theory compulsory, the law had never been enforced, and in any case there were not enough teachers to go round. There were no properly trained teachers. In view of this grim situation, and as one effect of the reforming zeal which spread throughout the country with the Enlightenment, a school commission was set up in 1789. Its report formed the basis of the School Law of 1814 which really did introduce a new era into Danish education. It provided for free schooling for all, though parents who wished either to teach their children at home or send them to private schools were entitled to do so. For failing to comply with the law, parents were liable to heavy fines, and in cases of non-compliance the law was to be enforced. The new schools were henceforth to be paid for out of taxation, not by the landowner on whose land they had been situated, as had hitherto been the case. In addition, provision was made for the training of proper teachers

by the establishment of training colleges, though decades elapsed
before the supply was sufficient to satisfy all needs. The nineteenth
century benefited from the new School Law, but it was essentially
a result of the eighteenth century's philanthropy.

On a different level it was also an offshoot of the peasant
reforms – one of the major achievements of the late eighteenth
century. Stemming from a happy combination of philanthropy, a
period of increasing prosperity, an enlightened monarch, and perhaps a touch of Rousseauist idealism, the peasant reforms saw a
reversal of the trend towards the oppression of the farming community which had been such an obvious characteristic of the past
three or four centuries. Now, as liberal thought spread wider in
ruling circles, a commission was set up in 1786 to consider peasant
reforms. Its first result was an act setting out a farmer's legal rights
vis-à-vis his landlord. So far lessees had been entirely at the mercy
of the landlord, and although many lords of the manor took a
genuine, if condescending, interest in their tenants, others were
less inhibited and looked only to their own gain. If a lessee died,
it was easy for them to demand compensation from the widow for
repairs to the farm, while on the other hand they never made any
allowances for improvements. The new law stipulated that the
question of increased or decreased values should be decided by a
disinterested party. Nor was the landowner any longer able to
inflict corporal punishment on a farmer, though he was still entitled
to do so in the case of smallholders and labourers. The following
year brought an end to *stavnsbaand,* the system under which
farmers had been tied to the estate on which they lived, and which
had been introduced in 1733 to ensure a plentiful supply of labour
for the landowners.

With this change the landowners lost their grip on their tenant
farmers, and thus some need for a statutory limit to the work a
farmer was forced to do for his landlord also became necessary. In
fact *hoveri,* as it was called, was now normally the subject of some
arrangement between a landlord and his tenant, and in many cases
the arrangement was for an annual payment. Thereby the farmer
was left in peace and the landowner was provided with funds to
pay for a labourer. Under the new system it also became common
for the farmer to buy back his farm instead of leasing it. The state
encouraged this, and by 1814 some 60 per cent of Danish farmers
were once more independent owner-farmers. They were not thereby made wealthy, and many had a hard time because of falling
prices, but they acquired a self-esteem which they had not had for
centuries. They were becoming a modern equivalent of the independent farmers of former ages, and it has been argued that the

new self-respect of these farmers coupled with the obviously growing influence which was to be theirs, provided the basis for the
modern democratic system.

Reforms such as these were only made possible by another
reform, introduced as early as 1781 by the otherwise conservative
Prime Minister Hoegh-Guldberg. Until then the basis of Danish
agriculture had been the strip system, which had made any real
improvements in agricultural methods impossible. In 1781 an act
was passed to encourage the parcelling-out of land and containing
the provision that if this was demanded by one single landowner
in a village, then it must be done. The problems of dividing the
land out justly, taking into account both the amount and the
quality of the land owned, were enormous, and it took many
decades to carry out the letter of the act – but it established the
basis for farmers to work in their own way instead of being limited
by the common policy of the village, and led to far greater efficiency once a farmer was freed from his duties to his landowner.
The scene was now set for the upsurge of agriculture which was
evident by the end of the nineteenth century, because land which
had previously been left untouched for common grazing, could
now be brought under ever more intensive cultivation.

Prosperity, War, and Poverty

The agricultural reforms had coincided with a period of increased agricultural and national prosperity. Thanks to the Industrial Revolution, England's population had risen rapidly, and from
being a corn-exporting country, England had started importing
corn. Denmark had been among those countries which benefited
from this turn of events, and such a turn, combined with the introduction of a corn monopoly in Norway, meant good news for
farmers. The reforms were in no small part due to the new opportunities and need for better organisation which followed this good
fortune.

Denmark's economy benefited also at first from the wars between Britain and France at the end of the eighteenth century
and from the American War of Independence, in all of which the
country declared itself neutral and set about trading with both
sides. Trade also prospered in the Far East, and Denmark earned
great sums there, while Copenhagen achieved its old objective of
becoming the centre of trade for the Baltic. By 1784 the new ideas
of the government led to the ending of trade restrictions – which
in their turn had led to smuggling – and Denmark was able to
enter the nineteenth century in a period of affluence and free trade.

Danish trading policy and the earning of such large sums in

foreign trade were not without their dangers. None of the belligerent powers was pleased to see Denmark trading with its enemies,
and in particular Britain sought to stop and search Danish ships
and confiscate cargoes whenever there was the slightest excuse. In
1780, therefore, Denmark joined with Russia, Prussia, and Sweden
in an armed neutrality aimed at safeguarding trading rights in
America, and was largely successful in doing so until the end of
the War of Independence in 1783. However, when Britain was
again embroiled in war with revolutionary France, Denmark was
less successful, and the decision to organise a convoy system met
with immediate British opposition. Denmark gave in, but went on
to join the second Armed Neutrality with Sweden and Russia.
After this apparent disrespect for an agreement just made, Britain
in 1801 sent a fleet to Copenhagen. The force found the Danish
fleet unprepared, and so won a resounding victory, despite stub-
born resistance. The Danes had to yield and accept the British
demand that they should withdraw from the Armed Neutrality.

The difficulties in which Denmark found herself, caught between
two major warring powers, were a sign of things to come, and also
an early indication of situations which were to emerge in the
twentieth century, when Denmark has suffered from being too
closely tied to each of two opposing powers. In particular the
situation became difficult when Napoleon announced the Continental Blockade in 1806, and even more so when Britain set in
motion a counter-blockade. Denmark, dependent as always on the
sea for communication, both between the islands and between Denmark and Norway, was at the mercy of the British fleet. Nor is it
surprising that the British government, after the events of 1801,
was scarcely sure of what Denmark's attitude was. In fact with
Napoleon to the south and the Royal Navy on the sea, Denmark
was mainly interested in keeping out of trouble.

After the signing of the peace treaty between France and Russia
at Tilsit in 1807, the position became even more difficult. Russia
joined in the Continental Blockade, and, although this was not
known, the intention was to force Denmark and Sweden to join in
too. Sensing this, Britain started pressing Denmark for an alliance,
a provision of which was to be that Denmark should deliver her
fleet to Britain as a pledge. The Danes were aware that if this
happened, France would invade Jutland, and there was no knowing what might happen. On the other hand, if a decision was made
for an alliance with France, the outlook for trade was bleak. In
the event, they played for time, and tried to work on the fact that
while the English were in Copenhagen making demands, the Crown
Prince was in Kiel with his army. But they wavered too long, and

the British lost patience. In order to force an alliance on the Danes they occupied Zealand and bombarded Copenhagen for three days, during which they laid parts of the city waste and killed hundreds of civilians. When at the end of it all the city gave in, the British confiscated the entire Danish fleet and sailed off with it.

Had they played their cards better and been less impatient, it may well be that they would have gained what they wanted, for on the whole the Danes sympathised with their cause. But by behaving in so high-handed a manner, and by cowing the city into surrender and then taking the fleet, they made themselves the object of hatred and loathing in Denmark for a long time to come. The bombardment of Copenhagen was felt deeply by the Danes as a national humiliation, and it gave rise to an upsurge of nationalism which, let it be admitted, had already been there in embryo since the domination of the court by German administrators in the middle of the eighteenth century.

In these circumstances an Anglo-Danish alliance was out of the question, and instead the Danes made an alliance with Napoleon. But it was too late, and it became obvious that they had joined the losing side, a side, moreover, that the average Dane did not love. Attempts to break with France and to join the alliance against Napoleon were thwarted by Sweden, where the new king, Carl Johan, himself one of Napoleon's generals who had turned against the emperor, had been promised Norway once the war was over, provided Denmark was on the losing side. Thus, in 1814, a year after a state bankruptcy had been declared, Denmark had to sign the Treaty of Kiel and found herself reduced from a medium-sized state to a minor and poverty-stricken one.

Chapter 2

1814–64

Liberalism, Nationalism, and the
Aftermath

IT IS A TRUISM to say that the explanation of the present century is to be found in the last, but the validity of this statement in the case of Denmark is perhaps more striking and of greater immediate significance than it is for some other countries. The nineteenth century saw the final transformation of Denmark from something approaching a major European power to a very small nation indeed, one so small that the possibility was mooted that she might be absorbed into the German Confederation.

This Confederation, formed in 1815, was itself a result of the Napoleonic Wars. Not only did it include purely German states, but also, in view of the sovereignty of some of its member states, it impinged on non-German countries. The King of the Netherlands was concerned as Grand Duke of Luxembourg, and the King of Denmark as the duke of Holstein and Lauenburg, both of which were members of the Confederation. The Confederation was a fairly loose association and its only military power was based on contingents from each state. There was no navy, though Prussia had plans for one. On the other hand, by the middle of the century the Danish navy bore some resemblance to its former strength, and the suggestion was made by the British representative at the Diet of the Confederation in a letter to Palmerston in 1848 that Denmark should be persuaded to enter the Confederation. This would head off Prussia's plans for naval strength and would also ensure that no Nordic union of any sort would be created, thus once more putting both coasts of the Sound under the control of one power.

Yet together with the rapid decline in Denmark's international prestige went, especially in the second half of the century, a determination to build up within her frontiers and to make good the wealth and power she had lost outside them. The two focal points

44

in this process were to be found in 1814 with the loss of Norway, and in 1864 with the loss of Schleswig and Holstein. At the end of this period Denmark was smaller than she had been for centuries, and would in fact have been smaller still if the Swedish negotiators in 1814 had realised that historically Greenland, Iceland, and the Faroes had belonged to Norway. As it was, Denmark was allowed to keep them and in place of Norway was given Swedish Pomerania and the island of Rügen by way of compensation.

In practice west Pomerania and Rügen were only held by Denmark for a short time, and were exchanged by Prussia for Lauenburg, a territory which suited Denmark better, since it bordered on Holstein. Subsequently, however, this was to prove more of an encumbrance than an advantage. Of more immediate benefit was the fact that Prussia paid Denmark a large sum of money as compensation for the difference in the size of these territories. Denmark was bankrupt, and the addition of between 2 and 3 million *rigsdaler* to her financial resources was only too welcome.

Discontent in the Duchies

Meanwhile, in a different field, the difficulties which were to face Denmark over Schleswig-Holstein and Lauenburg already began to make themselves felt. With the end of the Holy Roman Empire in 1806, Denmark had incorporated Holstein under the Danish Crown, carrying the ancient association between the duchy and the kingdom to its logical conclusion. Now, however, Frederik VI felt compelled to allow Holstein to join the newly established Confederation of German States, while himself remaining duke of Holstein. Thus the ambivalence in Holstein's position *vis-à-vis* Denmark became more pronounced. There were now direct ties with Germany as well as with Denmark, and in Holstein it was hoped that, as a result of the arrangement with the German Confederation, the Consultative Assembly, to which Frederik VI had agreed, would become a sort of local diet with increasing powers. In fact the assembly was not established until 1831, when the king allowed the formation of similar bodies in Schleswig and in the kingdom proper.

These were the direct results of the July revolution in Paris, news of which reached Copenhagen in August and was received with enthusiasm by the greater part of the population, though not by the king, who saw that the course of events could lead to the end of his absolute rule. There were no real revolutionary tendencies in Denmark, where absolutism was felt to have a restraining rather than an oppressive effect. The king was well intentioned, and this was appreciated by the people as a whole. The pressure to introduce reforms originated outside Denmark, and was originally directed at Holstein. Metternich, the leading spokesman of the German Confederation, had previously pointed out to Frederik that Denmark had agreed to give Holstein a constitution, and now Prussia, which had allowed a consultative assembly to be formed in 1823, added her voice and together with Hanover demanded the establishment of an assembly for Holstein.

In Holstein itself a movement began which was aimed at forcing the Danes to grant a constitution. The leader of the movement, Uwe Lornsen, had been a member of the Danish administration and had been attached to the central administration in Copenhagen. In September 1830 he applied for and was appointed to a relatively minor post in the island of Sild, where he was sufficiently close to events in Holstein to take a direct hand in and control them. It was his intention to separate Holstein from the central administration and to establish an administration within the duchy itself, probably in Kiel. At first he met with little popular response but the movement grew, and by the end of the year Lornsen was able to publish suggestions for a constitution for Schleswig-Holstein, providing for elections and the establishment of a legislative assembly. The king, however, should have the power of veto if he objected to any proposed legislation.

Although Lornsen's pamphlet was eagerly read by liberals in Kiel, it ran into opposition from both the moderates and the upper classes, who might well want an independent or semi-independent Holstein, but wished to run it themselves, not to see it in the hands of liberals and revolutionaries. In Denmark it was quickly appreciated that the whole idea ran counter to Danish policy. While the Danes saw both duchies as distinct entities and as having different historical relationships to Denmark proper, but none the less as part of Denmark, Lornsen's view was that Schleswig and Holstein formed an indivisible unity. He was arrested for activities prejudicial to the state, and subsequently sentenced to a year in prison. By treating him in this way, Denmark made him a martyr to his cause, which flourished more vigorously than it might otherwise have done. The idea spread that Schleswig and Holstein should be fused into one state independent of Denmark, and there was nothing Copenhagen could do to alter this. It spread despite the fact that the king, acting in fearful anticipation of events in the duchies, as well as under pressure from Germany, proclaimed his willingness to establish consultative assemblies in both duchies as well as provincial assembles in Denmark itself.

Provincial Assemblies and Reforms

In February 1831 he ordered legislation to establish four such assemblies, to the delight of politically mature Danes, but less to the liking of the Holsteiners, who saw this policy as running counter to their desire for a union between Holstein and Schleswig. Nevertheless, by the end of May preparations were completed and a royal proclamation issued establishing four assemblies, one each for Holstein and Schleswig, one for Jutland, and one for the islands. They were to be elected on a limited franchise, and they were to include representatives of the university and the clergy. Their functions were to be advisory and their spheres of influence limited. However, they were to have the right to petition the king for legislative proposals of their own. It was the object of the planners to make the four assemblies as similar to each other as possible, but they ended by giving those in the duchies greater rights to advise on local government.

Despite opposition it was decided not to place the budget before the assemblies, but in fact a statement of national finance was published the day before the first meeting of an assembly – and it gave ample scope for discussion. These four advisory assemblies were the first step in the process of moving from autocracy to democratic government. Even though it was only a modest step, giving the Danes nothing like the rights that the Norwegian people had been granted by Crown Prince Christian Frederik when he was regent there, it did mark the first occasion on which they had been able to have any say at all in the government of the country since the introduction of absolute rule in 1660.

Although the main lines for the assemblies were laid down in 1831, it took time to work out detailed proposals, and to arrange for elections. It was not until May 1834 that the final arrangements were made as to rules and eligibility for election. Only then was it announced that the assemblies would meet in Roskilde (70 deputies), Viborg (55), Schleswig (43), and Itzehoe (47), none of them major centres of population, and all of them removed from possible sources of trouble. The position of Iceland and the Faroes was solved by allowing them representatives in the Roskilde assembly, which was the first to start functioning, in October 1835.

There were no political parties, but delegates, who were more representative of the country than might have been expected from the limited franchise rules, soon divided into two broad camps of conservatives and liberals, with the liberals predominating. Under the leadership of Tage Algreen-Ussing the liberal faction demanded public knowledge of the workings of the state, especially of state finances, and they also worked for improved standards of education in schools other than grammar schools and for the abolition of press censorship. The farming community found champions in this group, but its views were not radical enough for some of the intellectuals and students under the leadership of Orla Lehmann. However, the division between the two liberal groups was not so big as to prevent co-operation between Algreen-Ussing and Lehmann.

Despite the agricultural reforms at the end of the eighteenth century, the farming community had not achieved anything like complete freedom, and moves got under way in the assemblies to improve the status of the farmers. On the whole the farmers were loyal to the king, remembering that it was the Crown which had granted their reforms. Now, however, they wanted more : greater opportunity to own their own land and complete freedom from *hoveri*. They also wanted to see conscription, which was still limited to the agricultural community, widened to include others than themselves. A petition to this effect was delivered to the king, but Frederik rejected it out of hand, thereby losing much of the support he had hitherto enjoyed. The farmers' sense of loyalty waned, and they turned to the liberal members of the assemblies for support, forming together with them the *Bondevennernes Selskab*, the Society of Friends of the Farmers, in May 1846.

In fact a limited reform programme was quickly carried out under pressure from this group. Although the main object – the enforced sale of land to those farming it – was not carried out until 1919, agricultural reforms were started in 1848. The condition of smallholders was improved, and conscription was extended beyond the farming community. In spring 1849 a commission was set up to look into further proposals for reform, the most important of which was perhaps the establishment of *Kreditforeninger* (Credit Societies), which attracted small savers and helped finance those farmers who by one means or another managed to buy the land they were working. These societies were one of the first expressions of the co-operative spirit which later in the century, and right up to the present day, was to be one of the main forces behind Danish agriculture. A similar venture to the Credit Societies was the establishment of the Zealand Farmers' Savings Bank in 1856, again intended to be run by the farming community for its own benefit, and partly with the object of freeing it from pressures from outside.

This increasing liberalisation in agriculture was accompanied by a liberalisation of trade and trading conditions in Denmark. In the 1840s the liberal trade principles of Adam Smith won increasing support in Copenhagen, where internal trade was still based largely on medieval principles, with the guilds and their anti-quated rules still predominating. The first politicians to put free internal trade in their programme were the Friends of the Farmers, who adopted it in 1846; but it was not finally put into effect until 1857. The new proposals were radical in scope and did away completely with the guild system and also with the old monopoly of trade in the market towns. Now anyone was free to pursue any trade anywhere, and the field was cleared for much-needed improvements.

Almost symbolically, the old-fashioned street-lighting by oil lamps was done away with that same year, and gas-lighting was introduced into Copenhagen, while the old Sound Dues were also abolished, thus making the use of Copenhagen more attractive for shipping than had previously been the case. The capital had rapidly been losing ground to Hamburg as a trading centre. Private banks were now being formed for the first time in Denmark and made a further contribution to the growth of trade under the initial leadership of C. F. Tietgen, who had first-hand experience of English methods and hoped to introduce them into Denmark.

Further help to trade within Denmark came from the opening of the railways, the first line, ironically enough, being that between Altona and Kiel in Holstein. This came into use in 1844, nineteen years after the first English railway and nine years after the first in Germany. By 1870 the railway system of today had in essence been laid out. Thus, it is true to say that by the 1860s both agriculture and trade, as well as industry, had been provided with the foundation for a period of expansion, so necessary for Denmark's survival after the loss of Schleswig and Holstein.

King Christian VIII, who succeeded Frederik VI in 1839, fulfilled much of his promise as a reformer. In addition to agriculture and trade reforms, his reign saw the overhauling of local government, a new charter for the government of Copenhagen, and a new law on the administration of rural communities. Yet although the reign of Christian was one of progress in these important, though limited, fields, it was one of *struggle* for reform in the wider constitutional field. Denmark possessed no real constitution, apart from the Royal Constitution (*Kongeloven*), which had established absolute rule in the seventeenth century. As Crown Prince and regent of Norway, Christian had granted that country the most liberal constitution in Europe. Danish liberals had looked forward to his accession to the throne of Denmark in the hope and firm expectation that he would do the same there. But Christian became more conservative with age, and aimed instead at maintaining the benevolent depotism which had developed over the

4—D • •

past 150 years. Consequently, although willing to introduce specific and limited reforms, he was not prepared to alter the traditional basis of government.

Towards a Constitution for All

However, the wish to rule autocratically was not the sole reason for Christian VIII's refusal of a constitution. By this refusal he was not merely seeking to perpetuate the internal *status quo* in Denmark, but also to avoid the complications over Schleswig and Holstein which would inevitably arise in any attempt to write a specific constitution spelling out the relationship between the duchies and Denmark proper. The king sought to maintain the existing relationship between them, to follow what was known as the *Unified State* policy, according to which the kingdom of Denmark and the duchies of Schleswig, Holstein, and now Lauenburg, should be unified under the one Head of State. This policy was opposed within Denmark itself by the *Ejder Policy*, the adherents of which wanted to incorporate Schleswig into the kingdom proper and make a break with Holstein and Lauenburg. Finding a reasonable compromise was made more difficult because neither of the Danish solutions suited Schleswig-Holsteiners now the movement for national independence had begun. Although many of the inhabitants of Schleswig were Danish-speaking, while the remainder of the population of the duchies spoke German, there was a sense of unity between them, and they refused to be partitioned. The two duchies must at all costs remain united, if necessary independently of Denmark. This solution, of course, found no favour in Denmark itself, and so any possible move was likely to cause intense dissatisfaction in one camp or the other. Yet the existing situation could not be maintained, partly because of the growing national feeling in the duchies and partly because of the demand of the liberal-minded Danes for a constitution. Consequently the constitutional struggle in Denmark became inextricably bound up with the Schleswig-Holstein question, and as no one would give way, an open conflict was seen as inevitable, especially later in the century when Bismarck began to develop his own aspirations in that quarter.

The question was further complicated at this stage by the dynastic problem. It was already fairly clear that Christian VIII's son, later Frederik VII, would be the last of the Oldenburg dynasty. In Denmark itself there was a possibility of a female succession, but the Holsteiners would not accept this, and the attitude in Schleswig was doubtful. The Schleswig-Holstein Assembly, in an attempt to avoid the danger that the Danish succession laws might be extended to Schleswig-Holstein, adopted a resolution demanding independence and indivisibility under the house of Augustenburg, to which the king replied by publishing an open letter maintaining the Danish succession laws in Denmark proper, Schleswig, and Lauenburg, but admitting some doubt as to Holstein. Again the seeds of discontent were not merely being sown, but were being given ample opportunity to germinate.

Partly under the influence of this pressure from the south, the Danes began to look to the other Scandinavian countries for support, and indeed Lehmann even went to the extent of suggesting a Nordic federation. The supporters of the *Pan-Scandinavian* movement could think of no reason why such a union as had once existed should not be revived, especially as the desire came this time from the people, in contrast to the original union which had been purely political. There was great enthusiasm among certain elements throughout Scandinavia, especially students and intellectuals, not merely because of pressure from Germany, but also because of a certain distrust of Russian motives, and there was a feeling that a united Scandinavia would be a power to be reckoned with. The first climax to the movement came at a meeting of students in Copenhagen in 1845, when there was almost ecstatic support for the idea, too ecstatic to be long-lived, as was plainly shown by subsequent events.

In the course of the 1840s, certain changes occurred in the attitudes of the politicians who dominated the assemblies. Until 1848, when the liberals organised themselves into a group, there were no real parties as such. Some of those individuals who had previously been radical in their approach had become more conservative, and in general the liberal group had become more nationalistic in their outlook and had earned the name of National Liberals. The Friends of the Farmers were still the radicals among the politicians. Outwardly the National Liberals were *national*, and inwardly *liberal*, and after making gains throughout the forties they prevailed upon the king to grant a constitution. He ordered a draft to be made, and it was his intention to discuss the recommendations on 6 January 1848. Before he could do so, he was taken ill and died on 20 January. Despite hesitations, his successor, Frederik VII, was persuaded to pursue the constitutional proposals, and signed a declaration on 28 January 1848 to this effect. The final result was to be a constitution – of strikingly liberal bent – which took effect on 5 June 1849, guaranteeing religious freedom, freedom of speech, and the general liberty of the individual. The legislative power was to go to a *Rigsdag* elected by popular vote, and this *Rigsdag* should consist of two chambers, the *Folketing* and the *Landsting*, the latter being elected on a more restricted franchise in order to give it a more conservative character. The king was no longer an absolute monarch, but he was given real political power, as his signature was necessary before any bill could become law, while he was entirely at liberty to choose his own Ministers, irrespective of the composition of the *Rigsdag*. The unity of the kingdom and the duchies was maintained, each being given equal status. The duchies, however, were far from being convinced that this equality would exist anywhere but on paper.

The Duchies' Reaction and the 1848 War

This distrust combined with the upsurge of national feeling that swept through Germany after the 1848 revolution in France, and there was a movement to establish a provincial government in Schleswig-Holstein and to include the whole area in the German Confederation. It was finally decided to send a delegation to Copenhagen to seek a common constitution for Schleswig and Holstein and to ask permission for Schleswig to join the German Confederation, which meant in effect that Denmark would be giving up control of Schleswig. The immediate Danish reaction was to maintain the old Unified State policy, but this led to a ministerial crisis brought about by the National Liberals, which was only resolved by the appointment of a new ministry consisting of a coalition of conservatives and National Liberals intent on forcing through the Ejder policy. More significant than the change of policy was perhaps the fact that King Frederik VII on this occasion, 22 March 1848, declared that he would henceforth consider himself to be a constitutional monarch. Absolutism was finally at an end in Denmark.

The new ministry now made a final offer to the Schleswig-Holstein delegation. Holstein and Lauenburg would be granted a free constitution and be free to join the German Confederation. Schleswig, meanwhile, would be united to Denmark, but would be allowed its own diet and freedom in its internal administration. This proposal was not acceptable to the Schleswig-Holsteiners, who, in an attempt to break away, hastily formed their own provisional government in Kiel. War was clearly imminent, and Denmark mobilised.

Left to themselves the Schleswig-Holsteiners had no hope. By weight of arms the Danes gained the upper hand, and Frederik VII entered Flensburg. At this point, however, Prussia, spurred on by the desire for German unification, sent an army of 12,000 men to the north, and this, together with forces from the other German states, faced the Danish army with an enemy 30,000 strong. There was nothing for it but to withdraw to Funen, and a Prussian army entered Jutland.

Although Britain and France had guaranteed the status of Schleswig in 1720, and Russia had done the same in 1773, Denmark sought support only from Britain. It was refused, and an offer of mediation made instead. Meanwhile Russia succeeded in her insistence on a Prussian withdrawal, and after a sudden attack on the remaining German troops, made with the help of a contingent of Swedish soldiers sent as a symbol of Pan-Scandinavian sentiments, Denmark accepted a cease-fire, together with Britain's offer of mediation.

Britain, together with most of the other major powers, saw a partition of Schleswig along the language border as a reasonable solution, but this the Danes would not countenance, and they even went to the length of drawing up a new constitution including Schleswig as an integral part of Denmark. It was still their intention to unite the two realms, and on 26 February 1849 Denmark announced an end to the truce. At the beginning of April hostilities recommenced. By now, thanks to universal conscription, the Danish army had been increased to 41,000 men, which had to face a German – Schleswig-Holstein force of some 65,000. After an initial defeat the Danes withdrew to Fredericia, but on 6 July they broke out and inflicted a resounding defeat on the enemy.

The battle of Fredericia has gone down in history as a glorious Danish victory. In one of his novels M. A. Goldschmidt refers to it as 'that glorious battle, one of the few known to history which almost seemed to be the work of a poet : an epic single combat in vast dimensions with a personal enmity between the 16,000 on the one side and the 16,000 on the other....' And Goldschmidt sees the victory as 'a dawn which after the passage of centuries once more sees the Nordic character rugged and indomitable, warriors who "without tactics" tramp, crawl, strike and bite their way to victory'.

Four days later a new truce was signed, and a commission consisting of one Prussian, one Dane, and one Englishman was set up to govern Schleswig, the southern part of which was occupied by Prussian troops, the northern part by Norwegians and Swedes. Provisional agreement was reached to give Schleswig its own constitution and not to tie it more closely either to Denmark or to Holstein. This was unacceptable to the Schleswig-Holsteiners, and when an unconditional peace was signed between Denmark and Prussia in 1850, they decided to fight on alone, despite the London Protocol of 4 July acknowledging the indivisibility of the Danish kingdom, and signed by Russia, Britain, France, Sweden – Norway, and subsequently Austria, a declaration which in theory re-established the Unified State policy. Without the active support of Prussia, Schleswig-Holstein could not hope to win against Denmark, and its army was defeated in the bloody battle of Isted and subsequently again when it tried to make a stand at Dannevirke, the ancient fortification west of the town of Schleswig. Under pressure from Russia, Prussia agreed not only to refrain from fighting, but in fact to oppose Schleswig-Holstein nationalism, and accordingly the provisional government was dissolved in New Year 1851.

A Dual Constitution – and Its Results

Thus Denmark, on the face of it, had won a great victory, although this final outcome was to a considerable extent the result of Russia's fear of nationalist movements and the pressure it exerted on Prussia. Moreover, Prussia herself, considering both Schleswig and Holstein to be German territory, and knowing Holstein to be already a member of the German Confederation and thus susceptible to German influence, preferred to see them both under partial Danish control rather than have Holstein outside and Schleswig completely within Danish jurisdiction. In any case Prussia was not sympathetic towards the radical nationalism in Schleswig-Holstein itself. Thus there was in effect a return to the original position, to the old Unified State policy, which for so long had been hateful to the Schleswig-Holsteiners, and which after the bitterness caused by the fighting was to prove even less palatable to them. The settlement was enshrined in the *Agreements of 1851 and 1852* which laid down that Denmark should henceforth consist of three parts : the kingdom, Schleswig, and Holstein with Lauenburg. Nothing should be done to tie Schleswig closer to either Denmark or Holstein; Holstein and Lauenburg should be free to continue membership of the German Confederation; the Danish constitution should not be valid in the duchies, which should each have assemblies with legislative powers. The following year the Treaty of London decided on the inheritance of the Danish throne : if Frederik VII should die without a male heir, Prince Christian of Glücksborg was placed next in line for the succession, which was to continue in his male line.

The agreements of 1851 and 1852 were not expressed in a new constitution until 1855. It was obvious that the liberal constitution of 1849 would have to be limited in some way, as it could no longer, according to the agreement, be valid for Schleswig and Holstein as well as for Denmark. The duchies were promised regional assemblies to settle their internal affairs, and then, after lengthy negotiations, and to the consternation of the liberals in the *Rigsdag*, the 1849 constitution was limited to internal matters in Denmark proper, while arrangements were made for a new common constitution for the duchies and Denmark – in other words, a constitution covering foreign policy and general finance and defence. The legislative body for this common constitution was to be called the *Rigsraad*, to consist of eighty members, of whom eighteen were to be elected by the *Rigsdag*, twelve by the Schleswig and Holstein diets, thirty by popular vote, and the remainder appointed by the king. Thus Denmark was for a time in the peculiar position of having two national assemblies, the *Rigsdag* for internal affairs and a more conservative *Rigsraad* for foreign affairs and for matters common to the kingdom and the duchies. The hope was that this constitution would unite the entire realm. It did not, and national differences emerged clearly at the outset when the new *Rigsraad* met and was immediately found to include Holstein members who spoke no Danish. To make matters worse, the Holstein Assembly refused to recognise the constitution.

Outside Denmark, the new constitution was accepted by Prussia and Austria, but opposition grew throughout the other German states. In 1856 Prussia and Austria complained that the 1851–52 agreements were being broken, and that the new version of the Unified State policy was linking Holstein too closely to Denmark. A change of Prime Minister in Denmark in 1857 was intended to symbolise a more accommodating attitude and a move away from the Unified State, but the Holsteiners were still not satisfied. The matter was brought up at the Diet of the German Confederation, and in 1858 the deputies issued a declaration to the effect that the common constitution was not valid for Holstein and Lauenburg. In May an ultimatum was served on Denmark and the common constitution was annulled for the two duchies – an action which quietened the Germans for the time being. This was in effect a move back to the Ejder policy, which found support among both the National Liberals and the Farmers' Party, and was the obvious solution to the adherents of the Pan-Scandinavian movement.

Meanwhile proposals and counter-proposals on the status of Holstein were made and rejected, and in 1860 Schleswig complained of Danish pressures. Again Prussia complained that Denmark was not keeping the 1851–52 agreements, and threatened to intervene in the dispute. In 1861 an ultimatum was served on Denmark, giving her six weeks to arrange affairs to the satisfaction of Prussia. The great powers also exerted pressure on Denmark to reach a settlement. Denmark refused, but did agree to direct negotiations with Prussia. This concession, however, was marred by the fact that bowing to the nationalism of public opinion the Danish Prime Minister, C. C. Hall, made the Ejder policy official. He was not impressed with Bismarck when he met him, though even then Bismarck knew what he wanted, and consequently gave no ground. At the same time Britain, whose assistance Palmerston had promised in July 1863, announced her support for the German demands, thanks to the pro-German policy of Queen Victoria.

Relying now on support from Norway and Sweden, Denmark rejected all complaints, prepared for war, and in March 1863 incorporated Schleswig into Denmark proper and separated Holstein and Lauenburg from the kingdom. The hope was that Prussia would be too occupied with the Polish rebellion against Russia to intervene. The German reaction, however, was to threaten to occupy Holstein and Lauenburg if the constitution were not restored. But the Danes had now gone too far to retreat, and consequently a new common constitution for Denmark and Schleswig was passed in the November of 1863, though by only three votes more than the required two-thirds majority and in the face of grave warnings. Even then it almost lost the royal assent, as Frederik VII died two days later, to be succeeded by Prince Christian of Glücksborg as Christian IX. The new king was not sympathetic to the new constitution, but finally signed it, though he was perfectly aware of the probable consequences.

Bismarck again demanded a return to the 1851–52 agreements, and as Denmark received no support from other sources, not even from Sweden – where the government was less eager than the king to embark on military adventures – Saxon and Hanoverian troops entered Holstein on 24 December 1863. Denmark was not prepared to fight there and withdrew to Schleswig. The Danish Prime Minister, D. G. Monrad, played for time, but Prussia refused to wait, and invaded Schleswig without warning. The Danes were outnumbered and their equipment was inferior. They retreated to and then beyond the Dannevirke fortifications, much to the dismay of the general populace, who had been convinced that Denmark would win as she had done before.

Danish intransigence was partly responsible for the failure of a peace conference called in London, and in June 1864 Prussia invaded Denmark proper. Denmark had little support from outside, and even Pan-Scandinavian enthusiasm led to nothing but limited support from Swedish – Norwegian volunteers. Hopes for official support from Sweden remained unfulfilled.

Monrad was blamed for the Danish failure and dismissed. The new government under C. A. Bluhme sued for peace and accepted humiliating conditions from Prussia. Denmark had to renounce all rights to the three duchies, which meant that about a third of the territory was lost, together with a third of the population. Denmark had shrunk to her smallest ever size since the formation of the kingdom many centuries before. The process of humiliation which had begun with the Napoleonic Wars was now complete and all dreams of glory were dashed.

The Economic Situation

Although by 1864 Denmark was politically at a lower ebb than at almost any time in her history, economically the country was considerably better off than at the beginning of the century. After some years of prosperity at the end of the eighteenth century, the years of the Napoleonic Wars had been accompanied by raging inflation, so much so that by 1812 the currency had dropped to one-fourteenth of its face value. Money was now supplied by the expedient of printing more, and although some effort was made to stem the inflation by increased taxation, this was not entirely effective. Because of the prospect of the imminent fall of the currency, speculation in foreign currencies increased, and attempts to stop it were scarcely successful. Indeed, the king himself indulged in it.

As a consequence, on 5 January 1813, Frederik VI proclaimed the bankruptcy of the kingdom of Denmark. The nation's bank, the *Kurantbank*, established during the period of mercantilism in the eighteenth century, was closed and replaced by the *Rigsbank*, and all paper money was called in to be exchanged. For six *kurantdaler* one *rigsdaler* was issued, and even then the value was fixed at only five-eighths of par. In other words, the real reduction in money was to be to about one-tenth of its former face value, in addition to which property-owners had to pay a proportion of their property values to the state, if necessary by taking out state mortgages on hard terms. In 1818 the *Rigsbank* was again replaced, this time by the *Nationalbank*, an autonomous institution outside the immediate direction of the state. Despite further falls in value – at one time to only 6 per cent of par, corresponding to only one per cent of the old currency values – the new *Nationalbank* succeeded by means of a strict control of the amount of paper money in circulation in bringing the *daler* back up to par by 1838.

Meanwhile the country had suffered. In particular agriculture had at an early stage got into serious difficulties, and a full-scale agricultural crisis developed around 1818 and lasted for a full ten years. This was a direct consequence of war, and corresponded to increasing agricultural production throughout Europe as troops returned to more estimable work than shooting each other. With increasing output came falling prices, and in their wake came the English Corn Laws in 1815, which hit Danish exports badly. This was especially a disaster for Denmark, as Danish corn was of low quality. The farmers' position was further complicated because many of them were in debt, having taken advantage of the eighteenth-century reforms and bought their own land. They were faced with enormous problems in paying off their debts, and many went bankrupt, while some few returned to a leasehold arrangement. Ironically, leaseholders came out of the agricultural crisis better than freeholders, as many of the dues were still paid in kind.

The repercussions of the agricultural crisis spread quickly throughout the community, hitting first shopkeepers and merchants in small towns, and then spreading to the larger towns. There they merged with crises which had reigned in Copenhagen business circles since 1816, and a series of bankruptcies rocked the business world.

The state did its best to help. Taxes on agriculture were reduced and then farmers were allowed to pay some of their taxes in kind. Next the price of corn paid in tax was raised to above market level, and finally paper money was accepted instead of silver for taxes paid in currency. The state also arranged for loans to farmers, but even then some went bankrupt, the state taking over their farms, only to have to sell them at a loss. Help for industry came in a relaxation of duty on many raw materials, with the object of enabling industry to start moving and to be self-supporting. But it all took a desperately long time. Nevertheless, the agricultural crisis was eventually overcome, and the economic situation was eased. The first sign of a change came with the liberalisation of the British Corn Laws in 1827 and 1828, which gave Denmark access to an important foreign market once more. At the same time the price of corn and other commodities in Europe began to rise with increasing demand based on the rise in population which became evident after the Napoleonic Wars. In the wake of the rising prices came a new optimism, which resulted in the gradual increase of land prices in Denmark. Between 1830 and 1845 prices rose by about 160 per cent in the richer agricultural districts. By 1863 they had doubled again.

There was also a change in attitude on the part of the farmers, the younger members of the community being the first generation to have benefited from the school reforms introduced in 1814. However imperfect the working of the system had been, owing to the economic difficulties, it had met with limited, yet increasing, success, and its effects were now being felt. The farmers were more receptive to new ideas and were willing to adopt new methods of culti-

all his activities are enclosed.
community, all the individual
to the predominant social int
economic, intellectual, æsthetic
vidual are included in the stoc
controlled by it. Every cultu
through the mediacy of this
character of the relations betw
primary and fundamental com
tinually referred to this comp
character directly from this re
education in such a group is
object from the standpoint of tl
Every situation is first of all t
ondarily as an economic, religi

The adaptation of the indivi
fore, that all his attitudes be s
itself becomes for him a criteri
attitudes are the *desire for res*
in the primary group-organizat
sponding to the traditionally s
which the social opinion of th
desire for response is the tenc
reaction to an action whose o

vation and accept modern implements. They had also realised the necessity of improving the quality of their products if they were, in the long run, to maintain the rise in exports. It should also be remembered that this new and more enlightened generation of farmers was expressing itself through the Friends of the Farmers in the provincial assemblies. They were the transitional generation, marking the change from the eighteenth-century peasant to the highly skilled farmer of the end of the nineteenth century.

Agriculture still accounted for more than half of the working population in Denmark, and as its increasing difficulties twenty years before had affected the remainder of the community, so better conditions now brought about an improvement in trade and general living standards. Industry benefited too, but it must be noted that there was relatively little organised industry as such in Denmark. It has been said, and with some reason, that Denmark was comparable more to central European countries at this time than with western Europe. There was no real industrial revolution there, and while the country lagged behind the major industrialised countries, it was free from the social problems brought about by the industrial revolution in England, Germany, France, and Belgium. When the change did come, relatively late, those responsible for dealing with the problems had gained in worldly wisdom and could learn from other countries' experience. The consequence was a very advanced means of dealing with the problems of industry, from which Denmark emerged in the forefront of industrialised countries. This late and sophisticated adaptation to the industrial age has doubtless had far-reaching effects on Denmark in the twentieth century.

Little wonder then that the years from 1813 to about 1840 were a period when Denmark was without a foreign policy. There was no energy and no resources to do anything except improve the country's financial status. The national outlook was limited by this, and it was a period of *petit-bourgeois* conformism, during which Frederik VI became as restricted as his people, an absolute monarch with narrow ideals, who was dutifully applauded by his loyal subjects when he was rowed around the canals in Frederiksberg Park on a Sunday afternoon. This was indeed symbolical of his position and outlook, and of those of his subjects. For despite misfortunes, he remained by and large a popular king who seemed to reflect his age. As well as being an absolute monarch, he was a citizen king who was close to his people and loved by them. 'Only one feeling really united high and low alike, both sexes and all ages : respect for the king', wrote the dramatist Thomas Overskou in his autobiography.

The Position of the King

Just how close he was to them is also reflected in Hans Christian Andersen's autobiography, *The Fairy Tale of My Life*, when he tells how in his early days in Copenhagen he had tried to find, and succeeded in finding, patrons who would help him on his way. One of them, Jonas Collin, seeing in Andersen not a writer of future international fame but a boy who, given a decent education, would be able to make a contribution to the life of his country and become a useful citizen, went to the king for financial support for Andersen – and got it. This was the action of the absolute king, and the populace at large preferred to view him in this light rather than dwell on his political ineptness. Bishop Mynster, the Primate of Denmark, was probably giving voice to the general feeling on the king's death in 1839 when he wrote :

> None of us was left alone on earth as long as we had him. What comforted me was the fact that difficult times were ahead, which, weakened by old age, he would have been less able to meet : and it would have given me great pain to see my old king as a mere shadow of what he had been, guiding the state with an uncertain hand in face of the breaking storms.

The bishop's doubt as to whether the king would have been able to rule successfully in the coming years is obvious, but what is equally significant is the feeling that 'none of us', none of the Danes, was friendless as long as Frederik was alive. He took a direct and personal interest in his people's life and conditions, read criticisms of his administration in the newspapers, and if on starting investigations, he found the criticism justified, he took action. He was his own *ombudsman*. When he discovered corruption in the civil service in these difficult years, he stepped in and personally saw to it that it was dealt with. He was the absolute monarch, and he felt his people's wellbeing to be his personal responsibility. As the Swedish poet Geijer said of him, 'In his person Danish absolutism is almost certainly the most paternal on earth'. Yet Geijer linked this with the narrowness and lack of vision which certainly distinguished everyday life in Denmark at that period, and which were reflected in many aspects of Copenhagen life.

Life in Copenhagen

Copenhagen was in many ways a city of paradoxes. It was the capital city, but with a population of under 120,000, scarcely bigger than a provincial town in countries larger than Denmark, and, having lost its monopoly of overseas trade because of post-war reorganisation, was giving way in importance to the Danish provincial towns themselves. As far as size was concerned, however, there was a considerable margin : Odense was next with only 8,700 inhabitants, while of the other towns only Elsinore, Ålborg, Århus, and Randers exceeded 5,000. Nevertheless, their influence was growing because of their significance as trading centres, not least with Copenhagen's main rival, Hamburg, where credit was easier to come by. Yet in Copenhagen, the centre of Danish absolutism, the home of the civil and military authorities, the seat of the only university in the country, the ideas of liberty and equality which swept through Europe after the French Revolution were gradually making themselves felt. So far they were less obvious in the political field than in the realms of literature and religion.

The concept of individualism was asserting itself : the individual's right to his own ideas and beliefs, the literary swing away from the universality of Classicism to the Romantic cult of genius and individuality. There was the attempt to find a different metaphysical explanation to the problem of existence from that implicit in orthodox Lutheranism : Hans Christian Ørsted, the discoverer of electro-magnetism, tried to find a scientific-metaphysical explanation, while N. F. S. Grundtvig sought to combine patriotism with a personalised religion. Sectarian movements were also in evidence. Within the field of orthodoxy itself, Bishop Mynster sought to introduce a new spirituality after the barrenness of eighteenth-century rationalism. The transition to individualism is to be seen no less in the architecture of Copenhagen itself : after the fire of 1795 and the British bombardment of 1807, the ruined areas were gradually rebuilt. Whether through lack of funds after the state bankruptcy of 1813 or a predilection for the strict, unadorned lines of neo-Classicism – or a happy coincidence of both – the original task was assigned to C. F. Hansen, who planned the entire centre of Copenhagen on a neo-Classical pattern. The old City Hall (now the Law Courts), the adjacent prison, the Cathedral, and the Metropolitan School behind it, were the outstanding achievements in this genre, though there were many town houses of less impressive dimensions as well. Hansen was, however, unable to finish his work, and his successor Peder Malling, one of his pupils, introduced a more individualistic style of neo-Gothic, and juxtaposed it to Hansen's buildings in his design for Copenhagen University. In architecture the transition from the controlled lines of Classicism to the bolder inventiveness of individualism came later than in other spheres, but its evolution followed the general pattern, and the outstanding buildings of the 1840s are varied and individualised, like St Ansgar's Church and the Synagogue in Krystalgade.

It was not, however, until the middle of the century that the transition from the old city to the modern capital really began to gather impetus. Until 1870 Copenhagen was still a city within its ramparts, as it had been for centuries. Permanent buildings were not allowed outside the gates within the immediate vicinity of the ramparts, and thus housing for the denser population had to be packed into the area which Copenhagen had occupied for the past 200 years. The result was a bewildering number of flats and houses packed together in a labyrinth of passages and courtyards, and overcrowding was appalling. In many cases two families are said to have had to live together in a single room.

The four gates to the city were shut at night until 1821, when Nørreport was left open to pedestrians – against payment of a toll. Carriage and coach could neither enter nor leave, and all wheeled traffic was forbidden in the city at night.

Even during the day few people drove to their destinations, as distances were short, although there were cabs for those who wanted them and, in a time of poverty, could afford them. Relatively few people went out at night to seek entertainment, and when they did so, they found the streets, already filthy and without drainage of any sort, ill lit by oil lamps. Even these were not lit on moonlight nights. Watchmen, in dress which corresponded to the antiquity of their task, patrolled the streets and called out the hours, as they had done since the seventeenth century :

Three O'clock

Now hastes black night away,
And morning fast approaches.
God, keep from us alway
All evils and reproaches.
　　The clock has now struck three.
　　Oh, Saviour bless'd,
　　Give grace and rest.
Let us keep faith with thee.

Klokken tre

Nu skrider Natten sorte,
Og Dagen stunder til,
Gud, lad dem blive borte,
Som os bedrøve vil :
Vor Klokk' er slagen tre.
　　O Fader from :
　　Vend Due os om
Din Naade os bete.

Entertainment

Entertainment was largely limited to private visits. People were fond of company, even though the entertainment they could offer was modest in proportion. At the same time some sort of café life was beginning to emerge, and though somewhat sordid at first, it began to brighten up and offer a more attractive and reputable form of diversion by the middle of the century. Restaurant life had been unknown in Denmark in the eighteenth century, but in the last decades what were known as *Schweizerkonditorier* – cafés serving cakes, liqueurs, punch, and chocolate – had begun to appear, and their numbers increased in the first decade of the nineteenth century. They were given impressive names, such as Gianelli, Pedrin, Pleisch, but according to the politician Orla Lehman, the names were their only charm as late as the 1830s :

> You entered an unpleasant murky room. On a series of small tables there were tallow candles in brass candle sticks, each accompanied by a small pair of iron scissors. They were not lit until a customer sat at the table, and then they were put out again as soon as he left. The customers sat with a glass of punch – and regular guests would have a long pipe which the waiter kept for them on the premises. They sat with a newspaper in their hands, or carried on halting conversations in a half whisper. It is impossible to imagine a less elevating sight than this sleepy finish to a sleepy day's work.

In the 1840s, however, with the opening of Kehlet's café, things improved, and cafés gradually became a recognised part of Copenhagen life.

There was little else in the way of public entertainment for the average Copenhagener, and when the weather was good he found his pleasure in walking about the capital – in the park on the eastern side of the city, in Kongens Have, the colonnades of Christiansborg, or on the ramparts themselves until they were demolished in 1870 – all well away from the stench of the overcrowded districts. In 1822 the Royal Art Gallery was opened, and in the winter this, together with the various museums, attracted a considerable number of visitors.

In good summer weather many citizens would walk outside the city boundaries, probably to Vesterbro, which became a popular place of amusement, and where a theatre for light entertainment was opened in 1801 by an Englishman named Price, who was later joined in the venture by his two brothers. One of the attractions of this theatre was Italian pantomime under Giuseppe Casorti, but when, in 1833, the Price brothers tried to introduce the more lavish

English pantomime, it was a failure. A walk beyond Vesterbro brought one to Frederiksberg Park, where a café was opened in 1813; but few went further than this unless they were going on what was a traditional annual outing in the forests around Copenhagen. Even then most people walked, and the route they followed was the inland road. The coastal road was little used in those days, and in parts it was covered by thick sand and virtually impassable. There are accounts of groups of trippers hiring a farm waggon to go that way, and all having to climb out and push the waggon along. It was not until relatively late in the century that this road was improved and made into the main road to the north of Zealand. There was little demand for improved communication along it, as pleasure-seekers by and large preferred the inland route. The sea did not have the romantic attraction in the nineteenth century which it has since acquired : it was considered cold and insensitive, and the Danes preferred the more idyllic surroundings inland. The cult of the idyll, perhaps thanks to Rousseau and the eighteenth century, held a great attraction for them, and those who had the opportunity spent the summer 'in the country', renting houses or rooms, depending on what they could afford, in the most idyllic spots available. A few wealthier families owned summer residences.

The pleasures of nature were, however, reserved for the summer. In the winter the people of Copenhagen were left to their own devices, to entertainment in the home, song and dance, and, occasionally for the more well-to-do, a private chamber concert. Interest in music was widespread, and these chamber concerts played a part in the lives of many cultured families, and gave Romantic composers such as Gade, Hartmann, and Rung a welcome outlet for their talents both as composers and performers. It was Hartmann who in 1850 founded the Copenhagen Music Society and thereby gave the Copenhageners their first opportunity of hearing classical orchestral music. Previous to this there had been sporadic performances of opera by an Italian group from 1842, which had proved popular, and in 1843 Jenny Lind had made her first appearance and carried the city by storm.

There was meanwhile one well-established source of public entertainment which enjoyed enormous popularity : the Royal Theatre. Then, as now, it put on a mixed programme, and it was the centre of Copenhagen cultural life. It enjoyed a social function also, attracting everyone who made any pretence of belonging to the cultured classes, and there was considerable competition to obtain tickets. As Hans Christian Andersen points out in *The Fairy Tale of My Life* :

At a time when politics played no part at all in Denmark, the theatre was the 'public interest', the most important theme of conversation for the day and the evening : the Royal Danish Theatre was probably also to be considered as one of the foremost in Europe : it certainly was in possession of considerable talent.

And he goes on :

Meanwhile, if I may be allowed to say so, the theatre was my club-room each evening : I still went there regularly. Just that year I had been given a seat in what was known as the 'Court Stalls', which were only separated from the rest of the stalls by an iron bar : it was the custom that every author who produced one play for the theatre was given a free seat in the pit : two plays gave him a seat in the pit stalls, and three gave him admittance to the 'Court Stalls' . . . the part of the stalls where the king gave seats to his courtiers, diplomats and leading officials . . . I, too, gained this honour. Thorvaldsen, Oehlenschläger, Weyse, and several others were there as well at the time.

Through Andersen's complacent-cum-childlike delight at being admitted to the Court Stalls, the reader perceives something of the esteem in which Copenhagen's major artistic talents were held. Perhaps this was the final expression of the patronage of an absolute monarch, but the populace as a whole derived a genuine and personal pride from the artistic achievements of the age, and in a city as small as Copenhagen the artists and literary figures themselves were as well known as television has made their modern counterparts in a more diffuse and impersonal society. It is a fact that when writing his pseudonymous works Søren Kierkegaard used deliberately to take regular short strolls through the streets of Copenhagen to give people the impression that he was wasting his time and to convince them that he could not possibly be writing. As for national pride in the achievements of one man, the return of Thorvaldsen from Italy was a national occasion on which the entire population of Copenhagen went to greet him – the sort of greeting reserved in this present age for lone sailors.

The Royal Theatre, a meeting-place for Copenhagen society, had nurtured the leading talents of the Danish literary scene. Adam Oehlenschläger, the first and in many ways the greatest of the Danish Romantics, had had his heroic dramas of the Ancient North performed there. Carsten Hauch, Oehlenschläger's contemporary, had seen his plays acted on the same stage. In the second generation of Romantics, Johan Ludvig Heiberg had been one of the leading attractions, and Hans Christian Andersen himself had both light plays and operas, for which he had written the libretti, produced there. To have a play performed in such surroundings was the token of success, of acceptance as a writer of talent, and – as Andersen also points out – it was the writer's best source of income.

The Literary Scene

The catastrophic economic conditions and the difficult political situation in the first half of the nineteenth century, when its new and impotent role forced the country to turn its gaze inwards, nevertheless formed the background of an unprecedented burgeoning of Danish literature. The period from 1803 to about 1830 is known as the Golden Age – an era of grandiose achievement, high Romantic tragedy, rolling verse, historical novel, and deeply felt and inspired hymns. If any period can belie the theory that literature cannot flourish in a period of national collapse, it is this epoch of Danish history. As it is possible to consider Copenhagen as a city of paradoxes, so it is possible to talk of the great cultural paradox, the fact that this age of political humiliation gave birth to one of Denmark's supreme literary achievements – a process to be repeated later in the century.

The apparent paradox hinged, however, on the coincidence of a number of factors : first, the arrival of the Romantic philosophy of Schelling, brought to Denmark from Germany by Henrik Steffens. This in itself had an immediate liberating influence after the constrictions of the end of the Enlightenment. It gave the philosophical foundation to a new attitude to literature and enabled writers to indulge in new literary forms and to renew the literary language. It taught, among other things, the idea of the unity of nature and the spirit, of past and present, the unity indeed of all things; and as examples of this unity, writers treated Nordic themes in literary forms which belonged to the South, while historical themes suddenly took on a new significance for the present time. Accordingly dramas and epic poems appeared dealing with the heroic age of Scandinavia, written by Oehlenschläger, Grundtvig, and Hauch, while Ingemann wrote his historical novels in the manner of Walter Scott. This movement was accompanied by what is known as the Aladdin motif, after the idea which Oehlenschläger expressed in his play *Aladdin*. This deals with the theory that certain people are chosen by nature, or God, or the gods, to achieve greatness, and that nothing can succeed in stopping them, however weak and ill-suited they may otherwise seem. Thus Aladdin is shown not to deserve the greatness which is thrust upon him, but all the machinations of Noureddin, the sorcerer, in fact the representative of eighteenth-century rationalism, cannot prevent him from winning the princess.

The twin themes of former national greatness and of the possibility of being chosen to be great, despite all appearances, assumed a special significance for Denmark after 1814. Romantic-patriotic drama dealing with the heroic past appealed to a population looking for an escape from the sordid present, and served as a source of inspiration for many years. At the same time the Aladdin conception also took on new proportions : it was not only of use as a literary theme, but it could be applied to individuals – Oehlenschläger felt that he himself exemplified it, as did Hans Christian Andersen – and it was also possible to apply it to a country. Denmark began to see herself as an Aladdin, especially after 1848 when Prussia was forced to climb down. The fact that this was largely due to the pressure of more powerful nations was ignored, and some romantic and patriotic Danes saw themselves in the role of an Aladdin, chosen to be great, and not to be prevented even by such a powerful nation as Prussia. There is little doubt that this upsurge of national self-assurance and implicit faith in what nowadays might be referred to as a country's destiny was largely responsible for the climate of public opinion which forced events towards the catastrophe of 1864. The final defeat then, coming after a period of growing self-confidence, gave a staggering blow to national self-assurance and had an effect which can only be described as traumatic.

Meanwhile, although the Aladdin theme had certainly survived as long as this, the other, escapist, aspect of the Romantic Age had gradually been replaced in the 1830s by what is known as poetical realism. The new generation of writers concentrated more on a mixture of fantasy and realism based on contemporary Denmark, and especially on life in Copenhagen. This process coincided again with the emergence from the financial doldrums and the approach to parity of the currency, reached in 1838. With this increasing affluence, and the retreat in time of the Napoleonic Wars, nationalism and escapism, typical of the Golden Age, became less attractive and less relevant, while the present began no longer to seem something to escape from.

Thus Poul Martin Møller could write his character poems *Scenes from Rosenborg Have* and his unfinished novel *The Adventures of a Danish Student*, both of which are distinctly and firmly based on contemporary Copenhagen, and written with a deftness of touch and a humour long absent from Danish literature. The first generation of Romantics, filled with an awed sense of their divine calling, had taken themselves very seriously : but the second generation felt themselves less as chosen tools of the gods and could thus use a lighter style. Even J. L. Heiberg, the chief exponent of Hegelian philosophy in Denmark, and a man who took his philosophical work with extreme seriousness, built up a reputation on his light and charming plays which he called vaudevilles – again an elegant fantasy, inspired by recognisable elements of everyday life in Copenhagen. Although he transcends this school, Hans Christian Andersen really belongs to it, and many of his fairy tales, and even more so his novels and plays, are closely tied to the Denmark and Copenhagen he knew – witness the Copenhagen of *Ole Lukøie* and parts of *The Tinder Box*, and the quite specific and recognisable mansions described at the beginning and end of *The Ugly Duckling*. Even Søren Kierkegaard had close affinities with the school in the novels which form part of his work – notably *The Diary of a Seducer*, in which the Copenhagen scene is an integral part.

N. F. S. Grundtvig and the High Schools

Outstanding among all these writers in his significance for contemporary and subsequent Danish cultural life was Nicolai Frederik Severin Grundtvig. In international stature far slighter than the other two giants of his day, Kierkegaard and Andersen, Grundtvig was a baffling mixture of poet, theologian, educationalist, and prophet. Theologically speaking, he was something of a sectarian, but he was never excluded from the state Church and was able to found one of the two main wings of the Danish Church as it exists today; though in another country he might well have suffered the fate of a Wesley. Certainly Grundtvig was at one time placed under state censorship for his criticism of the rationalist teachings of some leading theologians, and attempts were made to limit his freedom to preach. In his Romantic mixture of patriotism and Christianity he also expressed that trend towards individualism which was an essential aspect of Romanticism in Denmark as elsewhere, and which in Danish minds was linked with the idea of genius. The search for the individual and the desire to give to the individual the opportunity to express himself was also one of the motive forces behind Grundtvig's idea of the high school, a product of Danish Romanticism which has played a formative role in the life of the ordinary people difficult to overestimate. Having suffered from the old grammar-school tradition of education, Grundtvig was determined to work for a school of a different type. During a stay in England in 1829, he was fired by the dynamism he found there, and which he saw as springing from the English ideal of freedom, which he could only contrast with the passiveness of the benevolent autocracy of his native land. One feature which particularly impressed him was the growth of liberal studies and learning in the newly-founded London University (now University College London), itself an expression of the achievement of freedom from tradition. This, combined with the community spirit which he found in the Cambridge colleges, was instrumental in inspiring Grundtvig with his vision of a 'high school in Sorø'.

There was no thought of establishing a new Danish university on the lines of either Cambridge or London. Grundtvig, for all his learning, had too much patriotic and missionary zeal to be interested in establishing an exclusive academic institution. His idea was to start something which could be a seat of general learning divorced from the examination-ridden grammar schools, the 'black schools' as he called them. The original intention of founding such an institution at Sorø was shelved and finally abandoned. Instead, the first high school was opened at Rødding in 1844, as part of the effort to support Danish culture in the areas close to the German border – a move connected with the reaction to German encroachment after the Danish–Prussian wars, and as such a symbol of the true function of the high schools : to foster Danish patriotic sentiments and combine them with a liberal Christian outlook : 'Man first : then Christian', as Grundtvig himself put it. Not merely this, but the schools were intended largely to attract students from the rural areas and give them some feeling for cultural values.

Under the leadership of Christen Kold rather than Grundtvig himself the schools were a great success, and attracted large numbers of young adults from country districts. Although the movement was originally Grundtvigian, the idea was taken up by the more extreme evangelical wing of the Danish Church, Inner Mission, and a number of Social Democrat institutions have also been added to the list. To this day the high school is a flourishing institution, with a much wider horizon than in the nineteenth century; although the new educational opportunities offered by mass media and by university extension courses and evening classes in most parts of the country have caused numbers to diminish.

It is perhaps difficult to estimate the influence of the high-school movement on Danish life as a whole, however easy it is to produce statistics and figures. Nevertheless, it may not be hypothetical to suggest that it is responsible for the genuine interest in culture and art, so strikingly widespread in modern Denmark, and ultimately responsible for the proportionately large number of books read by Danes. Together with this interest in what may be termed 'artistic' culture goes the popularity of folk art, also a striking feature of the Danish scene today and probably connected with the good taste

of which the Danes are so justly proud. For Romantic though the
Grundtvigian movement was – and still is in essence – the Romantic view of history and its relevance to the present fostered
a real sense of the unity of Danish culture throughout the ages,
which has found its ultimate expression is much new Danish design
combining modernity with tradition.

Ecclesiastical Strains

Theologically speaking, Grundtvig was an individualist in a
rather different sense, in that he was one of many at that time who
rebelled against the conformity of the previous age and sought to
find a new and more living expression for the Christian faith. During the eighteenth century, rationalism had succeeded in removing
all truly metaphysical aspects of Christianity and reducing it to
little more than a moral code. The move away from this came with
Romanticism at the beginning of the nineteenth century, and
while Bishop Mynster sought to preserve the unity of the Danish
Church at the same time as he introduced a more spiritual element
into it, Grundtvig and others like him sought to introduce completely foreign elements. The ordinary people had found the
Lutheran Church unsympathetic and drifted towards these new
teachers and others whose teaching was further removed from
the Lutheran orthodoxy – Baptists and Methodists were perhaps
chief amongst these, but there were also Moravians and numerous
other small sects, some of which, being run by laymen, were put
down with a hard hand, as laymen were by law not allowed to lead
religious movements. Søren Kierkegaard was representative of this
tendency to go against the state Church, except that he was not
disposed to try to create a sectarian community. His significance
was rather that of religious individualism taken to its logical conclusion, and precisely because of this he can be firmly placed in the
Romantic individualist tradition.

By 1864, then, Denmark had progressed to the point at which
she could begin to be transformed into the Denmark we know
today. Her frontiers were much shorter than they had been half
a century before, and her population had shrunk to little more
than half of what it had been. Yet, counter to the catastrophes in
the field of foreign policy had gone the preparations for a period
of expansion at home. Most of the remains of the former systems
had been removed within a noticeably short period of time. The
age of absolutism was past, the limitations on trade had been removed, and the means were beginning to be put at the disposal of
industry to enable it to establish itself in the forefront of the Danish
economy. Although Denmark was basically an underdeveloped

country in the period around 1820, by 1864 things were looking very different. In agriculture, too, new methods of cultivation had been introduced, drainage had improved, and, perhaps fundamentally of more importance, the financial means needed to expand were available. And so was the will to improve matters. The farmers had experienced an age of liberation. The smallholders had not, but their turn was to come later in the century with the emergence of the working classes as a power to be reckoned with.

Chapter 3

1864–1901

Towards a Transformation

DENMARK'S INTERNAL POLITICAL AFFAIRS during the period up to 1864 had been concerned largely with the abolition of the absolute monarchy and the related problem of a suitable constitution. There had been an almost monotonous series of constitutional crises. Politically speaking the period which ends in 1901 with what is known as the change of system, is concerned with the continuation of that struggle and of the related phenomenon : the emergence of political parties. The battle now was not against the absolute rule of the king, but against rule by cabinet, the cabinet being appointed by the king. In face of an increasing liberal majority in the lower house of the *Rigsdag*, the upper house had a built-in conservative majority and was backed by the cabinet. It was only in 1901, after a period of bitter conflict which at one time led to violence, that the parliamentary system was finally established with the understanding that the government must be drawn from the majority in the lower house.

Reaction after Defeat

Whether they deserved it or not, the National Liberals were given the blame for the defeat of 1864, and there could no longer be any question of their forming a cabinet. The king looked for new men to lead the country, and found them in a class which had been largely out of politics for many years, the great landowners. They had been eclipsed by the farmers and their representatives because they had been unwilling to enter into public debate with them and had accordingly not fought elections in great numbers. It was their view that Denmark should no longer be governed by the academics who formed the discredited and by now reactionary National Liberals, but that they should be replaced by landowners and the upper-middle classes. They wished to replace the November constitution (forced upon Denmark by events in Schleswig-Holstein and already removing some of the freedom granted in 1848) by one far less liberal in content. In this they were opposed by the farming classes, expressing themselves through the Friends of the Farmers, who wanted to leave the 1849 constitution untouched. A return to this constitution in its entirety was one of the main objectives of the farmers and the party that emerged around them throughout the whole of this period. However, the election of 1866 gave a narrow majority of members of the *Rigsdag* in favour of revising the constitution, and after protracted negotiations between the parties most directly concerned, it was decided to leave the *Folketing* untouched, but to introduce new arrangements for electing the *Landsting*. The franchise for this was to be severely limited, and based on land and money, in addition to which the king was himself to appoint twelve of the proposed sixty-four members. Despite attempts to dissuade him, Christian IX signed the new constitution which came into force on 5 June 1866 and remained in force until 1915. He then chose to appoint his Ministers, as was his prerogative, from the *Landsting*, completely ignoring the wishes of the *Folketing*, although it was a body considerably more representative of the wishes of the people.

The first Prime Minister under this new constitution was the largest landowner in the country, Count C. E. Frijs, the owner even then of over 500 farms, an enlightened patriarch who accepted appointment from a sense of duty rather than from political ambition. As his Foreign Minister he chose J. B. S. Estrup, a consummate and determined politician who was subsequently to become a symbol of aristocratic rule. The only gesture to the National Liberals was the appointment of a professional civil servant as Minister of Justice. Nevertheless, the landowners were prepared within limits to work with the National Liberals, partly with the object of withholding influence from the farmers' representatives, whom neither considered to be sufficiently well educated to have a say in government. Thus even at this early stage there were signs of co-operation between the landowners and the intellectuals in what was the beginning of a political structure based on class.

What followed was a period of relative political stagnation. However, a number of much needed social reforms were carried out and a catastrophe in foreign affairs was avoided by the unwillingness of the government to accede to the emotional demands of the people, the way thus being cleared for a period of expansion after the advent of democratic government in 1901. It was at the same time a period of internal conflict, as improved educational standards and a changing social pattern made people unwilling to accept a form of aristocratic, semi-authoritarian government from a group which came to represent a diminishingly small section of the

Rigsdag. There was also considerable resentment at the system of representation. The electoral law allowed for single constituency members to be elected. This gave a built-in majority to the wealthier rural interests at first, as about three-quarters of the population still lived in the country districts, while many of the wealthier townspeople also owned land in the country and could thus be counted as belonging to that class. The working classes, on the other hand, were almost entirely disenfranchised.

Yet it was precisely this upper-class government which contrived to keep Denmark out of the Franco-Prussian War of 1871. The temptation again to intervene in international politics had already emerged in 1866, when Denmark had considered taking sides in the conflict between Prussia and Austria in the hope of regaining Schleswig and Holstein. The French government had then advised Denmark to remain neutral, and were able to include in the final treaty between the two powers a clause allowing the northern part of Schleswig to return to Denmark when the local population showed its desire to do so by means of a free vote. This clause was, of course, couched in such vague terms that Bismarck was able to ignore it completely, and he proceeded after the Peace of Prague to incorporate the duchies completely into Prussia.

It was hardly surprising, therefore, that the Danes were inclined to join forces with France when events started to lead up to the Franco-Prussian War. The Danish army had been modernised, and the romantically tinged, rather unrealistic, patriotic spirit which had been decisive in 1848 and 1864, and which had since been fostered by the Folk High Schools, again began to make itself felt. However, the government was now less inclined to be swayed by popular sentiment and stood firm. France wanted an alliance, and sent the duc de Cadore to Copenhagen to negotiate. The Danish government, however, was sufficiently hard-headed to demand that France should show some sign of success before Denmark would commit herself to entering the war, and when news of a French defeat arrived in Copenhagen, Denmark decided to remain neutral and to maintain indefinitely the provisional declaration of neutrality which had been issued when the war began. Some Danish politicians hoped that because of this Bismarck would return at least part of Schleswig, but they were soon disappointed. Bismarck had no such intention. He merely received no excuse to annex yet more of Denmark. 'Le Danemark est si peu de chose', the duc de Cadore is said to have remarked in an unguarded moment – and Bismarck's behaviour indicated that he thought likewise. The duchies were to remain in German hands for a further fifty years. Prussia set about tying them closer to the German states, and Prussian administration was introduced, as was conscription into the Prussian army. Even in the face of significant emigration to Denmark, this policy wts carried through.

Although annexed by Prussia, and thus for a time outside the direct control of Denmark, the duchies continued to exercise the Danish mind, as indeed Schleswig does to this day, though to a much lesser extent. Yet the effect of losing the duchies was a blow to Danish national pride rather than the economic disaster that the loss of Norway had been only fifty years before. Denmark was not ruined by the wars with Prussia, and was quickly able to recover from the financial strain which had inevitably accompanied them. Indeed, in a country reduced in size it was easier to concentrate on the task of reforming and modernising, and on the constitutional and political internal problems with which she was faced. In one sense there was a direct economic gain from the loss of Holstein : Hamburg, the old trade rival of Copenhagen, was less accessible, and the balance of trade altered significantly.

Conflict in the Rigsdag and the Emergence of Political Parties

During its first years the new 1866 constitution worked relatively smoothly, despite the unabated opposition of the farmers' representatives. This was in great part due to the able government of Count Frijs, who managed to mediate between the different points of view and especially between the two chambers of the *Rigsdag*. He avoided issues that might lead to a direct confrontation between them. In 1870, however, he resigned, and his successor, Count Holstein, was not a man to continue the policy. Indeed this very choice was sufficient to bring about a consolidation of the opposition forces, who felt that they were in truth the spokesmen of the people. The resultant increased tension caused the loose political groupings which had so far dominated the *Rigsdag* to change into embryonic political parties.

Broadly speaking, there were four more or less distinct groups in the *Rigsdag* in the early 1870s :

(i) The landowners and their supporters, who dominated the indirectly elected *Landsting* and represented the views of the upper classes.

(ii) The old National Liberals, the second main group in the *Landsting*, made up largely of intellectuals and academics.

(iii) The so-called Centre Party, which was akin to the National Liberals, but opposed to their increasingly conservative outlook. It drew its support from a less limited class than the

National Liberals, and was considerably more liberal in its social and economic outlook.

(iv) The farmers' representatives who, while putting forward a show of unity in their opposition to the present government, in fact contained a number of disparate elements ranging from radicals to Grundtvigians, whose national aspirations were akin to those of the National Liberals.

It was these peasant representatives who first formed a true political party under the name of *The United Left*, the name itself indicative of the reforming aims with which the party began. And indeed, it soon produced Denmark's first political manifesto. It aimed first and foremost at government by the people, with a return to the 1849 constitution, and also produced a series of demands for political and social reforms : a more equitable taxation policy; universal suffrage in local elections; freedom for the farmer from the remains of the leasehold system; and greater independence for the state Church. In two other fields the party's spokesmen were less radical and more national. In Schleswig they wanted to see a border drawn up based on the wishes of the people living there, a solution, in fact, similar to that agreed upon in 1920. They also called for a strengthening of ties between the Scandinavian countries, though this part of their programme was left vague because of a division of opinion within the party. It was a demand close to the hearts of the Grundtvigians, but which failed to fire the imagination of the rest of the party. In general the Grundtvigians among the party's supporters – nationalistic and financially well placed – were rather more conservative in their attitude, knowing full well their disagreement on fundamentals with other factions within the party, factions whose far-reaching demands for social equality were based, they felt, on hatred rather than on Christian charity. The seeds of dissent existed within the Left from its very inception, and the disparity of its various groups was in time to lead to new splits within the party, the formation of new groups, and finally to its split into two distinct and separate parties. Meanwhile 49 members of the *Folketing* (with a total of 102) belonged to the United Left. The demand for parliamentary democracy was not entirely unselfish, for the deputies of the Left saw a *Folketing* majority within their grasp. And they achieved it in 1872.

This parliamentary opposition was in essence the voice of the farmers large and small. It was not the voice of the smallholders and farmworkers, nor was it that of the increasing urban working population. Indeed, although the demands for equality of some factions within the Left would have favoured the workers, they were not really interested in them. The Social Democrats did not so far exist as a political party within the *Rigsdag*, though socialist ideas had begun to gain ground in Denmark in 1871. Pamphlets had been distributed opposing the rather patronising ideas that the workers should be educated. Significantly enough a parliamentary commission set up in 1874 had the task of examining 'how and to what extent the state can help to raise the workers' spiritual and material conditions and, more especially, protect them against undeserved poverty, particularly in their old age'. When the commission published its report in 1878, one of its suggestions was connected with the gulf which the commission saw between employer and worker :

If the gap is to be closed, and if dissatisfaction and conflict, which by the nature of free competition must be created between capital and labour, are to be avoided, then it must, in the view of the undersigned members of the commission, be through a new pattern of conciliation in the arrangement of the industrialised society. The conflicting forces must be reconciled : the worker can be related to the concern for which he works in such a way that he wishes for its success : his courage, his loyalty, and his hope must be strengthened by the prospect that by means or orderliness and thrift he can progress from his position as a wheel in the machinery, to one where he can be in control of it.

These were far-sighted words for a commission in 1878. However, in 1871, this was not the way along which the thoughts of the socialists were directed. Instead, they were arguing that their aim should be to unite the workers and to achieve political power. It was their belief that they could win two-thirds of the seats in the *Folketing*. The pamphlets gradually achieved a circulation of some 3,000. The editor was anonymous, but was in fact a certain Louis Pio, who on seeing the success of the venture, started to organise a Danish Internationale. He won 700 members in Copenhagen, was in touch with Marx for a time, and proceeded to organise a series of strikes. In April 1872 he organised a strike of 1,200 bricklayers, and his daily newspaper, *The Socialist*, which developed from the original pamphlets, called a mass meeting for 5 May. The government, aware of Pio's violent statements and foreseeing trouble, banned the meeting, and when Pio made it clear that he would ignore the warning, he was arrested. The meeting was cancelled, but it was too late : workers assembled as planned, and were dispersed by force, though without any loss of life.

The government now banned the Danish Internationale, and Pio and his colleagues were imprisoned, in Pio's case for five years, though he did not serve the whole sentence. Meanwhile the workers reorganised themselves in workers' associations and trade unions. By the time Pio was released in 1875 there were some thirty trade unions in Copenhagen, and between seventy and eighty in the rest of the country. Pio again took an active part in the movement, but was scarcely suited temperamentally to the changed conditions, and in 1877 he emigrated.

As yet neither the Left nor the Social Democrats appealed to the radical intellectuals. The previous generation's intellectuals had gone to the National Liberals, and some still did so, but those who wanted to see new ideas introduced into a backward Denmark had nowhere to go. They found their solution in a movement which originated in 1871, but which to begin with did not have connections with a political party. However, the Modern Breakthrough, as it came to be known, had such direct political implications from the start, and as time went on developed such a close connection with the radical wing of the United Left, that it cannot be omitted from any review of the emergence of political parties in Denmark. In the autumn of 1871 a young academic, Georg Brandes, began a lengthy series of lectures at the University of Copenhagen on Main Currents in European Literature in the Nineteenth Century. He contrasted what he saw as the dynamic literature of other countries with the uninspiring products of contemporary Denmark. (The 1860s had been a period of decline in Danish literature.) He sought now to infuse literature and intellectual life in general with a new desire to examine, to debate, to query. The ideas were not all new : they had been current elsewhere for years; but they all fell at one time upon a Denmark which had been cut off from such ideas in the rest of Europe, and they made an enormous impression on the young people who were looking for some new channel for their idealism.

In literature, in philosophy, in private discussion and public debate, the new ideas were expressed vehemently. Honoured institutions were attacked as irrelevant to modern society : marriage, chastity, piety, were condemned, and efforts were made to introduce a new morality based on the materialist conception of man. More conservative members of society saw the very foundations of Danish culture threatened, and they fought hard to stem the rising tide of radicalism.

It was not surprising, therefore, that these conservative forces, sensing the political implications of the various opposition movements within and without the *Rigsdag*, should also seek to organise themselves. In 1875 J. B. S. Estrup was appointed Prime Minister. In 1876 he and the landowners, the National Liberals, the Centre

Party, and a small number of independent conservative members came together in *The United Right*. The party sought to defend its conception of Danish culture, by military means in face of threat from abroad, and by opposing radicalism in all its forms within the country. It was prepared to supervise a gradual organic development, and to work for an improvement of the condition and moral standing of the working class – an aim quite different from that of the Left. Its position was essentially defensive from the start, and as part of its system of defence it aimed at a co-ordinated organisation at local level. The Right became the first of the parties to develop a close-knit organisation, though in this it was closely rivalled by the Social Democrats.

J. B. S. Estrup and Autocratic Government

In appointing J. B. S. Estrup as Prime Minister, the king was aware that he was giving the task to a man who only had the following of a minority in the *Folketing*. His majority in the *Landsting* did not promise to make life easier for him, as there was no real provision in the constitution for what should happen in the event of a serious clash between the two chambers. However, Estrup was thought to have the strength necessary to carry through a conservative policy in face of a Left opposition. He was a man of culture who from the start had been critical of the liberal provisions of the 1849 constitution, and when elected to the *Landsting* in 1864 he had played a leading role in working out the less liberal 1866 constitution. He saw it as his duty to defend Danish society as it had evolved so far, and to prevent any radical incursions into the *status quo*. Basing himself on the idea that the ownership of land gave rise to independence of mind and love of country, he argued that the ownership of land should be accompanied by political privilege, and so his political aim became and remained that of maintaining the supremacy of the upper classes. A further argument in favour of political privilege for landowners derived from the fact that taxation was based on land, and the more land a man owned, the greater the weight of taxation he had to bear. Thus, the argument went, he should get something for his money. The Left answered by maintaining that the tax system should be altered.

With the changes then taking place in the country's economic structure and the emergence of a new, wealthy urban middle class, so far untaxed, it is not surprising that taxation was to become a major factor in the coming parliamentary struggle. On the one hand, the more or less unprivileged farmers, represented by the Left, wished to see taxation extended to include the urban middle classes by the introduction of income tax. On the other hand, the landowners were unwilling to remove one of the arguments in favour of their own privileges, while the urban middle classes for purposes of their own had no interest in seeing income tax introduced. Both groups were represented by the Right.

While taxation was thus one bone of contention between the two major parliamentary factions, the issue was complicated and given greater significance by antagonism of a completely different nature. It is not an uncommon phenomenon that together with the ownership of land and such privileges as almost inevitably go with it, there may well develop a special type of patriotism, a sense of duty towards one's own country, and a feeling that only property owners are really worthy of being entrusted with government. Estrup was typical in holding to this point of view, and he was typical, too, in his resolve that Denmark must be able to defend herself in any eventuality.

He wanted to fortify Copenhagen. The Left opposed him on this, not so much because they were pacifists – the colourful and radical Viggo Hørup and his group being the exceptions – but because they saw the opportunity of using the defence question as a means of bargaining their way to parliamentary democracy.

The immediate clash between the two parties came over the budget. According to the constitution, no bills could become law until passed in identical form by the two chambers. The Left saw this as a possibility of stopping any bill of which they did not approve. For their part the Right pointed to another clause in the constitution empowering the government to legislate by decree in an emergency if the *Rigsdag* were not in session. In strict legality, therefore, it could legally dismiss a recalcitrant *Rigsdag* and enact temporary legislation by extra-parliamentary means. The Left, on the other hand, maintained that such an act was illegal, and fought for years for the re-establishment of 'legality'.

Trouble started in the 1876 session, when the government presented a defence plan costing 71 million *kroner*. (The currency had changed from *rigsdaler* to *krone* in 1875.) The Left suggested an alternative plan costing 30 million, to be coupled with the introduction of income tax. The government refused, and it proved impossible to reach a compromise. Estrup therefore dissolved the *Folketing,* and new elections were held in April 1876. The result was typical of many thereafter : the Left increased its representation, this time to seventy-four of the 102 seats, but there was no change in the parliamentary situation. The government was, and remained, the Right.

The Left now consistently refused to assist the passage of government legislation, and when 1 April 1877 was seen to be approaching without any signs of a compromise agreement on the budget, trouble was obviously brewing. On 4 April the *Folketing* session was closed. On 12 April there followed a provisional budget by decree, though it did not include points on which no agreement had been reached with the opposition during budget negotiations. These were in any case not important and had only been used as a weapon. The Left exhorted people not to pay taxes on this basis, but in fact there was no popular resistance.

Dissension in the Opposition

After this expression of anger by the Left, disillusion set in when the *Folketing* reassembled and the majority of Left members showed themselves to be in favour of co-operation with the Right. Indeed, feelings ran so high that a dissident group under the leadership of Berg and Hørup broke away from the main party and formed the Radical Left group.

Faced with the Left in disarray, Estrup saw an opportunity to strengthen his position, and dissolved the *Folketing* once more. His judgement proved correct, and the Right won nine extra seats in the election, giving them thirty-five, while the two Left factions were left about equal in strength. Estrup, using his considerable political skill, manipulated the two Left groups, and by so doing succeeded in pushing through more reform bills than had been passed for many years : Smallholders' Credit Societies were formed to give financial aid to smallholders; an act was passed establishing savings banks; and another by which the state bought up the Zealand railways. In order to do this Estrup had leaned heavily upon the support of the Radical dissidents, but he then unexpectedly reached a compromise agreement with the Moderates on a new army act, according to which the army was increased in strength, but the period of service reduced. However, the passing of the act brought to an end the co-operation between the Berg – Hørup group, strongly anti-militarist in outlook, and the ruling Right Party. It was the Moderates who now seemed in favour of compromise.

The year 1880 saw the election to the *Folketing* of Edvard Brandes, brother of the radical literary spokesman Georg Brandes, and one of his most ardent supporters. Edvard Brandes thus forged the link between the radical literary movement outside the *Folketing* and the Radical political movement within it. An outspoken atheist, he was an admirer of radical movements throughout Europe, and tried to introduce their ideas into Denmark – as did his brother Georg in a different field. It was natural that he should join the Berg–Hørup group. They became the vehicle for the new ideas and in time attracted a new class of intellectuals into the party. The difference which existed between them and the Moderates was such that it was obviously only a matter of time before a fundamental split developed, sufficient to start off an independent radical party.

The Right saw a dangerous enemy in Brandes, and an attempt was made to prevent him from taking his seat, because he was an atheist and thus would not take the oath. The same attitude was adopted by the Moderate Left, which was hostile towards him, both on account of his atheism and Jewish background, and also because of his connections with the literary radical movement, which it detested. In the event, he was accepted and allowed to take his seat. Meanwhile, although he signified an immediate strengthening of the Left, he was fundamentally the cause of a new and deepening split within the party, a split between the 'Europeans', with their ideas of freedom going back ultimately to the French Revolution, and the 'Danes', with their roots in Danish agriculture and Grundtvigianism. These two groups were essentially the Radicals and Moderates, but the advent of the 'European' ideas of Brandes served to aggravate the difference between them. For the time being, Hørup succeeded in uniting the various factions within the Left.

Brandes became a central figure in the Radical Left, to which he began to attract the younger generation of intellectuals. The literary radicalism of Georg Brandes had given them a satisfying meeting-point, and the progression to the Radical Left as represented by Edvard Brandes was a natural one; though here, too, there was a split between the types and the intellects attracted to the two wings of the Left Party. Nor were things made easier, when the Moderate intellectuals also showed signs of moving towards the Radicals.

An Impotent Left and Dictatorial Rule

When trouble arose over the budget again in May 1881, Estrup repeated his former tactics and dissolved the *Folketing*. This time he did himself no good, and the Right was reduced to 32 seats. The Left consisted of 29 Radicals, 22 Moderates, and 18 Independents. With progress still impossible, still further elections were called, after which the Right was reduced yet further to 26 members in the *Folketing*. By June 1884 they were down to nineteen. The Radicals, on the other hand, shot up to forty-six, with the Moderates at twenty-three. A completely new factor in the 1884 election was the appearance of two Social Democrat members representing

Copenhagen, a city which had so far been dominated by the Right.

With a result such as this it was doubtful whether Estrup could carry on : a minority government of nineteen against eighty-three was scarcely likely to be effective. Moreover, it was felt that the likelihood of a Left government was increased by the fact that one now existed in Norway without immediate chaos being apparent. Yet the Danish Left was as disunited as ever, forming at best a 'Danish' group consisting of the Moderates and those of comparable national sentiments, numbering about 50 members, and the 'European's on the Radical side, making up between twenty-five and thirty. Even though some co-operation was possible between them, it was of a nervous sort in which cultural as well as tactical and political differences were becoming increasingly apparent.

Under these conditions there was virtually a stalemate in the *Folketing*, with the result that it was dismissed and a provisional budget proclaimed in April 1885. Under the terms of the proclamation, the government was enabled to collect taxes, though not in excess of the original estimates on which negotiations had been carried out. However, there was a great difference between this and the previous provisional budget in 1877 : this was not limited to such clauses as had already been agreed between the parties.

The Left reacted furiously, and there was open talk of revolution by many of its members. Their leaders, however, were not in favour of such extreme action and merely advised farmers not to pay their taxes. Some did refuse for a time, but to little avail. Others joined together to form 'rifle clubs' – 'to combat enemies at home and abroad'; and the formation of co-operative ventures and stores, already proceeding apace, was speeded up as a political gesture towards the Right.

No government could ignore such widespread agitation, and a fresh provisional law was proclaimed forbidding the importation and distribution of weapons for the rifle clubs. Teachers were forbidden to take part in political agitation, and Folk High Schools agitating for the Left lost their state subsidy. A close watch was kept on public gatherings, and when Berg, immediately before delivering a speech, had the chief constable of Holstebro removed from the platform, he was condemned to six months imprisonment.

Yet nothing happened. The Left threatened to boycott the *Rigsdag* session of 1885–86, but when it came to the crunch they attended as usual. When the Right suggested taking the entire question of the provisional laws to the Supreme Court, the Left refused on the assumption that the judges would almost inevitably take the side of the Right. There was a deadlock again over the budget, and when an unsuccessful attempt was made on Estrup's life, the entire *Rigsdag* was dismissed and a series of new provisional laws were issued by decree. These established an armed gendarmerie run on military lines to maintain order, expanded the powers of the police, placed a limitation on the freedom of the press, and laid down penalties for the spreading of false rumour or the exhortation to violence. The most violent protest against the régime came in 1887, when there was a minor riot at Brønderslev. It was put down without bloodshed, though many of the rioters were thrown into gaol.

Yet still nothing was achieved, and the campaign by the Left began to lose momentum. Had its leaders been men of sterner calibre, there might have been a different outcome, but for all their fury, none of the leaders, not even the fiery Viggo Hørup, was prepared to accept the responsibility of leading a revolution. Seen in retrospect, at least from one point of view, their protests against the dictatorial régime were pathetic, a fact with which the novelist Henrik Pontoppidan makes great play in his scenes from the age of provisional laws. Yet there is another side to the picture. Come what might, the Left leaders decided to keep within the constitution – how could they do anything else when their perpetual cry had been that the Right was acting in conflict with the constitution? They knew they had legality on their side and they were determined not to undermine that position.

Nevertheless, since the policies of obstruction and protest had failed, a change in tactics was called for. Accordingly it was decided to embark on a policy of negotiation, to force the government to keep the *Rigsdag* in session in order to discuss a whole series of suggestions for reform. But the Right countered by dissolving the *Folketing* and calling elections. There was a record turnout of 70 per cent (in 1884 only 59 per cent of the electorate had voted, and even that was considered satisfactory), and the Right increased its representation to 27 seats against a combined opposition of seventy-five. Of the members who had gained seats from the Right in Copenhagen during the previous session only one Social Democrat remained. The Left was now even more willing to negotiate than before, but still no agreement was possible. So resort was again had to a provisional budget by decree.

In 1889 the Left published a comprehensive programme for reform, demanding reductions in customs duties and in military expenditure; the proclamation of neutrality; old-age assistance; financial aid in sickness and disablement; a limitation to the hours of work; the right of the workers to organise themselves; the provision of state aid to smallholders in order to enable them to buy land; women's right to vote; a reform of the legal system; and

greater freedom for the churches in Denmark – an enormous programme, which provided the basis for legislation for years ahead.

Whether or not under the influence of this programme, the
election of 1890 led to a new reduction in the strength of the Right
to 24 members, while Left members tended to be radical at the
expense of the Moderates. Two Social Democrats were also elected
to the *Landsting*, again a landmark in Danish politics.

The Social Democrats were now becoming more and more of a
power in Danish political life. They were well organised and were
making demands for reform which went beyond those of the Left.
Moreover, they were at last beginning to make progress among the
farmworkers in the rural areas, a preserve which had hitherto belonged to the Left, who were worried by this new development and
moved more towards a policy of negotiated reform. In fact during
the years to come both the Right and the Left were interested in
pushing through a reform programme, not so much out of reforming zeal, but from a desire to maintain their positions. The Left
Party was now under the leadership of Frede Bojsen, Grundtvigian
by inclination – and thus a moderate conservative in outlook – but
willing to go far in the field of social legislation to stop both the
Social Democrats and the European Radicals under Hørup. Hørup
himself, though a member of the Left Party, held views which were
closer to the Social Democrats than to his Moderate colleagues of
the Left, who despite their name were in practice becoming a liberal
Centre Party.

The Left Achieves its Object

Berg died in 1891, and with him went one of the main obstacles
to negotiation between the Moderate Left and the Right, who
together passed a law on Sickness Benefit Societies in 1892 and
also co-operated to prevent the payment of a state pension of 2,000
kroner a year to Georg Brandes, as was suggested by the Radicals.
Collaboration between the two factions went as far as an electoral
pact in the *Folketing* elections of 1892, when the Right maintained
its position with 32 seats, against the Moderates' thirty-eight. The
Radicals won a total of 30 seats, though Hørup himself was beaten,
while the Social Democrats remained at two.

The policy of mutual concession was continued, with the immediate result of further reform legislation and subsequently an attempt
at a true political reconciliation. A compromise was reached on
the fortification question and it was agreed that the remaining
provisional laws should be repealed. Briefly, the terms of the
reconciliation agreement were that while some defence plans were
to be continued, the aim of all defence measures was to be the

establishment of Danish neutrality, for which the government was to try to obtain the recognition of the great powers. It was duly accepted by 54 votes against forty-four. Edvard Brandes resigned his seat at this, and Hørup refused to consider further nomination. Estrup, who had symbolised the struggle between the parties, carried out his threat to resign in August 1894.

This was not, however, the end of rule by the Right, though the new government, under Tage Reetz-Thott, consisted chiefly of men who had worked for the reconciliation, and who were keen to co-operate with the Moderates. The country as a whole, however, was not so keen on the arrangement, and in the *Folketing* election of 1895, which took account of twelve new constituencies, both the Right and the Moderates, acting in concert, lost seats. The Right now had 25 seats, the Moderates twenty-seven; Left members opposed to the reconciliation numbered fifty-four, the Social Democrats eight.

Those Left members who opposed the reconciliation agreement were themselves not a homogeneous group; but, under the leadership of J. C. Christensen, the three factions into which they could be divided came together to form the Left Reform Party. Their object was to delay legislation and thus to tire their opponents, and to gain influence in a quiet way through their everyday work. As editor of *Politiken*, Hørup, still outside the *Folketing*, supported this new party. Its demands were much the same as those of the Radicals after 1889, though to these were added new ones occasioned by unfavourable economic and social conditions : subsidies for agricultural exports, for instance, and provisions for arbitration in industrial conflicts.

The Right government itself pursued a moderate policy and sought to gain the widest support possible. But the Right Party disagreed with this policy, especially when the Prime Minister declared that he would not issue any more provisional laws under any circumstances. Now it was the Right Party's turn to split, because of varying views as to what the future course for a party with so little popular support should be. In the *Landsting* the Right was still the major party, still with Estrup as its leader, but in the *Folketing* it was more and more in favour of coming to terms with the Left. The split went so deep that the Right of the *Landsting* was not without responsibility for the government's resignation in 1897. It was replaced by a government further to the right, a government which would not maintain the promise never to resort to provisional laws again.

But the Right had had its day, and after the 1898 election, while still forming the government, was reduced to 16 seats. The Left

Reform had sixty-three (an absolute majority), the Moderates twenty-three, and the Social Democrats twelve. That same year the Right in the *Landsting* was further depleted by the loss of 3 seats in a *Landsting* election. Estrup resigned. Many members even of the Right were now in favour of a Left government, not least when it was announced that the government had used half a million *kroner* on defence for which funds had not been appropriated. It had hoped for the money to be voted in retrospect, but the *Folketing* refused.

Although the Smallholdings Act was passed, together with a new Primary Education Act, in 1899, there remained the great stumbling-block of taxation. The Right was itself disunited on this also and the government had to resign because of pressure from the rebels within its ranks. The new government could not rely on their support, and it only succeeded in getting the bill through the *Folketing* by leaving out all controversial clauses. The *Landsting* split on the taxation issue, and in 1900 eight rebels left the party and joined a ninth, who had left previously, to form a new group known as the Free Conservatives.[1]

The *Folketing* election of April 1901 was held under different conditions as, to discourage political pressure-groups, a law had been passed introducing the secret ballot. The result was a resounding victory for the Left Reform Party and an almost total eclipse of the Right, now reduced to 8 seats, the smallest group in the *Folketing*.

In July the king, as expected, asked the government to resign, and requested the formation of a Left cabinet, under the leadership, not of a parliamentary politician, but of a university professor of law, J. H. Deuntzer. The demands of the Left had been met at last and 1901 thus saw the introduction of parliamentary democracy – the principle of rule by the majority party. This event has become known in Danish as the Change of System. The struggle needed to achieve it had been long and complicated, and accompanied by a bewildering number of splits and new groupings within the two major parties. Yet it has been necessary to follow these internal party problems, because the emerging factions form the basis of the major political parties in Denmark today. Their true role – and even their names – can only be properly understood if their origins are also appreciated.

The Industrial Scene

Politics were not the only sphere of Danish life to undergo a development of some significance in this period. It was a time of

[1] See below, p. 107.

rapid change outside the *Rigsdag*, in almost every sphere of activity, and some of the most important took place in the field of industry and industrial relations.

The industrial change which took Denmark once and for all away from the ancient pattern of industry and production came late. When it did come, it was partly the result of changing industrial patterns and methods elsewhere, but also the direct consequence of the liberalisation of internal trade in 1862. Before that, the guild system had been in full operation and the way in which trade had been carried on had been strictly limited. Now, with liberalisation, people were free to carry out any trade as and where they pleased. The guilds no longer had any significance, at least not beyond running such activities as sickness benefit societies. There had been some apprehension about the effect of this radical change of system, but the worst fears were not realised, although competition, now considerably stepped up, did have adverse effects on some workers.

Although a thousand or so industrial firms had been founded before 1864, these were small concerns and there had so far been little that one could call industry proper. By 1872 the number had risen to 1,400, but of these 800 still employed under ten men each, while only fifty-four were big enough to employ a hundred men or more. The increase was significant, however, and the new freedom to pursue any trade, together with rising prices in the 1870s, led to a further rapid increase. A few concerns in Denmark were now so big as to be beyond the resources of individuals, and the formation of limited companies began. Burmeister and Wain, the shipbuilders and the largest establishment in Denmark, went public in 1872 and was followed by many others: seventeen in 1872, sixty-nine more by 1875. Many of the companies thus formed are still in existence today.

At the same time, commercial activity increased. There was a move to expand international trade and the free harbour was built in Copenhagen. Communications improved internally with the expansion of the railway system and both internally and externally with the changeover from sail to steam. Easier transport meant that industry could develop in the provinces as well as in Copenhagen, and the period saw an increase in the populations of the provincial towns as well as Copenhagen, though the capital grew more rapidly.

This increase was due not merely to a marked growth in population, but also because workers were drifting from the villages and the countryside. The intensification of mechanised farming as well as the industrial breakthrough were behind this, and the growing proletariat had to be controlled and organised.

The workers had their representatives, or would-be representatives, in two fields. The Social Democrat Party sought to gain, and gradually achieved, political influence. On a different level the trade union movement emerged and grew parallel with industrialisation. Although in Pio's day there had been a close connection between trade unions and politics, it was now decided that the unions should not engage in political action or be directly connected with the Social Democrat Party.

They set about improving working conditions and wages, and encouraged a wave of strikes, mainly in Copenhagen, but also elsewhere in the country. By 1898 the various unions agreed, for the sake of the movement as a whole, and also in order to avoid hurting each other as a result of their activities, to join together in the Association of Trade Unions (*Det Samvirkende Fagforbund*) with the object of co-ordinating their efforts.

They were presumably also spurred to this move by the fact that in 1896 the employers had organised themselves into the Employers' Association (*Arbejdsgiverforeningen*). This new association was obviously created to protect the employers' interests in the face of growing union strength, and the possibility existed of a conflict between the two major organisations. It came in 1899. Before this, individual employers had reacted to strikes by introducing lock-outs, and one major example had taken place in 1885, involving the locking-out of 1,300 workers from twenty-four factories. Now, in 1899, one strike led to the locking-out of 40,000 men for a total of nineteen weeks, an event of such seriousness that many experts were concerned for the long-term effects on the economy. In the end the dispute was settled largely because of near-exhaustion on both sides, but the basis of the settlement has had great significance for industrial relations since that time. The workers gained recognition of their right to organise themselves, a right that some, but not all, employers had sought to deny them. Meanwhile the other clauses of the compromise settlement were just as important to subsequent peace, as they drew up terms for relations between the two sides of industry. No strike was to be called without a vote in favour by three-quarters of the executive of the union involved. A week's notice must be given. No strike or lock-out was to be supported by the unions or employers' organisations if called contrary to the rules. Agreements between unions and employers should be binding, and three months' notice must be given of intent to terminate agreements. It was also decided that efforts should be made to establish a compulsory arbitration tribunal, and this was in fact achieved in 1910. Thus the arrangement after the great lock-out at the turn of the century laid foundations for the civilised

standard of relations which has existed in Danish industry ever
since. It has been suggested that this one agreement outside the
Rigsdag has been of more significance than any signed within it
during the period at present under review.

Living Conditions

The transition from old-fashioned industry to the beginnings of
modern capitalism, the change from a small society where each
trader made and sold his goods, to one in which those with capital
financed trade, while the others worked for them, brought a change
not only in the pattern of trade and industry, but also in the pattern
of society. The move from the countryside to the towns, occasioned by industrialisation, led to the building of potential slum
areas, in which the new workers had to live – large blocks of flats –
and the stress seems to have been more on cheapness than on
quality. Many workers and their families lived in one-room flats
with no toilet facilities; the luckier ones had two rooms, of which
one was kitchen-cum-living-room, the other the bedroom. The
blocks in which these flats were built were large, and behind the
block facing the street came yet another block with possibly an
even less attractive exterior and no view of any sort – the so-called
baggårde, back-yards. This system of building persisted for many
years and was only done away with when local authorities began
to take a greater interest in building standards and town planning
after the turn of the century, and either refused to sanction these
large complexes or insisted on better and wider roads, which automatically put a stop to this kind of development. The structures
themselves were flimsy in the extreme, which precluded any pretence of private life, as everything could be heard from one flat to
another. Although social histories tell of these flats, the best description is probably to be found in the social literature of the day, first
and foremost in Martin Andersen Nexø's *Pelle the Conqueror* :

> Up through the narrow courtyards the entrance porches hung
> drooping and decaying towards each other, leaving a narrow
> opening where clothes lines glided backwards and forwards with
> children's clothes and floorcloths. The dark wooden stairs ran
> in zigzags against the walls, popped into the entrance porches
> and went right up to the attic. From the porches and balconies,
> doors gave access to the flats or to long corridors which led into
> the interior of the massive block. But on *Pipmandens* side there
> were neither entrances nor railings from the second floor up-
> wards. Time had devoured them, so that the stairs hung alone
> on their moorings : the ends of the beams still stuck out from

the walls like rotten teeth stumps. A rope was hanging from above which could be used for support : it was shiny and black from many hands.

Nevertheless, buildings of this sort were not all that Copenhagen or the other major cities possessed, for together with the growing proletariat went an up-and-coming middle class – those who in one way or another had managed to keep up their independence or who had a sufficient income to maintain appearances. They, too, lived in apartments, though of larger dimensions, usually with a kitchen, though probably still not with toilet facilities. Mains' drainage was still unknown.

Despite the lack of hygiene which marked the lower classes and many of those not so low, the standard of health in Denmark was improving at this time, owing partly to the discovery of new medical knowledge and techniques of treatment and partly to the greater provision of health insurance associations, especially after the legislation in the 1890s. Many of the trade guilds, which had died out after the introduction of the Free Trading Act in 1862, had themselves organised a form of sickness insurance, and although the guilds themselves disappeared, this particular service was continued in the form of health insurance societies connected with individual trades or branches of commerce. Membership was, of course, voluntary, and in many cases limited to members of the particular trade; and consequently a large section of the population was not covered at all. In cases of sickness, these people were either forced to accept poor-aid, with all its legal consequences – or to find a doctor willing to treat them without a fee. This was by no means as uncommon as might be supposed, and it was an accepted fact that many doctors varied their fees according to the means of their patients. This was also true when, as often happened, the doctor was paid a regular retaining fee covering any necessary services for a family and its servants throughout a year. The 1892 law on health insurance societies, while maintaining the voluntary principle, made provision for membership for all citizens whose income was below a fixed level, and consequently there was a rapid increase in membership, with, in the course of time, an improvement in standards of health.

Treatment also improved and new hospitals were founded. Finsen pioneered his light treatment for certain diseases and founded his institute, and at the very end of the period, in March 1900, Vejlefjord Sanatorium was opened in a first bid to end tuberculosis. As certain types of illness were being brought under control, other types appeared, some of them, such as poliomyeltis, apparently

aided by better dwellings and attention to hygiene. Along with
the founding of hospitals went the need for suitable nursing
staff, and in the 1880s the question was raised as to whether it was
fitting for a young lady to undertake the work of nursing others,
especially men, to health. Yet nursing became a profession open
to young ladies of good family who for some reason or other had
to fend for themselves. On the other hand, the fact that such young
ladies had their difficulties emerges from Herman Bang's novel
Ludvigsbakke, where the 'heroine', Ida Brandt, although left a
considerable fortune after the death of her parents, does not feel
constrained to live a life of leisure, and instead seeks to make a
contribution to society by becoming a nurse. Her position is scarcely
appreciated, for while the snobs of her day consider it beneath her
dignity to have a profession, many of her fellows, learning of her
small fortune, grumble that she has taken a post which could well
have been filled by someone in more need of the money.

Drunkenness posed a difficult problem. It was said at the turn of
the century that one man in seven died of drink, and although this
is probably a considerable exaggeration, there is no doubt that
alcohol caused many deaths in Denmark, and the figure of 23 per
cent of male deaths being *partly* due to drink is in itself frightening – and statistically more accurate than the first figure quoted.
Another impression of the problem can be derived from the fact
that in Copenhagen alone there were approximately 300 cases of
delirium tremens a year – and by 1910 about 700 – against an average of sixty-five to seventy a year now with a vastly increased population. The cause of this drunkenness was not beer, but *snaps,*
which was then extremely cheap, known even as the poor man's
drink. Just how much was drunk it is difficult to say, but there are
many examples in Danish literature from this period which indicate
that workmen, especially those engaged on outdoor work, were
provided with a bottle of *snaps* each day to keep them warm in
much the same way that a workman nowadays might take a
thermos flask of hot tea or coffee. The annual consumption of *snaps*
around 1880 is said to have averaged about 17½ litres per head of
population, or 67 litres for every man over twenty years of age.
The figure today is 3 litres. Even if doubts should be raised about
the accuracy of the figures, these early statistics are staggering, and
it is obvious that alcoholism must have been a serious social blight.
It is not surprising, therefore, that a movement aimed at total
abstinence got under way and attracted support from various classes,
especially the lower classes. It is estimated that at one time almost
7 per cent of the population belonged to the movement.

The obvious step which the government could have taken to

reduce the consumption of *snaps*, that of taxing it, was not taken because of the political struggle in the *Folketing*. A compromise was reached by taxing beer, though it was pointed out even at the time that this was in fact taxing the lesser of two evils.

Rural Conditions

Chaotic as was the situation in the towns during this period of transformation, it was no better in the country districts. The change from the old patriarchal society to a class society was accompanied by inevitable strains and stresses. Despite the superficial unity between the farmers and the smallholding-labouring class, a widening gap had existed between them since the end of *stavnsbaand* almost a century before. While the farmers had developed from a community which rented its land into one which normally owned it, the smallholders had been left behind. A revolutionary change in the relationship between these two groups had become apparent. Whereas previously the farmer had benevolently allowed his workers to dine in the same room as he did, now, after the prosperous period in the 1830s which enabled him to improve his house, the farmer built a special room for his workers and ensured that they no longer entered the house proper. A class system sprang up, and if by any chance a farmer and his employees did eat together, they sat at table in strict order : the farmer and his family; the resident workers; and lastly the day labourers and the smallholders who were doing chance work on the farm. These latter were always given the worst treatment, just as the most difficult work was left to them. This was the normal state of affairs by the 1880s, though things had not gone so far in some of the more backward parts of the country, where the patriarchal system was still maintained.

Not only is it quite certain that the farmers began to treat their labourers as an inferior class, but it is also quite evident that they sometimes looked on them as little more than slaves. Their labourers were housed in filthy rooms to which access was gained through the stable or cowshed. Several men might have to share a single room, some having to share their beds with each other or with the children who, from the age of about eight, acted as gooseherds or cowherds. Hygiene was almost non-existent and sickness was rife. The farmer had the right to beat the children who worked for him, and there is ample evidence that many took advantage of this if the child failed in his duty. There is some difficulty in discovering just how widespread this ill-treatment was, probably because, as is to be expected, the cases where it did not apply were not given prominence. The composer Carl Nielsen, for example, talks of his days as a gooseherd as a very happy time, though others who had lived the life talked of the frightening responsibility of looking after a herd of cattle all day long and the utter loneliness of life out in the fields.

Just as some farmers tended to exploit their workers, so local councils adopted an unsympathetic attitude towards families in need of financial help and treated paupers in the most humiliating manner. Whereas the poor had hitherto been helped by individual initiative, in the 1860s and 1870s a number of poor-law institutions were built, probably not so much out of a desire to be humane, as a wish to dissuade people from resorting to the parish. Many of the workhouses had the appearance and atmosphere of prisons, and it was said that many people committed suicide rather than be sent to them. There were obviously, says the novelist Skjoldborg in his memoirs, some good wardens as well as cruel ones, but he considered the whole system to be wrong and maintained that such institutions had awakened his feelings of social injustice.

After a good deal of discussion, the Ministry of the Interior decided in 1889 to revise the Poor Law, but not to change its basis completely. Comments were invited from all manner of qualified people throughout the country, and it emerged from their reports that there were two widely conflicting views. Officials and laymen with high humanitarian ideals looked objectively at the existing situation, while the local authorities consisted largely of well-to-do farmers who did not nourish tender feelings towards the less fortunate members of society in any case, and their chief interest was to cut down communal expenses as much as possible. Since taxes fell on those owning land, it would inevitably be the farmers themselves who had to foot the bill. This state of affairs explains, too, some of the abuses which had been current and were now stopped : the 'auctioning' of paupers, particularly children, to those who would take them into their homes for the lowest payment; and the system of the 'round' (*omgang*), by which paupers were forced to go from one farm to another, staying in each for a couple of days and working there for a meagre living. Then there was the practice of 'maintenance marriages' (*forsørgelsesægteskaber*), which was also prevented by the new Poor Law of 1891 – and which had in fact never been favoured by the authorities. When people had been living in a parish for a number of years they were entitled to receive poor-aid there. Women were entitled to it in the parish to which their husbands belonged, and so it was by no means uncommon for one parish to pay a man from another parish to marry some woman (often with a large illegitimate family) who was a burden on it. The Poor Law of 1891 stated that illegitimate children remained the responsibility of the parish to which the mother had belonged before marriage, thus denying the local authorities the chief advantage to be derived from marrying off their pauper women to men from elsewhere.

The other main provisions of the new Poor Law were to clarify the question of where people were entitled to receive aid, to limit the power local authorities had over them, and to define just when a man could have cancelled his debt for any poor-aid received, and thus receive back the civil rights he had lost by accepting it. Five years were to be the norm : after five years' residence in one parish without poor-aid from another, people were entitled to assistance there; after five years without receiving poor-aid a man could be counted free from debt; and only after five years without poor-aid was a man free to marry without permission.

While, in retrospect, the Poor Law remained harsh, some provision was certainly also made for more humane treatment of paupers, and another bill was passed the same year providing assistance for old people who fulfilled certain conditions, the chief of which was that they had not received poor-aid for the ten years prior to their sixtieth birthday. It was left to the local authorities to decide what form the old-age assistance should take and they were able to put applicants into special homes if they wished – though not in poor-law institutions. There was some resistance from those most directly concerned, but the increasing number of beneficiaries can be deduced from the fact that payments made under the act rose from just under 3 million *kroner* in 1893 to almost 5 million in 1899. The payments were very modest at first, on average only 69 *kroner* per head in 1894, rising to 168 *kroner* by 1914.

Parallel with these early attempts to help the needy went a series of efforts to put smallholders on a new footing. These culminated in the first Smallholdings Act of 1899 which introduced the principle of state loans to smallholders to enable them to buy a certain amount of land for themselves. The aim was typical enough of the attitude of the better-off members of rural society, as the size of the plots which the smallholders could buy was not to be sufficient for them to live off them exclusively. Yet they were to be too big for the owner to take a full-time job in addition to running his smallholding. Thus those in need of labour were still assured of a plentiful supply.

With all its deficiencies, this act was used to provide some 1,900 lots during the five-year period 1899–1904. Its renewal in 1904 brought no major changes, but when it again came up for renewal in 1909, provision was made for the purchase of bigger plots, and thus the smallholder was enabled to take another step along the road to complete independence from his more wealthy colleagues.

The provision of 'state smallholdings' had from the start a far-reaching influence on the morale of the smallholders. They were now for the first time enabled to buy land for themselves, and the very fact that this meant to them a financial tie encouraged them to give of their best. It was sometimes said that the best models for agricultural methods were to be found in the smallholdings, not in the farms, such were the eagerness and determination with which they undertook their new tasks. As time went on provision was made for 'smallholders' tours', in which competent smallholders were taken to see the best results of their colleagues, so that they could learn from their methods. Evil tongues argued, perhaps with some justification, that smallholders going on these tours were often too old to benefit from what they learned, but there is no evidence to suggest that this was the normal run of affairs. With enhanced abilities and economic independence came a widening sense of social pride, which led to the formation in 1910 of the Federation of Danish Smallholders' Societies, an organisation which was the living expression of a new class. Thus the period had seen the emergence and establishment of two distinct classes in rural Denmark : the modern farmer, progressive in outlook and well able to look after himself; and the smallholder, freed from the final traces of serfdom which had still been apparent at the end of the century. The term 'peasant' could scarcely be used of them any more.

The farmers themselves had undergone a transformation which in its way was just as radical as that experienced by the small-holders. But such a transformation did not serve to bring the two classes closer together, for while the farmers were determined to free themselves from the influence of the wealthy landowners, they were equally determined not to lose the use of the smallholders. Nevertheless, the reorganisation of farming which took place to-wards the end of the last century was started at least as much by economic factors as by social and class pressures. It just happened that the means chosen by the farmers to overcome financial problems could also be used as a political weapon.

The change originated in the mid-1870s in the appearance of cheap corn from the United States. Denmark had so far been a corn-exporting country, but could no longer compete. At the same time, Britain, thanks to the Industrial Revolution, had seen a transformation resulting in an increased import of animal products. The Danes saw their opportunity in this market and within the twenty years from 1875 to 1895 more than doubled their exports of animal products. At the same time Denmark went over from being a corn-exporting country to a corn-importing country, thanks to the increased quantities needed to feed the growing numbers of livestock. This happened despite the energetic efforts of the Danish Heath Society to cultivate the Jutlandic heath and grow corn on it. Between 1871 and 1914 the number of cattle in Denmark went up from 1·2 million to 2·5 million, pigs from 400,000 to 2·5 million, and poultry from 4·6 million (in 1888) to 15·2 million. Only sheep production dropped, owing to increased competition from Australia which resulted from the introduction of refrigerated ships.

Increases such as these were bound to bring about problems of distribution, while another problem was the quality of some of the products, notably butter. Danish butter at that time varied much in quality and had a poor reputation in England. That of farm butter especially was poorer than that of butter made on the larger estates, and so in trying to improve and standardise the quality of farm butter, there was at the same time the political motive of competing with the landowners. In 1874 an Århus merchant called Hans Broge suggested the formation of co-operative dairies in each village. In 1880 the first common dairies were established, in which the owners bought milk off the local farmers, but not on a co-operative basis. The first co-operative dairy proper was opened in 1882 in Hjedding, Jutland. The principle was that each farmer using the dairy should have a share in it, though the amount of capital required of each was minimal. Each farmer, whatever the size of his farm, was to have *one* vote in running the dairy and profits were to be shared according to the amount of milk delivered. The skimmed milk left after butter production was to be returned in proportion to each farm and used for pig rearing. This system was so democratic as to enable smallholders to take part on the basis even of their limited production, and also to have an active share in the running of the dairy, a system which tempts one to hear another echo of Rollo's men maintaining their equality.

The co-operative dairies were a success, and the following years saw a rapid increase in numbers: by 1885 there were eighty-four dairies, by 1890, 684, and by 1895, 832. In an effort to stabilise quality, the state provided consultants who travelled round the country advising on the best methods and adopting a strict line with the inevitable few low-grade dairies. After 1888 a consultant was sent to England to keep a watch on what happened to Danish butter after import and to try to prevent adulteration – a not uncommon practice. In 1906 the Lur mark, the reproduction of the Viking horns (*lur*), was introduced as a trademark on the English market and in 1911 legislation was introduced laying down the quality of butter required before the Lur mark could be used – guarantee of quality at a very early date.

The same trademark was used on bacon, the export of which had increased along with that of butter from the early 1880s. Prior to this Denmark had exported live pigs to Germany, but in 1879 one Magnus Kjær had decided to produce bacon for the English market. He imported Yorkshire pigs and crossed them with pigs from his own district, and succeeded in producing the type of bacon acceptable to the English consumer. This new trade was given a boost in 1887 when the Germans prohibited the import of live pigs, and of bacon and sausages, because of an outbreak of swine fever, and was further helped when they placed an import duty on live pigs in 1889.

The co-operative principle was adopted here, too, and the first co-operative slaughterhouse was opened in Horsens in 1887. More capital was obviously needed to start a co-operative slaughterhouse than for a dairy and this problem was solved by allowing the slaughterhouse to serve a wider area, thereby attracting a larger number of farmers. By 1890 there were ten co-operative slaughter-houses, by 1895 seventeen, and by 1900 twenty-six. In addition a few were privately owned.

Through the dairies and slaughterhouses the co-operative principle had become firmly established in Denmark, and this method of distribution was extended to cover fodder, seed, cement, and machinery. A different aspect of the same principle was also to be found in the co-operative stores which began to open all over the country, until there were 900 by 1900. They were inspired by the first English co-operative store in Rochdale, founded with the aim of securing commodities for the working people. Thisted Workers' Association, founded in 1866, had the same object, that of improving the workers' conditions by buying more cheaply and dividing the profit amongst those who took part in the venture. However, one great difference arose between the English and Danish co-operative stores, in that while they originated in England as a working-class movement in the towns, they were established mainly in the country districts in Denmark. This was because while the country people saw the advantages of the system, the workers from the towns were dissuaded from forming or joining co-operatives by the Social Democrats who feared that lower prices would ultimately lead to lower wages. Thus, until 1900 the co-operative movement in Denmark remained almost entirely rural, and did not acquire the working-class image that became part of the parallel movement in England, and which has since become its bane.

The growth of these stores was helped by an anomaly in the trading laws dating from earlier in the century. These had defined areas around the market towns where shops could not be built. But as the co-operatives were societies, not shops, the law could not prevent them from opening, and in these belts around market towns they were a great success because of the lack of amenities arising from the trading laws. There was certainly also some political motivation, as the co-operatives often aimed at opposing the grocers, nearly always supporters of the Right Party, which by 1885 was ruling by decree, while the farmers nearly always supported the Left.

The main difficulty encountered by the co-operative stores was the lack of expertise. They were in fact run by amateurs and consequently some of them went bankrupt. A move to counter this came in 1884 when the co-operatives in Zealand amalgamated, while those in Jutland followed their example in 1888. An amalgamation of all the co-operatives in the country took place in 1896 when the Danish Co-operative Wholesale Society, which has been described as a co-operative within a co-operative, was formed.

The Arrival of 'Modern' Literature

At a time which saw so many changes in so many fields, most of them in some way concerned with contemporary society, it is not really surprising that the critic Georg Brandes should have made an impression with his assertion that literature only shows signs of life when it debates problems. These words, uttered in 1871, came at an abundantly favourable time, a time when society was ready for a change after a period of relative stagnation, thanks to the aftermath of the wars earlier in the century, and at a time when new techniques and new ideas at all levels were capable of ensuring an end to that stagnation. Brandes made his original impression not only because of what he said, but also because of when he said it. The result was a close affinity between the literary radicalism of Georg Brandes and the political radicalism of his brother Edvard and of Viggo Hørup. Little wonder that while the political Radicals became known as the Radical Left, the literary and cultural movement for change under Georg Brandes was dubbed 'the Literary Left'. Neither, however, was popular with the Moderate Left, with its Grundtvigian affinities and its Christian and nationalist overtones.

Romanticism, or its echoes, had persisted until after the 1864 war. Some of its great figures had lived until the mid-1850s, while others, notably Andersen and Grundtvig, lived on until the 1870s, even if they could no longer be said to be figures of literary influence. Literary criticism had also remained in its Romantic stage, not least thanks to the influence of Heiberg in the 1840s. Literary eyes were in fact almost all turned inwards, and in a society which itself was more or less indifferent to what was going on outside, it was natural that few new ideas should be introduced. Then, after 1864, came the transformation of Danish society and a gradual realisation that the civilisation hitherto obtaining had not been valid for all time, that other countries had progressed both materially and intellectually. Thus, when Brandes started introducing new ideas from all over Europe, the time was ripe for progress. With him came the modern English and French philosophical ideas of John Stuart Mill and Auguste Comte; with him, too, came an upsurge of Darwinism, though Darwin's *Origin of Species* had already been translated into Danish by J. P. Jacobsen. In the field of theology, the liberal, radical ideas of Strauss and Feuerbach were introduced. Marx was also brought into the picture, though his importance for Danish literature was limited. All these ideas were in conflict with the established outlook in Denmark and they led people to question all accepted conventions – marriage, religion, political institutions, family life, the position of women in society – nothing was left untouched. It was clear that in introducing the discussion of contemporary society into literature, Brandes was forming a link between political and literary radicalism – hence the name 'the Literary Left' – to go hand in hand with the other Left groups. In this he was ably helped by Edvard, who was politically more active at the same time as he was acknowledged to be almost as redoubtable as a critic – 'the best hated man in public life', Georg Brandes admiringly called his brother in 1883.

The fact that the time was ripe for Brandes' arguments and his attempts to reintroduce a new, European, radical dynamism into Danish literature did not, however, mean that he had all his own way. Indeed, although the youth of his day was attracted by him, the older generation saw him as Lucifer and as of one accord sought to stop him. He was opposed by the entire establishment, whether on political, religious, or moral grounds, and when the chair of literature became vacant at the university in 1872 and Brandes was nominated for it by the retiring professor as being the only man qualified, he was kept out. Feelings ran extremely high throughout the 'cultural debate', possibly higher than they have run since, and book after book dealing with this period, be it fictitious or biographical, indicates the intensity of the struggle. In his autobiography, Johannes Jørgensen, an opponent of the idea of this movement, subsequently known as the Modern Breakthrough,[2] told how as a child he was kept away from conversations concerning modern literature, and how the new literature was received :

[2] See below, p. 134.

They spoke of 'this Ibsen', 'this Brandes', 'this Drachmann', and sometimes of 'this Zola'. . . . Most of what they wrote was supposed to be of little value : admittedly, Ibsen had previously written valuable works, such as *The Pretenders,* and to some extent *Brand,* but his latest plays – now that Nora or whatever her name is, who deserts her husband – is there supposed to be anything beautiful or elevating in that?

The new revolutionary ideas undermined the boy's views of life, given him by his parents, and caused a break with them as happened in countless other homes. Jørgensen tells also how his ideas led him to take part in workers' demonstrations in Copenhagen – and thereby lose the support of the kindly but conservative families who had given him patronage as a student. (It was quite common then for a student to have a number of families who 'adopted' him, so that he could always be sure of a free meal.)

The same situation is to be sensed in the work of Henrik Pontoppidan, a loyal admirer of Brandes, who depicts him in his novel *Lucky Peter* as a certain Dr Nathan. There 'Dr Nathan' is referred to as 'this much fêted and much attacked man who more energetically and determinedly than anyone else had cleared the ground for a Denmark of the future and started a stir in the country, the likes of which had not been seen in any intellectual or spiritual movement since the "Reformation" '. Dr Nathan (Brandes) had attracted followers and created opponents, and the split between them was deep :

In a way the extent of Nathan's significance could temporarily best be measured in his opponents. In several of them he had really succeeded in awakening that active passion, that fanatical fire which he in vain had sought to inspire in his comrades in arms. The religious counter-movement was still not very apparent in the capital, where minds were too concerned with the newly created stir in business life. But in the provinces, especially out in the country, it was quietly growing strong, gathering together in parsonages and high schools like an army around its fortresses.

As it was, the Modern Breakthrough provided Denmark with an upsurge of new literature aimed at carrying out Brandes' demand for contemporary interest, and philosophically based on Darwinism and a new pagan humanism : 'There is no God, and Man in his prophet', remarks one of the characters in Jens Peter Jacobsen's novel *Niels Lyhne,* the story of a man who throughout his life fights with himself and with others for his atheist faith, and who

finally, mortally wounded in the war of 1864, refuses the ministra-
tions of a priest and 'dies the death, the difficult death'.

J. P. Jacobsen, the first and internationally the most influential
of the writers of the Modern Breakthrough, points to something
of a paradox in the movement. While many of the most thoroughgoing Brandesians are now relegated to the histories of literature –
and only the larger ones at that – those writers who have achieved
a lasting place in the Danish literary consciousness are all in varying degrees exceptions who only within certain limitations can be
said to be representative of the movement. The medium of this
kind of movement must obviously be prose, probably rather colour-
less prose. Yet Jacobsen started his career as a lyric poet, one of
startling originality even, and during this time provided the cycle
of poems which in their German translations Schönberg took as
the text of his *Gurrelieder*. Even here, however, with the thwarted
Valdemar cursing God and being condemned to hunt the forests
of Zealand until the end of time, there is discernible the anti-
Christian tendency of the Naturalist movement, the Modern Breakthrough. It was a traditional story, of course, but one which must
have had a special appeal to a budding atheist.

After Brandes entered the arena Jacobsen abandoned poetry in
favour of prose, and his prose is among the most finely chiselled
language ever produced in Denmark, a language which at its best
is rhythmic and almost poetry, but which at its worst is artificial
to the extent of being mannered. In his attempt at finding the
mot juste, Jacobsen reminds one very much of Gustave Flaubert,
and in fact his first major novel, *Marie Grubbe*, is almost a Danish
version of *Madame Bovary*. Based on historical fact, it is the story
of a woman who belongs to the very highest strata of society, but
gradually sinks, until she ends by eloping with a farm labourer, a
potential criminal, and ferrying people across the straits between
Zealand and Falster. Such a theme had attracted other writers
before Jacobsen, but the interest here is the psychological motivation, based on Jacobsen's Darwinist conception of human nature.
Basic animal instinct is what drives Marie Grubbe to do what she
does. But the novel is an expression of faith, not an attempt at
discussing modern problems. Jacobsen's other novel, *Niels Lyhne*,
however, is an attempt at examining one 'problem' of the day in
its treatment of the theme of atheism – though one feels that the
author is looking at it from his own point of view rather than from
a general standpoint. He was dying, and he knew it, and the question of faith was of vital importance to him.

Because he was not concerned with the immediate problems of
Danish society, Jacobsen was able to give his work a more universal

quality than was the case with any of the other writers of this period. However firmly his work was placed against a Danish background, it was in each case a historical one, albeit in the case of *Niels Lyhne* a recent historical one, and this in itself is sufficient evidence that Jacobsen was not primarily interested in society in the sense of social conditions. His 'problems' are of an ethical-religious nature, and as such could still be appreciated outside the borders of his homeland. Whatever he has done with the text, it is perhaps symptomatic that Frederick Delius should have chosen just this novel as the basis for one of his operas, *Fennimore and Gerda*. It is this universality of Jacobsen's that distinguishes him from his contemporaries.

At the other end of the scale is Henrik Pontoppidan, who started life as an out-and-out social critic in a series of short stories dealing with the material conditions of the poor, and went on to produce a number of long novels in which material conditions play a smaller part, but, where Danish society is concerned, none the less is always of fundamental importance. As already indicated, *Lucky Peter* is concerned with Copenhagen at the time of Brandes, a city torn between the old and the new. On another level the conflict between old and new is reflected in Peter's struggle between his rural, Grundtvigian upbringing and the dynamic, materialistic outlook which he cultivates in Copenhagen. This is a novel which might possibly be acceptable to an English-speaking public without any particular knowledge of Danish affairs, but the earlier trilogy *The Promised Land*, concerned with sectarian conflicts in rural Denmark, is scarcely destined to be read outside its homeland. Perhaps this is reflected in the fact that the first two volumes were once translated into English, while the third never appeared. Again, the third of Pontoppidan's novels, *The Realm of the Dead,* is closely tied up with the political situation, and it will only be fully appreciated by a reader who knows at least a modicum of Danish history. At the same time the author is concerned to chart the social developments of the age, showing how the new, upstart families who had gained wealth from the new industrialisation were trying to assert themselves alongside the families whose culture was established, but whose wealth was diminishing. For all his radicalism, Pontoppidan obviously deplores the ensuing decline in cultural standards, as does Herman Bang in a parallel situation in his *Ludvigsbakke*. In his concern with social and political problems, and also in his discussion of ethical questions, Pontoppidan is well within the definition of the Modern Breakthrough. Where he differs to some extent is, however, in the ascetic solutions he finds to some of them.

Lucky Peter, the brilliant engineer, throws away his opportunities and finally dies as a road-mender in Jutland, materially a waste, but nevertheless finding a sort of peace of mind, a kind of Nirvana. And Torben Dihmer, the central figure of *The Realm of the Dead*, finally contracts out of life by refusing to take the medicine he needs to keep him alive : he symbolises a refusal to accept modern civilisation.

The other two figures of the Modern Breakthrough are also to some extent exceptions to the rule. In a time of prose, Holger Drachmann was a lyric poet who at first tried to use his lyrical gifts in support of the new movement, but gradually drifted into a more expressly Romantic view of life. And Herman Bang, the Impressionist, is far more concerned with individuals than with society as a whole, although the social picture is important to some of his work. He is mainly interested in depicting those whom life has passed by : the nurse who sacrifices herself to the man she loves, but who is rejected for someone with a larger fortune, or the gentle wife of a boorish stationmaster watching life slipping away and not being willing to make a break when another man appears on the scene. These are sad, muted stories, written with great artistry : they are worthy of a greater reputation, but are so unassuming that they have not made their mark outside Denmark. In their gentle melancholy there is something peculiarly Danish about them which has in general tied them to their land of origin.

These four men are the outstanding representatives of the Modern Breakthrough, even though literature with a social flavour has continued to be written even to the present day. One thinks in this connection of authors such as Aakjær, whose novels from the end of the nineteenth century and the beginning of the twentieth were fervent attacks on social injustice, or even of Jakob Knudsen who defended the *status quo* and discussed social and ethical problems from a conservative standpoint. Yet, within twenty years of its beginning, the Modern Breakthrough was spent and had to give way to a new form of literature, more lyrical and more abstract in character. In the late 1880s a new generation of authors appeared who, though at first Brandesian in outlook, soon began to tire of the grey prose which was the typical product of the time. And when they came across the French Symbolist poets, they found a literary form which appealed to their own deepest instincts. Social problems, and indeed society itself, were pushed into the background, and the new writers sought instead to establish something beyond materialism.

Thus the 1890s emerge as a decade of introspection and soul-searching, though this is only a partially true picture. The major writers of the breakthrough were still productive, while the second generation of realists – Aakjær and company – were also active. The lyric element, however, was the work of the most significant group among the younger generation, and the introspection of much of their poetry was echoed in their prose and in that of some of the younger writers emerging at the end of the 1890s. The two major writers in question, Johannes V. Jensen and Martin Nexø, have both achieved an international reputation for their later, more extrovert, work, but they both started off as typical products of the 1890s, exponents of the *fin de siècle* atmosphere which had developed.

Literature, society, and politics – and painting, with the social realism of a P. S. Krøyer and a Christian Krogh – had gone hand in hand in this final period of the nineteenth century, perhaps more noticeably than they had done for over a century. These final decades had brought about an awakening of the social and political conscience which had transplanted itself to literature, and for which literature had become a willing vehicle. It had been a period of immense drive during which Denmark, partly through reaction against the lingering Romanticism of the years up to 1864 and partly through the introduction of new ideas from other more progressive countries, had undergone a profound but relatively peaceful transformation. By the turn of the century Denmark was on the road to becoming the country we know today, a country with a social conscience, with an economic urge and, by 1901, a democratic system. She had been transformed from an inward-looking and backward country to an outward-looking nation rapidly catching up with her neighbours.

Chapter 4

1901–14

Reform within Limits

The First Democratic Government

IT WOULD BE USELESS to pretend that the king was enthusiastic in
his decision to give in to popular pressure and introduce the principle of parliamentary democracy. He was loath to relinquish rule
by the Right, and his basic dislike of the Left was apparent in his
decision to use his prerogative and choose as his Prime Minister not
the leader of the Left, J. C. Christensen, but an academic who had
so far played little or no part in political life. Deuntzer may well
have had Left views, but at least he was not a farmer. On the other
hand, he was quite aware that it would be impossible to form a
viable government without bringing in professional politicians as
his chief Ministers, and this he set about doing. J. C. Christensen
was naturally included, and so, after some hesitation, was the
mercurial Viggo Hørup, although he was not a member of the
Folketing. The new government was very different in character
from anything that had gone before : instead of the academics and
aristocrats of former times, it included schoolteachers, farmers, and,
in charge of military and naval matters, men from the services with
first-hand knowledge of the situation rather than professional politicians. There was a genuine effort to bring into the government
politicians and non-politicians alike whose views could be classed
as Left, and who were willing to devote themselves to spheres of
activity in which they were specialists. Deuntzer also made a show
of balancing in his government the conflicting views which were
held by the various factions of which the Left was composed,
factions with such strongly held principles that they were finally
to lead to the breaking-up of the Left as a single party. The views
of the Radicals and the Moderates were too incompatible for them
to belong to the same party once that party had achieved power
and had been given the opportunity of ruling and carrying out a
policy. The bond that had held them together – the desire to get

rid of the Right and the knowledge that concerted action could
best be expected to achieve this – was liable to dissolve at any
moment. Then, as time went on, the smallholders, on whose support
the Left had also depended, discovered that in power the farmers
were less inclined to look to the interests of the rural working classes
that had been expected. As the government became more obviously
a farmers' government, they withdrew their support from the party
and moved instead to the Social Democrats. Parliamentary democracy had certainly been achieved, but new divisions and new
struggles lay ahead.

In the *Folketing* the new government, within the limits laid down
by its own divergent opinions, could command a majority, but this
was not the case in the *Landsting*, where the Right still held sway.
As legislation could only be carried through if a bill was passed in
identical form in both houses, it appeared at first that Deuntzer's
colleagues might still have difficulty in carrying out any serious
programme of reform. However, they were helped by disunity
within the ranks of the Right Party itself. The nine members of
the *Landsting* who had broken with the Right in 1900[1] now officially launched an independent conservative party which they
called the Free Conservatives. Here the Left found the means of
achieving compromise agreements and forcing them through the
Landsting. With the help of the newly formed Free Conservatives
the Left managed to push through many of the reforms it had so
long desired. The first of these was to be tax reform.

The new taxation laws meant a reduction of land taxes in the
countryside and an increase in property taxes in the towns. These
were coupled with the introduction of direct income tax according
to a sliding scale, though to a modern eye the forms it took were
haphazard. It was not compulsory to fill in returns, and only about
60 per cent of those liable did in fact do so. The remainder were
content to accept the assessment of the taxation authorities, a sign
of how intimate Danish society as a whole was – the tax authorities
obviously knew sufficient of their immediate neighbours' means to
be able to tax them reasonably accurately. Symptomatically, a
greater percentage of townsfolk preferred to fill in their assessment
forms.

Change came in another field, too, where it was long overdue.
Tithes were still the rule in Denmark, though instead of going to
the Church, as had been the case before the Reformation, they
went to those people, and their successors, to whom church property had been distributed – in effect often the local pastors. Henrik
Pontoppidan, in his early satirical story *The Polar Bear*, gives a

[1] See above, p. 87.

clear impression of how deeply rooted the custom was in the rural population by telling how Thorkild Müller, an unconventional pastor, sees the poverty of many of his parishioners, and decides with true Christian charity to forego his tithes. He tells them so, but instead of being hailed as a man of vision, he actually loses prestige as his flock think he must be mad. The entire system was done away with in this 1903 tax reform, though provisions were made for compensation to be paid to those affected.

The other significant reforms introduced by the new government concerned education, and 1903 saw a new Education Act which remained the basis of education in Denmark until 1958. Until now schools by and large had been of two types: primary and grammar; and a grammar-school education had been reserved for those who could afford it. The grammar school led to the final Student's Examination, which gave access to the university. The new act made provision for free schooling not only in the primary stage, but also beyond it in what was called the middle school, with entry at the age of twelve. Entrance to a grammar school now came after the middle-school examination, with entry at about fourteen. The result of this new act was to make education available to classes who had previously been barred from it, and to make for greater uniformity in the educational pattern. It is generally considered that this reform was a major step to breaking down the class distinctions which had existed until that time, but which are so significantly absent today. The local authorities were keen to adopt the new line laid down by the act, and a great improvement in educational facilities was made, less marked, however, in the country districts than in the towns.

Nevertheless, the government did not in the main live up to its promises, and various sections of the community, especially the smallholders who did not benefit from the tax reform, felt that they had been let down. Moreover, there was the perennial question of defence. Hørup, as ever against spending on defence, had in practice little influence on the government, as he was already a sick man when appointed Traffic Minister, and in 1902 he died. He was not replaced by a man of similar views, and thus opinion within the government swung towards accepting expenditure on defence. The more radical members of the *Folketing* began to react against the increasingly conservative attitude of the government – though this was to some extent due to the need for co-operation with the Free Conservatives in the *Landsting* – and as a countermeasure they formed the Radical Club, which aimed at the same drastic programme of reform that had formerly been the Left's. In 1903 the Social Democrats increased their representation in the

Folketing and sought to cause a split within the government on the defence issue. They succeeded, as the Army Minister had gone beyond his mandate and built defences without authorisation – and the first Left government fell in January 1905.

Compromise and Conflict

It was followed by a new government under J. C. Christensen who had exercised a dominant influence even when Deuntzer was Prime Minister. He was a negotiator *par excellence* who understood the need for compromise in order to achieve any reforms at all. His programme was ambivalent on the question of defence, but tended to be conservative. So high did feelings run that a group of eight anti-defence members threatened to break with the party and were finally excluded from it. This coincided with agitation for a more radical party which would carry out the reforms previously expected of the Left. In 1905 a convention in Odense launched a completely new political party which called itself the Radical Left (Radicals), obviously indicative of its sympathy with the radical programme of many members of the Left Party. The eight Left rebels immediately joined the new party and a radical reform programme was published. An interesting side issue connected with the formation of this new party was the fact that it was formed outside the *Folketing*, and thereafter sought representation, as had also been the case with the Social Democrats. By way of contrast, the two older parties had originated from groups within the *Folketing* who had then sought recognition and support from the voters.

The new party aimed first and foremost at proclaiming Denmark a neutral state and reducing all armed forces to the status of border- and coast-guards. Other reforms demanded were more help to smallholders (who had been disillusioned by the neglect accorded to them by the Left and the realisation that the tax reforms had benefited them less than the wealthier farmers); taxation based on land values according to the ideas of the noted American economist and social reformer Henry George;[2] greater social equality, including women's right to vote; and far-reaching social reforms. These were in many ways a restatement of the old Left principles which were being forgotten and shelved as the party was moving towards a more conservative attitude. It was, of course, not the first time an effort had been made to maintain the radicalism of the programme originally formulated by the Left, but while the earlier breakaway groups had been short-lived, this new party had come to stay, and has played an important part in later

[2] See below, p. 134.

Danish politics. Although springing from the Left, and thus having
affinities with it, it has incorporated many ideas which are akin to
those of the Social Democrats, and has thus on many occasions
been able to form a coalition with both the other parties. Always
a small party, it has often held a balance of power. In the *Folketing*
elections following its formation, it already showed this ability to
co-operate by making an electoral pact with the Social Democrats,
an arrangement whereby the Social Democrats were to gain 8 seats,
and rise to twenty-four, while the Radical Left won 11 seats.

One of the points of contention in the election was again the
question of defence, though this was coupled with that of electoral
reform in local elections. Local authorities had been so far elected
on a limited franchise, but the Left Reform Party[3] was in favour
of extending the franchise. In the end, having lost its overall
majority in the election, the Left Reform co-operated with the
Moderate Left and the Right to force through its proposals. That
the more conservative members were willing to lend their support
was not due to any strong desire to see the old system reformed –
they were bound to lose by it – but to avoid the possibility of
Radical Left and Social Democrat thinking on defence gaining
ground. The result was something of a compromise, as the Conservatives introduced a clause laying down certain requirements,
which successfully kept numbers of itinerant workers off the electoral roll.

No immediate action was taken on defence, as the government
was waiting for the report of a commission on defence set up some
years previously. Nevertheless, the issue was a major one, even
though it was not quite clear against whom Denmark was trying to
defend herself. If the enemy was Germany, things would have to
be organised differently than against Britain and France. The rest
of Europe was dividing into the German or Anglo-French camps,
and it seemed that a decision must be taken. Germany was herself
seeking to gain Danish support, a desire reflected not only in
general contacts, but also in the more liberal attitude adopted
towards Danish sympathisers in the former duchies of Schleswig
and Holstein. Yet, while the government was inclined to seek a
modus vivendi with Germany – though not to enter into an alliance
– popular sentiment was anti-German and pro-British. J. C. Christensen's attitude, which was also that of King Frederik VIII upon
his accession in 1906, was to provide sufficient defence forces in
Denmark to act as a deterrent to anyone who might wish to carry
out a bloodless invasion.

When the defence commission finally produced its report, its

[3] See above, p. 86.

members were seen to be in as much disagreement as the politicians. The decision about what action to take seemed to be left
to J. C. Christensen, but then, unexpectedly, any action he was
contemplating was stopped by what was probably the biggest
Danish government scandal of all time.

For a good while rumours had been circulating about the affairs
of P. A. Alberti, the Minister of Justice. Questions had been asked
in the *Folketing,* but had always apparently elicited satisfactory
answers. Nevertheless the campaign against Alberti continued and
in July 1908 Christensen was finally forced to ask for his resignation. In May that year Alberti, who was a director of the Zealand
Farmers' Savings Bank, had asked Christensen for a loan from
state funds to save the bank from going into liquidation. At a
particularly difficult financial period the request was granted and
the state was given mortgage deeds as security. The deal was,
however, kept secret. New rumours developed about Alberti, news
of the transaction leaked out, and finally Alberti himself, no longer
a Minister, admitted embezzlement of a sum totalling 9 million
kroner. In the resultant examination of his affairs, this was in fact
shown to be a conservative estimate and the true total was 15 million. Alberti was disgraced and in 1910 sentenced to eight years
imprisonment, and thus disappeared from the political scene. But
Christensen was left to cope with the crisis which Alberti had
occasioned. He was himself entirely blameless – though perhaps he
should have seen through what was going on – but by the middle
of September 1908 he was forced to resign together with his
government, with the defence question still unresolved.

The succeeding administration under N. Neergaard aimed to
solve the question once and for all. The new Prime Minister was
a member of the relatively conservative Moderate Left, and as
such in favour of some defence arrangement. Finally he arrived at
a compromise with the Right and the Left Reform Party, whereby
the army and navy should be reorganised and the land fortifications of Copenhagen replaced by a limited number of outlying
forts. This, it was hoped, would satisfy everyone. But before the
plan could be carried out, an election was held in which the Left
Reform Party lost heavily, while both the Right and Radical Left
won seats. And significantly, in view of its attitude towards defence,
the Social Democrat Party won more votes than any other.

It still proved impossible to agree on the compromise, and consequently the government resigned after less than ten months in
office. Its successor lasted only six weeks, but managed to reach a
compromise agreement whereby some fortifications were to be

maintained until 1922, while plans for others were to be scrapped. This compromise came about not so much because of enthusiasm on anyone's part, but because it began to look as though the new democratic ways were not leading to effective government, and there was a sense of the need to achieve something in order to avoid undermining the system which had been so long preparing.

The Radical Left brought this short-lived government down and so it was only fair that the problems of forming a ministry should fall to the party. Even with the help of the Social Democrats, it was a minority government incapable of taking effective measures. Furthermore, the Radical Left refused to make the compromises which had enabled previous Left governments to rule, preferring to be a government of principle, and decided to hold an election in May 1910. Both the Radicals and the Social Democrats maintained their strength, but the position of the other parties altered decisively. The various factions of the Left had again combined and fought as one party under the simple name of Left, and by so doing had won 57 seats, while the Right had been reduced to thirteen. This new amalgamation of the various factions within the Left meant that the major parties which have dominated Danish politics in recent years had been formed : the Right, the Conservatives, which was subsequently to change its name to the Conservative People's Party;[4] the Left (*Venstre*[5] as it is still called to this day), a moderate liberal party, especially close to the farming community, variously referred to in English as the Liberal Democrats or Social Liberals; the Radical Left, now completely divorced from the original Left Party, known in English as the Radical Liberal Party; and the Social Democrats. Thus the parties had taken shape after a varied and even confusing history over a period of fifty years, and Denmark had achieved certain political maturity.

A Return to the Constitutional Issue

It was an old *Venstre* wish to return to the liberal constitution which had been replaced in 1866 and the new government under Klaus Berntsen, though more conservative in outlook than its predecessors, set about revising the constitution. In particular it looked into the role of the *Landsting* and suggested that in a case of disagreement between the two houses they should get together and

[4] See below, p. 121.
[5] With this stabilisation of the parties the English equivalents for the various factions of the Left will hereafter be dropped, the Danish name of *Venstre*, free from the overtones which the word Left has in modern politics, will be used. The term Right, on the other hand, must for the time being be retained, because when an official change was finally made, it was with a definite purpose in mind.

vote as one. The difficulty, of course, was getting this new constitution through the *Landsting* after it had passed the *Folketing*.
When the time came for new elections to the *Folketing* in 1913, no
progress whatsoever had been made on this issue. The election
results changed the balance of power in the *Folketing* completely :
the Right had only 7 seats and *Venstre* forty-four; while the
Radicals had thirty-one and the Social Democrats thirty-two. The
time seemed to have come for the radical parties to share power.

All was not plain sailing, however, for although the Radicals
themselves were willing to form a government, they did not wish
to show any unseemly haste, while the Social Democrats, not being
quite sure of the Radicals, and being more inclined to wait until
they were in a position to form a government alone, preferred the
Berntsen government to stay in office. It had gone to the polls on
the constitutional issue and the Social Democrats were themselves
interested in seeing the proposed amendment carried out. For a
time the two majority parties were arguing that the government
should remain at its post, while the government only wanted to
resign, J. C. Christensen arguing that the voters had given the
majority to the radical parties and that therefore it was their right
and duty to accept responsibility. The Social Democrats refused to
form a coalition with the Radicals, but finally the problem was
solved when they promised to support a Radical minority government under C. T. Zahle, who had held office for six months after
the Alberti affair.

The immediate concern was again that of a liberal constitution,
and it was originally the new government's intention to lay before
the *Rigsdag* the same proposals as had Berntsen's government. Yet
it still remained uncertain whether, even if the *Folketing* passed
them, the *Landsting* would not reject them again. The problem was
even more complicated when Christensen on his own account published some new proposals for a constitution, slightly more conservative than those of the Berntsen government. This conserva-
tism was especially to be found in his proposals for the *Landsting* :
it should be elected by indirect voting, the voters all being aged
thirty-five or over, and once elected its dissolution would not be
possible until the next general election. Moreover, he proposed
that any future changes in the constitution should require a two-
thirds majority in a general referendum. The proposals went counter to all that had been suggested so far, but they found favour
among the Right and among more conservative members of the
three parties which favoured altering the constitution.

In the event Christensen's *Landsting* proposals formed the basis
for the new legislation on the upper chamber. His suggestion of

indirect voting was accepted, but the suggestion that the *Landsting* should be indissoluble was rejected. Instead the procedure for dissolution was laid down quite precisely : it could only be done if the *Landsting* twice rejected an identical bill submitted to it by two *Folketings* chosen in statutory elections – it was no use dissolving the *Folketing* merely for the purpose of resubmitting a bill. It was fairly plain that although the *Landsting* could in theory be dissolved, in practice it would be hard to do so. The deputies of the Right, however, sought to make the best of a bad job by co-operating only at a price. They wanted proportional representation and finally got their wish in Copenhagen and three major cities. In the remaining constituencies a second ballot was to be held if no candidate were elected with an absolute majority of the votes cast.

But the proposal had to go through the *Landsting* according to the constitution then in force, and although Estrup chose to die in 1913, to be replaced by Deuntzer, thus giving a majority of one in favour of the new proposals, the Right boycotted the sessions and thus prevented a quorum. There was nothing for it but to dissolve the *Landsting* and hope that the ensuing election would show a majority in favour of reform. This did in fact happen, so that the new constitution seemed assured of an easy passage when the new *Rigsdag* met on 20 July 1914. But before the necessary procedure could begin, the First World War had broken out and the constitutional crisis was completely overshadowed. Not for the first time, constitutional issues in Denmark were swept aside by external events.

Attention was now turned to Denmark's international relations, with the aim of keeping the country out of the conflict which was obviously going to engulf most of Europe. Denmark was in the difficult position of being on good terms with all the belligerents, but while relations with Germany on the official level were good, there was a distinct anti-German sentiment in the population at large. The events of 1864 had not been forgotten, and emotions similar to those that had agitated for intervention in the Franco-Prussian War were widespread. The Germans were aware of this, and one of the worries of the Danish government was whether Germany in the final analysis would feel able to rely on Denmark's protestations of neutrality.

In the country as a whole, while war had been unthinkable, there was a feeling of approaching disaster : not merely a fear for the safety of Denmark as a country, but the feeling that the world was seeing the end of an era. After a period of unbroken peace and increasing stability and prosperity, upon which had been founded a civilised and increasingly humane society, Denmark found herself facing a catastrophe of unknown dimensions. News-papers of the day tell plainly of the confusion in Copenhagen, while Jacob Paludan, in his novel *Jørgen Stein,* shows how the news of the assassination in Sarajevo broke on a typical upper-class dinner in the Danish provinces. On a different level there was the contrast between the widespread anti-militarism in Denmark and the desire for revenge in other sections of the population, a com-bination which was subsequently to have its effect on public morale.

Chapter 5

1914–18

Between the Belligerents

The Immediate Effect of the War

BECAUSE OF THE LOSS of Schleswig and Holstein in 1864, and, even more, the repressive measures which had periodically been enforced by Prussia against Danish sympathisers in the former duchies, there was no doubt where the sympathies of the Danish people lay in 1914. Official policy was to keep out of the conflict, but there was some heartsearching in Danish official circles in case the German government should have such doubts about the Danish will, or ability, to avoid taking sides that they might decide to invade. As long as the war was fought on land Denmark was of little significance, but in any naval hostilities she would hold the key to the Baltic, a position which in the old days had been an enviable one, but which has since on more than one occasion brought her into conflicts she would rather have avoided. Consequently, on this occasion the government went to considerable lengths to convince the Germans of neutral intentions, proclaiming their strict neutrality and promising not call up the security forces, although the navy was put on an alert and the sea forts manned as well. It should be noted that the British government had dropped a hint to Denmark that she should not rely on assistance in the event of an attack. The Danes had to do as little as possible and hope. Indeed, Edvard Brandes, the Minister of Finance, warned the people against demonstrating feelings at variance with the country's official policy of neutrality.

The first difficulties arose when Germany started mining the Langeland straits, south of the Great Belt, and put indirect pressure on Denmark to mine the Great Belt herself. The Danes were afraid that if they did not do so, the Germans would lay their own mines and then establish shore posts to guard them. Consequently after lengthy consultations the decision was made to mine Danish waters, and mines were in fact laid in both Belts and the Sound. King

Christian X sent a telegram to his cousin George V informing him
of the move, and received the reassuring reply that Great Britain
understood Denmark's difficult position. The Danes also informed
Germany that any attempt to break through the minefields would
be considered a breach of Danish neutrality, and that it would be
communicated to other belligerent powers.

The trade situation was more complicated. A large proportion
of Danish trade was carried out with Great Britain and Germany –
about 60 per cent of Denmark's agriculture exports went to
England, 30 per cent to Germany – and a difficult balancing act
was needed if trade was not to be seriously interrupted. Moreover,
Denmark was dependent on trade, especially with England, for her
supply of raw materials. At the same time it was in the belligerents'
own interests to continue trade with Denmark – England because
of her agricultural imports, Germany because of her desire to use
Denmark and Danish ports for the transit of goods from America.
In this peculiar situation – both the warring nations were in a
position to damage the other by cutting off Danish trade, but by
doing so they would also hurt themselves – an arrangement was
made by which Germany promised for the time being not to interfere with Denmark's exports to England, and Britain allowed
American goods to be imported into Denmark provided that certain of them were not re-exported to Germany. Restrictions were
immediately placed on some of these goods, but before the export
of horses was prohibited in November 1914, some 80,000 had been
sent across the frontier, and fortunes made in the process. Nor were
these to be the only ones made in Denmark during the war.

However, during the first few days of August 1914 most people
were less interested in making quick fortunes than in ensuring the
safety of such money as they then possessed. There was a run on
the banks and a demand for gold, which the National Bank was
by law forced to pay in exchange for paper money. That law was
very quickly changed, apparently only for a while, but in reality
for good. In this sphere as in so many others, the old order was
changing. Even silver money became scarce and the National Bank
was given leave to issue paper money for amounts down to one
krone. At the same time food prices soared, by as much as 30 to 100
per cent in the space of a few days, and it became apparent that
the government would have to do something to ensure the reasonable distribution of food and to keep prices within tolerable limits.
The argument that high prices would themselves ration food was
correct, but it overlooked the fact that everyday commodities such
as rye bread and potatoes were put out of the reach of precisely
those people who were most dependent on them. As a result of the

rapidly deteriorating situation the *Rigsdag* passed on 7 August a law giving the government very wide powers to regulate trade; to enforce maximum prices on goods; and to ensure a fair distribution of them. As a result of this new act, the government was empowered to interfere in fields which had traditionally been outside the sphere of its control, and here again it is reasonable to talk of the old order changing, for although these measures were only to be temporary, they were in fact the beginning of something new and permanent, something of which the Social Democrats were in favour, as were now other sections of the population who had not previously seen eye to eye with the Social Democrats. The government was also required to act on the insurance question. With the outbreak of war, shipping had come to a standstill from fear of submarine attacks or of minefields. Insurance companies refused to accept the increased risk, and thus the government was itself forced to accept a liability for compensation in the event of loss through hostilities. And losses there were – 236 Danish ships went down through submarine activities and thirty-eight were mined in the course of the war.

The decision to help to insure shipping during the war was taken by the new government Special Commission acting in conjunction with representatives of trade and commerce, a method of working which was to become more and more common during the war and to bear fruit in the years to come. From it came the realisation that by giving the representatives of trade and commerce some say in taking important decisions, their sense of responsibility also grew, and an increasingly close co-operation was fostered between the government and representatives of various branches of national life, including the trade unions. There is no doubt that responsible co-operation between these various parties has stood Denmark in good stead and brought about a sense of working together for the common good rather than working for sectional interests at the expense of others.

However, a sense of responsibility was not common to all sections of the community, and some of its members set about the task of earning – and losing – large fortunes overnight. As Denmark was neutral, and had her imports more or less guaranteed, she was able to produce many goods which the belligerent powers wanted to buy. In particular Germany began importing great quantities of Danish goods, and at one time bought some 50 per cent of Danish exports. Not least among these was tinned stewed meat (goulash), and so great was German demand for this that the traditional Danish quality was in some cases alarmingly reduced. This sale of low-quality goods became almost symbolic of the age, which has become known as the *gullasch* age, and the profiteers as the *gullasch* barons – their entire range of vision warped by the profits they were able to make thanks to the war.

The lack of competition from abroad, where all efforts went towards fighting and where manpower was scarce, and the demand for Danish goods from former competitors caused a remarkable drop in Danish unemployment figures. The percentage in the years before the war had varied between 6 and 13; but after an initial rise from 8 per cent at the beginning of the war, it fell to that figure again in 1915 and then even dropped as low as 5 per cent in 1916. Shares rose and there was widespread speculation in them. Denmark had for the first time in years a surplus in the balance of payments and ready money was plentiful among many sections of the population. The resultant rise in prices, however, led to hardship among those who had a five-year agreement on wages, workers and employees of state and local authorities. Counting 1914 as 100, the retail price index rose to 136 by 1916, but the workers were still bound by an agreement signed in 1911, and despite some slight adjustments by some firms, their standard of living fell. In the new agreement of 1916 a cost of living bonus was agreed, though this still did not reach the 1911 standard, and discontent was only to be expected among those who found themselves so severely restricted; while others were fast becoming rich, so rich, it was said, that they used 100 *kroner* notes to light their pipes – probably an apocryphal story, but illustrative of the age none the less.

The government found itself having to play an increasingly active part in regulating the day to day affairs of the Danes. More and more prices were fixed. So, in 1916, were rents, which were threatening to rise at an alarming rate and hit the already battered lower-income groups. The Statistical Department began gathering information on prices and costs, and on this basis it became possible to work out an accurate cost of living index, according to which it has since become customary to regulate wages and salaries, a system which has certainly led to difficulties, as it has had a direct inflationary tendency in the past twenty years, but which has helped to avoid much industrial discontent.

The Constitutional Issue Solved

The difficulties occasioned by the war contributed, however, to reaching an agreement on the constitutional problem. A new willingness to compromise was evident and the Right ceased to block the progress of the constitutional reform in return for certain concessions on voting procedures. Its following throughout the country was fair, though scattered, and thus it lost its chance of significant representation in the single-seat constituencies. Consequently, in order to maintain an influence corresponding to its total strength, it wanted proportional representation. In the end a complicated system was devised, with proportional representation in Copenhagen and Frederiksberg and 93 single-seat constituencies throughout the rest of the country, but with 23 supplementary seats spread throughout the country to be filled in proportion to the votes cast. Of these nine were for the islands, eleven for Jutland, and the remaining three to be divided for the country as a whole. It was a typical compromise which was subjected to considerable criticism, especially from the Radicals, who felt that the distribution of the 23 seats would favour *Venstre*. Another concession to the Right was the decision that one-quarter of the new *Landsting* members should be elected by the outgoing *Landsting* and that any subsequent alterations to the constitution should be approved by 45 per cent of the electorate in a referendum. Yet another concession was a clause stating that forced purchases could be delayed until the next elected *Rigsdag* if demanded by at least one-third of the *Folketing*. The voice of the landowners was very plain here.

Once these concessions were arranged, the remainder of the new constitution was plain sailing, providing for a lowering of the voting age for the *Folketing,* in stages, from thirty to twenty-five, while the voting age for the *Landsting* was raised to thirty-five. Women were also given the vote and made eligible for the *Rigsdag,* and so were the lowest-paid workers. The new constitution gave Denmark, true to her predominant democratic sentiments, a much more progressive form of government based on universal suffrage. The right to free schooling was made statutory, but likewise parents were entitled not to send their children to school, provided that they ensured an acceptable standard of private tuition for them. This clause of compulsory education, not compulsory schooling, is still a part of the constitution, though it is only invoked by very small numbers.

The new constitution was ratified by both houses, after which arrangements were made for an election. Then the newly elected *Landsting* also had to ratify it. By common consent, and with an eye to possible breaches of Denmark's neutral position in the heat of the debate, no election campaign was held. The new *Rigsdag* was elected and immediately ratified the new constitution, which received the king's signature on 5 June 1915.

According to the Constitutional Act, the new constitution did not come into force until one year after receiving the royal assent, and this period could be extended by legislation if necessary. Again with a view to avoiding the dangers of an election contest, the date was in 1916 postponed for a further year, largely thanks to the efforts of the newly formed Conservative People's Party, an amalgamation of the old Right and the Free Conservatives. It was a natural union and one which has lasted until the present day, but it was scarcely a case of the same old party under a new name. The old Right had realised that it needed to base itself on a broader popular appeal and sought to become the party of the middle classes, aiming at freedom from government intervention on the one hand and at a system of protective tariffs, to safeguard Danish industry, on the other. At the same time, with the Danish security forces reduced to 35,000 men, it placed defence high on its list of priorities. On the basis of this programme it was hoped to appeal to a wide section of middle-class opinion and, perhaps, even to take some support from *Venstre*; or perhaps to co-operate with that party in opposing the related principles of the Radicals and Social Democrats.

While the desire to avoid controversy had been a contributory factor in solving the constitutional crisis, wartime conditions helped on the solution of a further problem. Steps were now taken towards a thoroughgoing reform of the Danish legal system, which brought it much more into line with the system already in force in England. The judiciary and the executive were finally separated, and the principle of public trial by jury was introduced. Prior to this the executive and judiciary had often been one and the same thing – for instance, mayors were appointed by the Crown and their functions included those of both chief of police and magistrate. Thus what from a modern point of view was another anomalous situation came to an end and further democratisation of local government was duly promoted, as mayors could now be elected instead of appointed by the Crown.

Conditions in Denmark during the first two years of the war had been surprisingly good. Prices had risen, though government measures had maintained stability. Denmark had got into debt, but earnings in the country as a whole had been good enough to make higher direct taxation feasible. A form of supertax on high incomes was introduced and a tax on stock-exchange transactions – on the principle that it was here that many fortunes were being made as a direct result of the war. Nevertheless, Denmark had always been in a difficult position because of her need for overseas trade, and when in January 1917 Germany designated a number of areas as danger zones for shipping, the difficulties were considerably increased. They were intensified yet further when Great Britain demanded that a percentage of neutral ships carrying coal

from British ports should sail for the Allies. In order to ensure
sufficient supplies, 200,000 tons of Danish shipping were put at
the disposal of the Allies for this purpose. Something of the significance of these moves for Danish shipping can be seen from the
fact that thirty-three ships, totalling 26,000 tons, were lost in April
1917 alone, and still more the following month. After this ships
sailed in convoy, using neutral waters as far as possible, and losses
were considerably reduced. Nevertheless, total losses during the
war amounted to 282,000 tons and 667 lives.

The situation was complicated still further when the United
States declared war on Germany in 1917, for now, as a belligerent
power, the USA was less inclined to export fodder and industrial
raw materials to Denmark if there were any possibility of re-export
to Germany. Consequently there was soon a shortage in Denmark
of raw materials and animal foodstuffs: imports fell to half their
normal size and prices started to rise quickly. In July the retail price
index was 155 and a year later 182. Even these indices were only
held at this low level through government price control, and
wholesale price indices rose faster, reaching 302 by July 1918.
It was no longer possible to allow goods to regulate themselves
through prices, and so rationing was progressively introduced
through 1917, while other measures were taken to reduce the
amount of fuel used on lighting by closing restaurants and theatres
earlier than usual. Gas was cut off for several hours daily and
people learned to cook their food by means of 'hay boxes': food
was brought to the boil by means of gas and then placed in a box
packed with hay, which kept it hot sufficiently long to finish it off.
Special cookery-books were prepared to promote cooking by this
method, which was also used during the Second World War. To
some extent the difficulty of importing fuel from overseas was,
however, offset by increased imports from Germany.

This increase was due rather to commercial than to political
reasons, but the public suspected pro-German sentiments among
some members of the government, first in P. A. Munch, then in
Thorvald Stauning, the first Social Democrat member of a Danish
government, who as one of three 'control Ministers' had part
authority over wartime measures. Stauning attended a meeting in
Stockholm of a peace movement which was backed by Germany
but not by the Allies and therefore came under suspicion. Despite
demands for his resignation, he refused to go. His Conservative
colleague then tendered his resignation in protest, was subsequently
prevailed upon to withdraw it, and as a result excluded from his
party. Three other members now joined him – former members of
the Free Conservatives – and together they formed a small break-

away group within the *Folketing*. There were also other reasons for suspecting a pro-German policy in Denmark. Because of the difficulties of trading with Britain and the USA it was obvious that trade with Germany had to be stepped up. Special credits were arranged to enable firms to do this. At the same time, however, a historically more significant move came from the need to boost inter-Scandinavian co-operation. Exports of agricultural goods were increased to both Norway (independent since 1905)[1] and Sweden, and in return Denmark received saltpetre for artificial manure from Norway and industrial products and raw materials from Sweden. Mutual suspicion, long a feature in the relations between the Nordic countries and a legacy of the Swedish wars and the methods by which Sweden had acquired Norway in 1814, were by no means allayed as yet, but the first step had been taken on the road to Nordic co-operation and integration.

Under these conditions the Danish national debt grew considerably, reaching 420 million *kroner* by 1919. Increased taxation, including a new and very heavy tax on liquor, again helped to cover it, but the need for a reduction in government expenditure was also apparent, and this accounted for the decision by *Venstre,* and unwilling recognition by the Conservatives, that the security forces should be reduced still further : first to between 23,000 and 24,000 men in 1917 and finally to 20,000 in 1918. This number was obviously not sufficient to cope with any major invasion, and, taking the Radicals' defence views into account, it was doubtful whether anything more than even a token resistance was contemplated by the government should the occasion arise. At this particular juncture, however, no invasion took place, though contingency plans were drawn up by Germany.

The *gullasch* age of the first two years of the war continued more or less unabated, despite the economic difficulties in which the country found itself. Money was still in plentiful supply and profiteering was still rife. Even though an order was made restraining the amount of profit made on each transaction, the object of the law was avoided by increasing the number of middlemen between factory and retailer, thus forcing retail prices ever higher. Suspect companies were formed, holding companies with subsidiaries and subsidiaries of subsidiaries, so that it was easy to falsify accounts. It was therefore easy to persuade willing and naïve

---

[1] The union of Sweden and Norway as two theoretically independent states under one – Swedish – king, which had come about in 1814, had proved unworkable owing to the dominance of Sweden. In 1905 the Norwegians had voted for and been granted complete independence. They chose as their new king Prince Carl of Denmark (Haakon VII), brother of Christian X.

speculators into investing large sums of money. Profits in rural areas, too, were made, and a general fever for spending and investing money spread throughout the farming community. Many of the investments in modern equipment were sensible, but much of the capital was borrowed without any thought of repayments and the possible difficulties which might be facing farmers at a later date.

Yet the workers were not doing quite so well out of these doubtfully buoyant conditions, despite the fact that the negotiations in 1916 had led to increased cost of living payments, sufficient to maintain the standards they had been used to before war broke out. Unemployment was rising and reached the record figure of 18 per cent in 1918. Little wonder that the workers' thoughts now turned to more violent means of demanding their rights, now that they had the example of the Bolshevik revolution in Russia and other revolutionary movements within Europe before them. In contrast to the sober and responsible efforts of the trade unions – whose freedom of action was partly circumscribed with the Social Democrats now partners in government – the syndicalists came into their own, fomenting wildcat strikes and threatening sabotage. In 1918 they began organising major demonstrations in Copenhagen and on one occasion they set about sacking the stock exchange, symbol of the society they hated. They were not truly representative of the workers, but were rather symptomatic of vocal minority groups who take advantage of lethargy to get their way. All the same, they succeeded in gaining control of some trade unions. The official unions reacted by pushing up their wage demands, in the hope of winning back support among the dissidents, and the employers, only too eager to avoid any greater conflict, gave in easily. They too had taken account of events abroad and wanted to avoid parallel situations in Denmark.

Under these conditions the elections to the *Rigsdag* were due to take place. The previous ones had been in 1915 and according to the old constitution a parliament's life was three years. Accordingly it was decided that the new constitution should come into force immediately before this election. The Radicals, the governing party, and the Social Democrats, who had supported them throughout, entered into an election pact outside Copenhagen, where the system of proportional representation was not favourable to them. The remaining parties fought alone. The election result, however, was not decisive enough and the Radicals and Social Democrats had a majority of only four over all other parties – including the one member of the so-called Trade Party and the member for the Faroes, who voted with *Venstre*. The actual distribution of seats was: *Venstre* 44, Social Democrats 39, Radical 33, Conservative 22, Trade Party one, Faroes one. Thus the government was to be formed by the third largest party, with the support of the second largest, while the opposition was based on the two old enemies *Venstre* and Conservative: two radical parties against two middle-class parties. Thus the two antagonists were forced into some sort of co-operation, a position in which they have often found themselves since. In the *Landsting* the grouping was similar, but there the middle-class parties held the power, as they were to do for many years.

In 1917 Denmark had given up her West Indian colonies by selling them to the United States.[2] Now the government was faced with another problem concerning Danish overseas possessions. Iceland, it will be remembered, had been left to Denmark after the loss of Norway in 1814, but now, after the difficulties caused by the war, the demand for independence was becoming more strident. The idea of independent nationhood was then in vogue and as a result there was a generally conciliatory and tolerant attitude in Denmark to the aspirations of the Icelanders. A delegation in which the Conservatives, of the four major parties, alone refused to serve, went to Iceland in 1918 and came to an agreement for a federation, a personal union in which citizens should enjoy equal rights in both countries, and in which laws concerning both should be passed by a special committee consisting of an equal number of representatives from Iceland and Denmark. One of the clauses in the agreement was that in twenty-five years Iceland should have the right to complete independence if she desired it and could show this desire by a referendum in which at least three-quarters of the votes should be positive and at least three-quarters of those eligible took part. No one could then foresee that when the twenty-five years had elapsed, contact between Denmark and Iceland would be severed by another major international conflict.

The Wartime Atmosphere and its Literary Expression

The signing of the Armistice in November 1918 brought general relief to Denmark, even if the country had not been directly involved in the war, and the security forces were almost immediately disbanded. Yet the activities of the syndicalists, who continued to organise strikes and demonstrations, brought worries enough. A general strike, intended as a protest against an eighteen months sentence for the syndicalist leader, was a near fiasco, though a largish demonstration did take place in a revolutionary atmosphere. The genuine demonstrators were joined by the usual rabble and

[2] See below, Appendix D, p. 243.

Copenhagen was a city of turmoil for a few days before order was
eventually restored.

The atmosphere in Denmark had undergone a remarkable transformation during four years of war. The years immediately before
1914 had certainly been a period of change and renewal, but the
transformation had been an orderly one, reflecting the give and
take of an ordered society. Now, under the shadow of the Russian,
and later of the German, revolutions, Denmark itself was seething,
and the future looked bleak. The old values had gone and no one
knew what had replaced them, so that there was a state bordering
on moral confusion in the country. One of the best impressions of
this is to be found in Jacob Paludan's *Jørgen Stein* :

> The thunder was rolling in the south for the fourth year.
> People had already had a long time to accustom themselves to
> the thought that the civilisation to which they belonged had
> been built on sand. Many had difficulty in understanding. But
> new broods appeared and had their most receptive years marked
> by the knowledge that war was possible, and that it was indeed
> taking place. For them the word took on a new, natural sound;
> it was no textbook word, but ordinary everyday reality. Without
> any surprise at all the young people saw the publication of a
> work entitled *The Next War,* and cut open its pages in the light
> of the stinking carbide lamps which in many places had to
> replace electricity, which was in short supply, and paraffin,
> which had entirely disappeared. The future held no danger of
> boredom; this war, it appeared, was even now to be thought of
> as a grand, educational dress rehearsal. And accustomed as they
> were to war, their minds could contain the thought and their
> nerves stand it.
>
> The older generation had more difficulty. Most of them would
> have denied that the individual, thoroughly civilised citizen
> engrossed in his daily paper could possibly have retained any
> vestige of barbarism. Certainly there was some virtue in the
> courage which impelled a man to defend his country's frontier,
> but in this massive world-engulfing cataclysm it was soon for-
> gotten who was guilty and who the injured party . . . These
> elderly people had to learn in the afternoon of their lives that
> they had been sleep-walking in the forenoon. It was like having
> settled comfortably in a sunny vineyard only to discover that it
> was a nest of vipers. The concept of Man, the concept of Cul-
> ture, had to be understood and defined anew – but they were far
> beyond the age when their brains were supple enough to form
> a new view of life. The older generation became in a strange

way much older in these years; in some strange way they moved out of context – like false teachers who have to turn their heads away on being shown up. . . .

Between the two generations, the dethroned and the acclimatised, there lived a third – the generation which had just had a taste of the era before 1914, its atmosphere and its spirit, its faith in unchanging values.

It was as a member of this third generation that Paludan was writing, for he was looking back at the war from the early 1930s – and thus could scarcely be considered as a wartime author. Indeed the war played singularly little part in contemporary literature. How could it, when Denmark was not taking part? And yet it was a period during which some of the Danish authors who have achieved international fame were producing their best work. Johannes V. Jensen was engaged not on depicting modern events, but on writing his epic *The Long Journey,* in which he produced a poetic version of the descent of man, from the Ice Age to the discovery of America. It does not pretend to be a scholarly work, but within a framework of Darwinism incorporates inspiration from such diverse elements as the Bible, *Robinson Crusoe,* and Hans Christian Andersen's *Fairy Tales.* The theme of this large work is Man's ability to adapt himself to his surroundings and then conquer them, and it ends with Columbus moving towards the New World. Ultimately it is a question of Nordic expansionism, the Nordic spirit as the vehicle of progress, for it is the Scandinavians who originally brave the advancing cold of the Ice Age and adapt themselves to it, as it is the Scandinavians who as the Cimbrians move southwards and form the stock from which Columbus comes. From a scholarly angle it is easy to pull this epic to pieces, but as a work of poetic inspiration it possesses great beauty and power. Prior to this, in the years before the war, Johannes V. Jensen had written his *Stories from Himmerland* (the part of Denmark from which he originated, and from which it has been surmised the Cimbrians also stemmed) and his *Myths* (these latter being an attempt to express profound truths in short compass). In his movement towards myth Jensen was ahead of his time and in harmony with subsequent trends in literature outside as well as inside Denmark. As a poet, too, he made an original contribution to his country's literature, showing the same linguistic innovation and conciseness of expression as in his prose work.

At the other end of the political scale was Martin Andersen Nexø with his novels of proletarian life in Denmark: *Pelle the Conqueror* (1906–10) and *Little Ditte* (1917–21), the first showing

Pelle growing up as the son of a farmworker in Bornholm, moving to Copenhagen, and becoming engaged in the socialist movement there, the second a more sentimental novel about a proletarian girl who is ill-treated by society.

Nexø was continuing the realistic tradition from the nineteenth century, and he continued to do so until his death, though he employed it more and more as the vehicle for his communist ideas. These two early novels, however, represented the height of his achievement, and only in parts does he show any sign of a non-literary intention in his work.

Yet literature was beginning to change, and even though it did not reflect the war directly, in the shape of novels or plays dealing immediately with the conflict, the breakdown of the social order was reflected in the emergence of new and apparently less ordered forms. These were the work of poets singing in praise of modern civilisation, expressing their love of the twentieth century, with its violence, its terror, and its power. Foremost among the younger writers, the Expressionists, was Tom Kristensen, a poet who was born in London and wrote of these themes with greater perspicacity, as well as greater poetic insight and mastery of the language, than anyone else. In a poem such as 'Atlantis', he talked of the need completely to break down society in order to build up a new culture, while his novel *Havoc*, written a decade after the end of the war, is probably the most penetrating analysis in Danish literature of the demoralisation which the First World War brought about, the sense of frustration at being kept in the wings to watch the great events taking place in Europe at large.

Colour had been one of the major ingredients in the new Expressionist poetry. The new school of painters also emerged at this time and, under the general influence of a tempestuous age and under the particular impact of French painters, also produced works of new colours and new forms, breaking down traditional lines and traditional uses of colour. Painters such as Sigurd Swane, Harald Giersing, and Olaf Rude were the main representatives of this genre, while William Scharff painted more under the spell of Picasso. And while new colours and forms were emerging in literature and painting, new sounds, new sound colours, were making themselves heard in the music of Carl Nielsen, who betokens a complete break with the late Romantic music which had been the vogue hitherto. Each of his symphonies explores new ground, and indeed each of his major works represents something new and exciting in sound combinations and in musical structure. Yet this tempestuous writer is often referred to as being typically Danish, an appellation immediately most apparent in his songs, the sim-

1. The Union Document of 1397, according to which Denmark, Norway, and Sweden were united under one Crown

2. Part of the text of the Jutlandic Law of 1241

3. Ribe Cathedral, started *c.* 1125, is representative of the earliest Danish cathedral architecture

4. Roskilde Cathedral, also from the twelfth century, the burial place of many Danish kings, comes from the time when the Church finally established itself in Denmark

5. Spøttrup, an example of an early mansion, built for defence. Perhaps dating originally from the early fifteenth century, it was partly destroyed in 1534 and then rebuilt in the 1570s

6. Hesselagergaard, a mansion started in 1538, with more attention to architectural grandeur

7. Lerchenborg. Built in 1742, at a time of prosperity and internal security, this is now a miniature palace, designed without any thought of fortification

8. The Naval Church, Copenhagen – *Holmens Kirke* – an example of Christian IV's public architecture

9. The British bombardment of Copenhagen, 1807. Coloured print by C. L. Lahde after a painting by C. W. Eckersberg. (National Historical Museum, Frederiksborg)

10. Scottish soldiers encamped outside Copenhagen, 1807. (National Historical Museum, Frederiksborg)

11. *Nyboder* – Christian IV's domestic architecture; these houses, which were originally built for his skippers in 1631–41, are still in use

12. A working-class Christmas, 1905

13.   A cigar-sorter and family, 1906

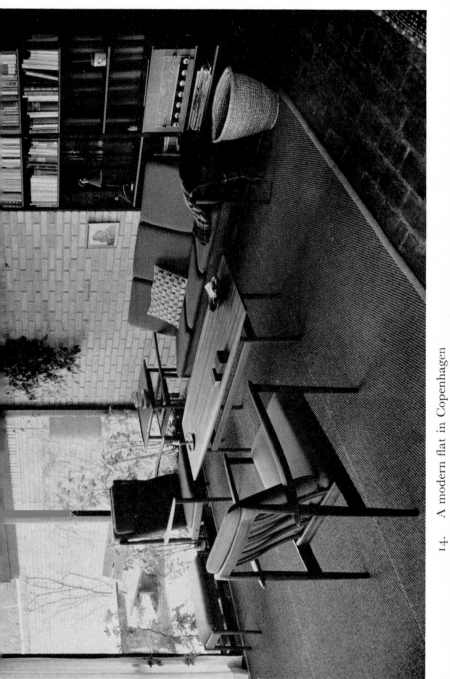

14. A modern flat in Copenhagen

15. Large-scale flat development from the 1930s

16. A typical back yard in slum tenements from the end of the nineteenth century

17. Modern flats in Gladsaxe, outside Copenhagen

18. The old City Hall, now the City Court, built 1805–15, is typical of the neo-classical architecture of the period. Note the quotation from the Jutlandic Law on the façade: 'The land shall be built on law'

19. St Ansgar's Church, a product of Danish architecture in the mid-nineteenth century

20. Thorvald Stauning (1873–1942)

21. The British attack on Shell House in Copenhagen, the headquarters of the Gestapo, March 1945

22.   King Christian X riding alone in Copenhagen, 1942

23.   The County Hospital at Glostrup, one of the most modern in Europe

24. Rural Denmark—Gunderslevholm in Zealand

25. Danish art. Woman setting her hair.
C. W. Eckersberg (1783–1853)

26. Danish art. Summer evening on the beach of the Skaw.
P. S. Krøyer (1851–1909)

plicity and melodiousness of which are in direct continuation of Danish song tradition, without being a slavish imitation of it.

There are many ways of looking at the years from 1900 to 1918. They can be regarded nostalgically as an age which saw the end of old values and the civilisation which had reigned, basically unchanged, for several centuries; or as the dawn of something new, something expressive of great power. The passage from Jacob Paludan's *Jørgen Stein,* quoted above, expresses all this in powerful terms, as it struck the people of the day. Yet whichever way one looks at the period, it was surely one of rapid, almost explosive, transformation in which not only society underwent a change and showed a new potential, but in which all branches of art followed suit. Traditional forms persisted and indeed persist until this day, but alongside went a longing for experiment, a willingness to cope with new forms and to look at art, and thereby at life, with an openness which had scarcely been there before. It is possible to talk of the advent of something epoch-making with Romanticism in 1803, or with Naturalism in 1871, but the general embarkation on untried literary forms, of which Tom Kristensen was perhaps the most outstanding representative, meant a striking and equally intense literary revolution. While Romanticism had brought the liberation of the individual, and Naturalism had introduced a new philosophical basis for literature, the results in each case had been readily related to what had gone before. Now, the move from Impressionism to Expressionism had meant the abandonment of an attempt at reproducing something approaching objective reality, and the surrender to complete subjectivism. The old reality had gone with the old society on which it had been based, and in Denmark as elsewhere everything was in a state of flux.

Chapter 6

1918–30

The Fight for Stability

The Return of North Schleswig

ALTHOUGH DENMARK HAD NOT BEEN ENGAGED in the war, the country was very interested indeed in the changed pattern which was bound to emerge in Europe after the end of the conflict. The Schleswig-Holstein problem began to raise its head again, not least because of the zeal with which Germany had gone about suppressing Danish sentiments before the war and even more so during it. Those of military age in the border area had been called up into the German army, as indeed was only natural, but it was less natural that these unwilling conscripts had been forbidden to speak or read Danish, or to write home in that language. Such measures were scarcely likely to help the German cause in the area, and some troops with Danish sympathies took the opportunity of crossing the border when home on leave. Pro-Danish politicians had also been arrested for various lengths of time and had only been released when consenting to refrain from working for the Danish cause. They were forced to maintain their own type of neutrality in their own country. Further complications had been caused by the fact that children of parents who had opted for Danish nationality but remained in German territory were in practice stateless, as German laws would not grant nationality to children of foreigners, while Danish law denied Danish nationality to children born abroad, even if they were the offspring of Danish parents. As a result of an agreement with Germany in 1916, these children were in fact given Danish nationality, but the resentment smouldered still.

The collapse of Germany, especially when one of the expressed objectives of the Allies was the right of people to choose their own nationality, provided an obvious chance to return to the thorny problems which had existed since the loss of the duchies in 1864. Yet there were varying conceptions in Denmark as to how this

should be done. The majority, including the government, subscribed
to the view that the border should be revised according to the
wishes of the local population, to be ascertained by referendum.
The historian H. V. Clausen had for years made a village by
village examination of national attitudes in the border area, and
could say with a fair amount of certainty where the border would
be drawn in this event. One of his conclusions, however, was dis-
turbing : the city of Flensburg, the largest city in central Schleswig
and once a centre of Danish sentiment, would be lost, thanks to a
thorough Germanisation over the half-century it had been under
German rule. Consequently there was a movement to have Flensburg included in Denmark in any border revision. There was also
the historical approach, giving rise to the opinion that the border
should revert to the Ejder and that Denmark should regain control of the entire duchy of Schleswig. There was a good deal of
support for this attitude, very reminiscent of the old National
Liberal stance, but there were fears that more trouble would ensue
in the future if this solution were adopted. Finally, after a lengthy
debate in the *Rigsdag,* it became official Danish policy that a revision of the border should be made on the basis of a referendum.
On the other hand, as Denmark herself had not been engaged in
the war, she could not make demands as part of any peace treaty,
and it was obvious that requests for frontier revision should come
from inside Schleswig itself.

This was done, and the Danish Schleswig representative in the
German Diet, H. P. Hanssen, pressed for the implementation of
Paragraph 5 from the treaty with Prussia. The reply was that
Denmark had no legal right to demand the return of Schleswig,
but that the request was in fact likely to get favourable consideration in its own right. Prior to this voices had been raised in favour
of the Danish demand by opposition members of the Diet. (It is
worth remembering in this context that this understanding was
reached at a time when it was apparent that Germany had lost
the war, but before the actual signing of the Armistice.)

The final decision about a referendum now lay with the Allies,
and attention in Denmark turned to the question of how to formul-
ate a policy which would be acceptable to them. The final outcome, after a period of disagreement and discussion, was that that
part of Schleswig which might be thought to want a return to Denmark should be divided into two zones, the northern zone corresponding closely to the part which Professor Clausen had deemed
to be Danish in sentiment and a second, southern zone, in which
the position was doubtful. The northern zone, which excluded

Flensburg, was to vote as one unit, while the second zone should vote parish by parish.

Flensburg was the sore point, and there was plenty of time for feelings to run high, as the peace treaty incorporating provisions for the referendum had to be ratified by the Allied governments and did not come into force until January 1920, until which time Britain maintained her blockade of Germany, including Schleswig. Demands were made for Flensburg to be incorporated into Denmark irrespective of the result of the referendum there, but the Danish government maintained its original stand and refused to work to this end. It seemed to be justified in its attitude when the referendum finally took place on 10 February in the northern zone and 14 March in the southern zone. In the north the vote was three to one in favour of Denmark, while in the south the ratio was almost exactly the reverse, with the exception of a few villages. In Flensburg itself 27,081 voted for Germany against 8,944 for Denmark.

Even now there were elements in Denmark who felt that it might still be possible to win Flensburg with a different government in Copenhagen. When a Radical deputy and one of the Social Democrats joined the opposition on this point, there was a stalemate in the *Folketing*.

A change in government led to little change in policy, and a new administration under N. Neergaard worked for the implementation of the referendum result and for internationalisation of the southern zone, by which was meant that the zone should be turned into a free state and removed from both Danish and German jurisdiction. These objects were never achieved, but first the northern zone was put under Danish control, then the parishes in the southern zone which had voted for Denmark. The final incorporation of northern Schleswig into Denmark took place through a law passed in the *Rigsdag* on 25 and 26 June 1920, and was given effect as from 15 June. A period of festivities followed, during which the king made his famous crossing of the old border on horseback – and a promise was made not to forget those Danes who still lived in German territory. Nor has this been done, though no efforts have been made to incorporate more territory into Denmark. As a further safeguard for the permanent status of north Schleswig the treaty contained a clause saying that sovereignty could not be transferred again without the sanction of the League of Nations.

Feelings continued to run high between the two communities in the border area for many years : indeed, it is only in recent years that they have subsided somewhat. In towns with a divided community, it was not the done thing for Danes and Germans to consort together, for the Danes to go to the German theatres and cinemas, or for the Germans to attend the Danish ones. By means of German schools in Denmark and Danish schools in the German border areas, attempts were made by both sides to foster and, if possible, develop their own culture in the country of the other. The Second World War did not help matters, nor did the resettlement of refugees from East Germany in Schleswig and Holstein after the war. So far, the Danish argument went, the Danish language had been largely understood and Danish culture appreciated in those areas, but the advent of new settlers from the east without any basis for the understanding of either, meant the suppression of Danish culture. And this was at first attributed to the desire of the Federal German government to intensify the movement to Germanise the region. The fact that this thinly populated area was admirably suited to resettlement was apparently overlooked. But with the passing years and despite the appearance of the East German refugees, strong feelings and tension have eased and a new spirit of co-operation appears to have asserted itself between the two peoples. There is probably more stability on the Danish-German border now than there has been for centuries, and the Schleswig-Holstein problem appears finally to have been solved.

Labour Troubles and Economic Problems

Meanwhile, the question of the return of north Schleswig to Denmark, although the one uppermost in many people's minds, and the one with most international perspectives, was by no means the only problem facing Denmark after the war. As has been seen in the previous chapter, the war ended to the accompaniment of syndicalist stirrings within Denmark itself and the inconclusiveness and dissatisfaction within the labour market continued. The problem demanded a solution. It was in the interests of neither the official trade unions nor the employers to allow the situation to slide into the grasp of the syndicalists, and so the search for a solution was an eager one. Even so, strikes were widespread, and particularly damaging ones took place in the docks, coping with the flood of trade after the war, and in the building industry, where an effort was being made to ease the housing shortage. All this was happening at the same time as wages in real terms were not only catching up with pre-war levels, but actually passing them. The 100 points of 1914 reached 95 in 1918, 137 in 1919, and 148 in 1920.

Attention was turned from wage levels, which, with the cost of living arrangements, could to some extent look after themselves, to the length of the working day. The year 1919 saw the intro-

duction of the eight-hour day, first in the civil service and then in
Copenhagen and other local authorities, while in May negotiations
between the employers' and workers' organisations in a joint committee led to the acceptance of the eight-hour day for all sections
of industry, though not for seamen and farmworkers. This arrangement was to take effect from January 1920.

Also in 1919 came the introduction of important legislation concerning land ownership. The original law on smallholdings of 1899
had been revised in 1914 and 1917, but still worked essentially on
the same basis of a state loan which had to be repaid, albeit at a
reasonable rate of interest. As a consequence of the general increase
in prices, not least in the price of land, it was becoming more and
more difficult for would-be smallholders to finance purchases even
on these conditions. So the government proposed legislation which
would radically alter the entire basis on which land was to be provided for smallholders. Instead of selling the land to them, the idea
was to lease it to smallholders for an indefinite period. The smallholder should pay no deposit, but should pay interest of $4\frac{1}{2}$ per cent
on the value of the land he worked, the value to be revised at
intervals in the light of current prices. In other words, if the value
of land rose, he would have to pay more; if it fell, he would be
liable to less interest. The buildings he put up on the land would
be his – and the state would be prepared to make advances for
this purpose. All equipment and livestock would be his to sell at
any time. The principles behind the idea were based on those of
the influential Henry George[1] : that the rise in land values, thanks
to the efforts of society, should benefit that society as a whole
rather than the individual. On the other hand, the individual's
own gains and profits through his private industry should remain
his and not be taxed. This idea had some appeal both to the Radicals and the Social Democrats, but neither party was willing to
base itself on an unmodified form of Georgism. Those who were
eager to do so formed a new party, called *Danmarks Retsforbund* –
normally known in English as the Single Tax Party – which has
had parliamentary representation and is still in existence. Georgist
ideas have also found other modes of expression in the country, not
least in the organisation now known as JAK (*Jord, Arbejde,
Kapital* – Land, Work, Capital) which arranges private financing
at low rates of interest and also runs a bank.

The question of how to provide the land necessary for the pro-

---

[1] In his main work *Progress and Poverty* (1879), George (1839–97) argued
that the increase in the value of land, in the hands of a small proportion
of the total population, tended to widen the gap between rich and poor. He
advocated easier access to the purchase of land and taxation gradually to
be exclusively based on the full economic rent of the land owned.

jected reforms was simpler to solve than might at first seem likely. Most parsonages in Denmark were well provided for, a situation dating from the day when the pastor had depended on the land for his living. This land actually belonged to the state, and it was decided to requisition it – though where pastors were still working it, the property should only go to the state with a change of incumbent. In addition there was still a good deal of entailed land dating from feudal times, and this, too, it was decided to take over, as indeed was expressly provided for in the constitution. Tenants were entitled to buy the freehold for 20 or 25 per cent of its value, depending on the exact terms of the entailment, but the state was to take over one-third of each estate at its market value. This would both ensure the availability of land for the new purposes and also provide the state with funds to finance the scheme. The proposals were passed, despite some misgivings: *Venstre,* for instance, was reluctant to introduce a new form of leasehold and was more eager to extend individual ownership, which had been a source of encouragement to farmers in the past.

These developments had taken place against a background of economic crisis – the aftermath of war. Trade had been slow to pick up and Denmark was still suffering from the effects of the blockade of Germany: there was still a shortage of goods in the country and the regulation of prices was still necessary to avoid inflation. Developments in world trade were also against her. Although there had been a surplus during the war, and thus apparent prosperity, Denmark had allowed stocks to run down, and now had to replenish them at current prices. This she was forced to do at a time of rising prices, while she was obliged to sell her agricultural produce at a low rate. As had happened before, and was to happen again, she had been caught between her two main trading partners, Germany and Britain. Germany could not yet afford to import, while Britain did her own price fixing – and Denmark had little choice but to put up with it. At the same time the speculation of the war years still continued, and this resulted in a further running-down of financial reserves. It was hoped that Denmark could become a centre for trade with the Baltic lands as soon as they were in a position to start trading again and consequently enormous quantities of goods were imported into Denmark to be stored for further use. There followed a financial deficit and the *krone* fell to as little as 48 per cent of its face value. The consequence was inflation, with soaring prices – taking 1914 as 100, the price index rose to 182 in July 1918, 211 in July 1919, and 242 in January 1920. Little wonder that the government felt the need to maintain some control of prices, and little wonder, too, that there was discontent among the workers, although their wages were now linked to the cost of living and the effect of rising prices thus minimised.

By March 1920 there was a general malaise in the country : a combination of the desire to have the Flensburg problem solved in a way satisfactory to Danish interests; a general dissatisfaction with the government's handling of the Schleswig question; discontent with the country's economic situation; increasing tension between worker and employer, which had led to the warning of an imminent lock-out. Within the *Rigsdag* there was near stalemate, coupled with the desire for a revision of the electoral laws before a new election, a suggestion opposed by *Venstre*, who stood to suffer most from any change. There had been intrigues, details of which are still not known, to have the government dismissed and replaced by a caretaker government of specialists who would introduce new electoral legislation and then arrange for a new election. Finally, on 29 March, things came to a head.

The king sent for Zahle,[2] the Radical Prime Minister, and demanded that an election should be held immediately. Zahle refused on the grounds that there had already been too many elections, that the electoral law was on the point of being revised, and that this would result in yet another election in the near future. By way of reply the king dismissed the government and did not at first ask Zahle to continue in office until the election. That there would be serious repercussions was quite apparent, and in order to avoid immediate trouble, the king was persuaded after all to ask the Zahle cabinet to continue for this short period. Zahle refused, and so a government of specialists, not politicians, was appointed, with the object of arranging an election.

In acting thus the king was within his legal rights and prerogative, though certainly against the spirit of the constitution, and the reaction among the Social Democrats and the working population was immediate and uncompromising. A meeting of the Social Democrat Party and the trade unions led to the demand for the reinstatement of the Zahle government, failing which a general strike would be proclaimed. The ultimatum was given to the king on the evening of the change of government. He rejected it, and the unions went on to make preparations for a general strike, due to start on 6 April, a strike, moreover, which had a political rather than an economic objective. The combination of what appeared to them as a right-wing *coup* and an approaching lock-out seemed to smack of a conspiracy aimed at the working classes. A statement issued on 29 March made clear the workers' demands, but as so often

[2] See above, p. 113.

happens in comparable situations, the immediate demand for the
reinstatement of the Zahle government was coupled with a demand
for improved working conditions. After demanding the recall of
the *Rigsdag* and the calling of elections, but no longer the reinstatement of the government, a further proclamation continued :

> At the same time, however, the situation of industrial conflict
> must be resolved, and lock-out notices must be withdrawn and
> the repeated demands of the Trade Union Association must be
> carried out – including the inception of negotiations between the
> organisations, the ensuring of cost of living increases in August,
> and the start of negotiations concerning the right of the workers
> to participate in management.

These aspirations were far removed from the political question of which government was to be in power, but they were
indicative of the increasing strength and ambitions of the unions,
and also of their fear of being weakened by the combined efforts
of the Right. Whatever the intentions of their opponents, the
Social Democrats were no longer willing to have the idea of
government by the people endangered. Although the Radicals
sympathised with the aims of the Social Democrats, they did not
approve of the means they proposed to adopt – as indeed was also
the case with some of the more moderate Social Democrat leaders
themselves.

No one at this stage could see what might happen. The Social
Democrats, most ably supported by the communists and other
extreme left-wing elements, arranged demonstrations in Copenhagen, and there were real fears that a revolution might take place.
There were certainly calls for a republic. The police were thought
not to be sufficient to control the situation if violence ensued – if
indeed they could be relied upon – and some troops were called in
from outside Copenhagen in case of trouble. It was obviously
essential that the government should go, and the king was finally
persuaded that in order to save the situation he should appoint a
fresh caretaker government consisting of men approved by the
political parties after mutual consultation. They should, moreover,
be men who had had nothing to do with the moves which had
given rise to the crisis. After long and difficult negotiations it was
announced on Easter Day that a government was formed and that
the *Rigsdag* was to be recalled immediately after the Easter recess
to pass the new electoral legislation. Elections would then be held
by 22 April at the latest. At the same time the threat of a general
strike was withdrawn and the crisis was resolved. As a by-product,

the trade unions achieved most of what they were demanding from the employers.

This Easter crisis, as it had become known, opened many perspectives in Denmark and had a far-reaching effect. It was generally greeted as a triumph for democratic principles, and no attempt has since been made by the sovereign to interfere with the elected majority principle in government. Yet it could not be denied that the government in the final analysis had been brought down not by the *Rigsdag,* which the Prime Minister had refused to recall, but by the pressure exerted by the Social Democrats – in other words, by extra-parliamentary activities. The Social Democrats were proud of their achievement, but the remainder of the population had a different perspective in this newly-discovered power, and they were to show their disapproval in the elections which all parties had been clamouring for and which were now based on the new compromise electoral law.

The swing to the Right which resulted from these elections was the culmination of many factors. There was the fear of left-wing agitation and the strike threat, aggravated by the fact that a dock and transport strike did take place, since the relevant unions were under the leadership of syndicalists who refused to be bound by the compromise agreements. There was also a reaction against the emergency powers which had been adopted by the Radical government during the war, powers which many had deemed socialist in essence, not least perhaps because the Radicals had had the tacit support of the Social Democrats. In the event, however, the Social Democrats won an increased number of seats, forty-two against their former thirty-nine, though the left-wingers of the party were routed. It was the Radicals who suffered most severely, their numbers being reduced to seventeen, the smallest of the majority groups. *Venstre,* the Social Liberals, were the real victors, increasing their representation from forty-four to forty-eight, despite the fact that the supplementary seats no longer worked in their favour, while the Conservatives also went up from 22 to 26 seats. The small Industrial Party was left with four. This put a completely new complexion on the new *Rigsdag,* which now had a clear majority of moderate to right-wing members, a living repudiation of the wartime measures and a symbol of hopes for a speedy return to peacetime normality. There was nevertheless no question of a *Venstre*–Conservative coalition, not least because the farming community, represented by *Venstre,* had not yet forgiven the dictatorial régime of Estrup, whose successor the new Conservative People's Party[3] was. So in fact a government was formed similar

3 See above, p. 107.

in principle to the preceding one : Neergaard formed an administration with the tacit support of the Conservatives and carried out a purely *Venstre* policy, though taking care not to antagonise the party on whose support he ultimately depended. His immediate concern was to put an end to the dock strike which was damaging national interests, and so he gave protection to volunteers who were prepared to work in the docks. The Social Democrats and trade unions were not enthusiastic, but on the other hand the strike was controlled by their opponents, the syndicalists. An end to the strike would be an end to the syndicalists, and so the Social Democrats looked the other way. The strikers were duly defeated and the syndicalist movement in Denmark disappeared from the scene.

Denmark Joins the League of Nations

The desire for elections in 1920 had been strong and there were to be plenty of them. The reunification with north Schleswig called for a modification of the 1915 constitution and this could only be done with the consent of two consecutive *Rigsdags*. So accordingly the new *Venstre* government introduced the amendment and carried it, after which the *Folketing* was dissolved and fresh elections held in July. The new *Folketing* again carried the amendment, as did a referendum which took place in September. Finally a new election had to be held on the basis of this amendment which gave representation to the population of north Schleswig. In this final, enlarged *Folketing Venstre* maintained its majority with 52 seats – though only because of support in north Schleswig – closely followed by the Social Democrats with forty-eight. The Conservatives had now twenty-seven, the Radicals made one gain to eighteen, and the Industrial Party one loss to three. The new German Party, representing the German-speaking population of north Schleswig, won one seat. Thus in the main the position was similar to that after the April election, though the Social Democrats gained most from the electoral process.

With its liberal views on the economy the new *Venstre* government set about dismantling the wartime controls, including rationing, which was abolished in 1921, though not including rent control. Yet it was unable to make any significant reduction in taxes on abolishing its price support policy because of the financial burden of the reunification of north Schleswig, where the economic position was disastrous. In fact taxation was gradually increased and new taxes on luxury goods and a restaurant tax were introduced in 1922.

Together with the other neutral countries, Denmark had been invited by the victorious powers to join the League of Nations and had decided to do so in common with the other Nordic states. It had seemed natural to accept the invitation, as membership of the League appeared to offer some sort of security to a small country, and Denmark had long suffered from being a small neighbour without any significant support abroad. Germany was certainly no longer a menace after the war, nor was Russia after the 1917 revolution, but there were plenty of influential Danes who even at that time foresaw that Germany would re-emerge as a dominant power in Europe. This latter feeling was one of the reasons why there was such widespread support for a Danish-German frontier based on the principle of nationality, as this would diminish the validity of possible future demands. At the same time Danes sensed that joining the League of Nations, which was so far essentially the instrument of the victors, meant sacrificing Denmark's traditional policy of complete neutrality. There was a definite conflict of principles and interests here, but the decision was made to abandon neutrality and to rely instead on a form of collective security, a stance which has been Denmark's ever since. The decision was made despite doubts in some quarters as to how much security the League did in fact offer Denmark.

Closely connected with membership of the League of Nations was the perennial problem of Danish military preparedness. The defence laws of 1909 were due for revision because they contained the clause stating that Copenhagen's defences would be dismantled no later than 1922. In practice they were discontinued in 1920 for obvious reasons. The question remained as to what should be done instead, and how future defence should be organised. The fundamental positions of the four parties were unaltered, the Conservatives being most inclined to maintain a fair-sized military force, the Social Democrats holding to their traditional anti-militarism. *Venstre* was in favour of some military forces and although the party did not go far enough for the Conservatives, its proposals were carried. Military expenditure was to be limited to under 50 million *kroner* a year and the army was to be centred on Jutland instead of Zealand. Conscription was to be limited to 8,000 men a year, in addition to which 1,500 were to do two months' service in the militia. No one was happy about this arrangement: the Conservatives wanted more, the Radicals no more than a militia, the Social Democrats only a police force; but the Conservatives were not prepared to bring down the government on the issue and risk the opposition's ideas being put into effect. So *Venstre* had its way and even when the Social Democrats came to power in 1924 they were unable to carry out their desire to disarm completely.

Venstre *Government and Further Economic Difficulties*

The hopes for a quick return to pre-war conditions, partly reflected in the election in 1920 of one of the parties most dedicated to the old standards, were not realised. Post-war speculation in buying produce with a view to re-exporting to the Baltic countries was unsuccessful and Denmark was left with vast unsold stocks and a large foreign debt. Prices on the world market began to fall, but as new materials were affected before manufactured goods, Denmark was not immediately hurt. Yet her day came with a general fall in prices and the value of money. The wholesale price index fell from 390 in 1920 to 223 in 1921, and further still to 171 in 1922. Farmers who had borrowed money some years previously to modernise their farms were hard hit, although they were to some extent helped when Britain started importing in larger quantities. But for industry there was little compensation and no encouragement. Production fell by a third within one year, and unemployment reached unprecedented levels, rising from 6·1 per cent in 1920 to 19·3 per cent in 1922 after a brief period when it had been at 34·2 per cent.

Extraordinary measures were obviously called for to deal with hardship resulting from unemployment. Under previous social legislation workers were insured against unemployment in their own insurance societies, in practice normally administered by the unions, but unemployment benefit was limited to seventy days. In many cases it was used up and in order to avert serious hardship the government created an extraordinary unemployment fund to benefit workers who could prove there was no possibility of employment for them. To the annoyance of the Social Democrats the government also insisted that workers so benefiting should have a control card regulariy stamped. (The system was scrapped in 1927.)

Even greater discontent was caused the following year, 1923, when certain categories of workers for whom such aid had been possible were declared to be no longer eligible because of the improved situation. An enormous demonstration was organised in Copenhagen, described as the biggest ever seen there – the procession is said to have taken two and a half hours to pass. But nothing was achieved. Nothing in fact could be achieved, because events were against the workers and their political fellows had no influence on the government. As wages were linked to the cost of living, they fell; but more than that, the employers had to cut costs, which they did by forcing down wages still further – so the workers suffered a real reduction in their standard of living. Where negotiations failed, resort was had to lock-outs, and where strike action was attempted, it was generally broken by the use of volunteer labour. A combination of these two expedients led to violence in Randers in 1911 which had to be put down by the use of infantry. A general strike was called there and it lasted a month, but the strikers had to yield in the end.

It would be unfair to argue that the *Venstre* government was not interested in the industrial workers, for it was perfectly well aware of their significance for the country's wellbeing. But it was in the field of agriculture that it made moves for improvements in the workers' conditions, and this was, of course, the mark of a party with rural interests at heart. *Venstre* had never liked the Radical government's bill making provision for state smallholdings in 1919, insisting that the desire to own land rather than lease it predominated in the country districts. And yet the new laws had had their effect in at least partially stopping the drift from the country to the town which had begun with the vision of higher wages. *Venstre* was convinced that more young people could be persuaded to stay in the country districts if more land were made available, and so in 1921 it passed a new act making provision for more state loans to be made available to those wishing to buy their own land, and these people were now enabled to buy plots big enough to live on without working for others. The two concomitant plans did much to stop the movement away from farming, although the percentage of rural workers continued to fall throughout the decade, dropping from about one worker in three in 1914 to one in four by 1930. Consequent upon this the mechanisation of farming, begun during the war, proceeded apace, and alongside the increasing number of smallholdings, on which the owner or lessee had to rely on his own strength and energy, the larger farms became mechanised and modernised.

Nor would it be fair to give the impression that *Venstre*, which had been inclined to leave society to look after itself and to avoid state interference, was indifferent to social legislation. Indeed at the beginning of the 1920s it introduced social legislation of some consequence which was also symptomatic of profound changes taking place within Danish society at the time. First, the principle of sickness insurance was extended to cover disablement insurance, an early and significant change which ensured a reasonable standard of living for those who were partly or entirely disabled. The amount of disablement pension was based on the degree of incapacitation, which was in turn determined by special tribunals. The funds were obtained in the same way as funds for sickness benefits – though this insurance was compulsory, whereas sickness insurance was still voluntary – by contributions from the employee and the employer and the local authority.

Changes were also made in methods of welfare for the aged. The legislation of the 1890s had introduced the principle of old-age assistance, but it still smacked of the Poor Law and people were still loath to apply for it. Now an old-age pension was introduced as a right, and rates of pensions were laid down by the state and no longer left to the judgement of the local authorities. Provision was also made for housing the old when they could no longer look after themselves. Old peoples' homes began to be erected in impressive, if not elaborate, designs, and care was taken to avoid the atmosphere of the poor-law institutions. The idea was to remove any stigma attached to living in a home, as changing conditions demanded. With the drift from country to town families had less room to house their old people : in the country there had always been the possibility of adding a small room or building some sort of cottage for the aged, but this could not be the case in the towns. There the new arrivals found a community of flat-dwellers, and although the size and quality of flats were better than they had been at the beginning of the century, there was still no room to spare. Provision was therefore made for some form of communal accommodation for the old. From this a social pattern which is perhaps typically Danish has emerged, where it becomes more and more the natural thing that old people should live not with their younger relatives but in communities and be well cared for. Subsequently the trend has been to build special flats for them as well, so that they can preserve their independence.

It is difficult to assess what the profounder significance of this development has been for Danish society. Ideally the system is designed to give independence to all, and there is no doubt that this is achieved to a greater or lesser extent. But it may be obtained at the price of the breakdown of the family as a unit and lead rather to a respect for old people than intimate ties with them. Against this, of course, must be balanced the inevitable stresses which arise when grandparents live with their children, stresses to some extent avoided by the Danish system. All in all, however, the trend does loosen the family unit, however much family feeling still remains. It is ultimately connected with a sense of the independence and freedom of the individual rather than the desire to sacrifice some of that independence for the good of the family.

The First Social Democrat Government

Social legislation and help to smallholders were not sufficient to save the popularity of the *Venstre* government in the financial crisis of the 1920s, and in the elections of 1924 the government was badly defeated. After the war people had turned to *Venstre* in the hope of something better; now in their disappointment they turned not to the Radicals but to the Social Democrats, who had never held power before even though Stauning, now chosen to be Prime Minister, had been a Minister in the Radical government after the war. In the same year the first Labour government was elected in Britain, at a time when the Social Democrats were already in power in Germany and had achieved power in Sweden. The Social Democrats had 55 seats, *Venstre* forty-five, the Conservatives twenty-eight, and the Radicals twenty, while the German Party remained constant at one. The situation was now the reverse of what it had been under the last Radical government proper, when the Social Democrats refused to join but gave tacit support. Now the Radicals played a similar role for the Social Democrats. In the *Landsting*, however, the governing party was still in a minority and had to carry on with this in mind.

Stauning, who at fifty was acknowledged by all to be an outstanding politician, started on a programme designed to achieve the support of the Radicals rather than on a narrowly Social Democrat programme. He talked of improvements in the existing social legislation, of educational improvements rather than reform, of medical and dental care for schoolchildren. But all this had to be preceded by the strengthening of an economy still in dire straits. The *krone* was at 62 per cent of par and measures had to be taken to strengthen it. The government made two major proposals: that it should introduce import restrictions; and that there should be a once-and-for-all wealth tax on all estates of 50,000 *kroner* and more. The Radicals successfully opposed this second suggestion, while their support for import regulations was of no avail, as the opposition majority in the *Landsting* rejected them. A law on land value taxation was the sole measure passed to alter the country's economic framework.

All-party agreement was vital before the obviously necessary action could be taken. In December 1924 it was agreed that the National Bank should back the *krone* at 65 per cent of par and gradually increase its support price, if necessary by means of foreign loans. The government would at the same time increase taxation and start paying off its own debt to the Bank, which would thus be enabled to withdraw some paper money from circulation. This process worked – indeed it worked far more quickly than had been foreseen, as foreign investors were quick to pour money into Denmark and to bring the *krone* up to 92 per cent of par within just over six months. It reached par within the year, and by 1 January 1927 the *krone* was again exchangeable for gold.

But this impressive result was only achieved at the expense of industry and agriculture which both suffered badly from increased prices. Unemployment, hitherto falling, rose again to 14·8 per cent, and in order to combat higher costs and diminishing profits, the employers tried to lower wages. The unions reacted sharply and a lock-out lasted from mid-March to early June. But the employers achieved nothing. By 1926 unemployment had risen to almost 30 per cent and remained on average just over 20 per cent throughout the year, the highest figure this century. In 1926, too, the effects of the situation became more apparent for agriculture, which also suffered from a series of extra difficulties, including foot and mouth disease and the imposition of import restrictions by Germany – again a symptom of how Denmark was exposed to the economic situation of other countries. It was clear that strong measures had to be taken and the government suggested a programme of direct aid to industry and agriculture, export credits, and a reduction of taxation. (A programme of public works was also suggested and, again, an extraordinary wealth tax.) The government threatened to resign if these measures were not adopted by the *Folketing*. They were not adopted. The subsequent election campaign, in which the Radicals and Social Democrats for the first time openly opposed each other, was the bitterest ever. The result was a slight but significant move to the Right, *Venstre* and the Conservatives winning a small but sufficient majority over all the other parties. The new Georgist Single Tax Party (*Danmarks Retsforbund*) won 2 seats.

Although *Venstre* was the largest party, it had no overall majority. But as Madsen-Mygdal, who was to lead *Venstre*, refused to compromise on the party's liberal principles, a coalition was seen to be impossible, and so a *Venstre* minority government was formed, with conditional support from the Conservatives and Radicals. Its object was to reduce state expenditure, partly by reducing civil service salaries, partly by reducing expenditure on social benefits, and by streamlining state services – for instance by combining the postal and telegraph services. With some modifications – mainly the decision to reduce civil service salaries by less than originally envisaged – these measures were agreed upon.

By 1928 some improvement was discernible in the economic sphere. Unemployment fell to 18·5 per cent, while a good harvest brought a breathing-space for agriculture. That year saw also a direct arrangement between the workers' and employers' organisations, providing for wage agreements to last for a number of years – an attempt to combat strikes and lock-outs.

Despite opposition to its liberal policies, the *Venstre* government
stood firm and even embarked on what was called 'a doctrinaire
liberal act', Radical and Social Democrat opposition and Conservative reservations notwithstanding. The general aim of the
bill was to allow the individual to follow his own conscience in the
industrial situation, irrespective of pressures from his fellows and
their representatives. He was to be entitled to work at a lower rate
of pay than that approved by the unions if it so suited him. He
was not to be forced to join a union against his will. Any kind of
victimisation was to be punishable under the law. The Social Democrats were eloquent in their condemnation of the act which they
rightly saw as an attempt at undermining the principle of strength
through solidarity.

Yet this liberal minority government succeeded in forcing this
law through because the Conservatives were not willing to vote
against it. Where trouble did arise to mar this traditional co-
operation was over defence. The defence law of 1922 needed
revision and attempts were made to reach an agreement with the
Conservatives on this issue. The Radicals and Social Democrats
were still agitating for varying degrees of disarmament, while the
Conservatives wanted increased spending on the armed forces.
Venstre itself was divided, but the aim of the government was to
reduce the scope of armaments while spending the same amount
on them – this amount not being enough to carry through the present programme. Although *Venstre* offered a slight increase, this was
not enough for the Conservatives and negotiations between the
parties broke down. As these had been in private, there was no
question of the government's resignation, but the Conservatives
decided to refuse to pass the budget – an ironic gesture in view
of what had happened in the 1880s[4] – and when their intention
came out, the Radicals also abstained, and *Venstre* was defeated
by the Social Democrats alone. The Conservatives had been aware
of what might happen all along, but under their new leader,
Christmas Møller, they had decided to show themselves as a party
truly independent of *Venstre*, with whom their constant and somewhat subservient alliance had identified them too closely. The party
was freeing itself from the old Right stigma rather than trying to
show any new identity.

Stauning's Return and Important Reforms

The Conservatives gained little in direct influence from this
move, and in the election following (30 April 1929) they slipped
from 30 to 24 seats. The winners were the Social Democrats with

4 See above p. 83 f.

sixty-one. Stauning led the new government almost as a matter of course; and as a coalition of Social Democrats and Radicals, it commanded a majority of five. Its aim was a reform programme within the area of general agreement between the two parties, touching on disarmament, social legislation, and reform of the criminal laws.

The armament question had been one of the main features of the election campaign, and here there had been the usual division of parties – Radicals and Social Democrats in favour of reducing expenditure, the others against it. Now Social Democrats and Radicals had their way, and the result was a reduction of 6 million *kroner* a year, brought about partly by reducing the call-up from 10,000 to 8,000 a year and partly by increasing efficiency within the armed forces – by appointing more permanent commissioned officers for example. The result was a modest but quite efficient army, considered reasonable in an age which foresaw little danger of renewed war. Hitler and his Nazi freebooters were no more taken seriously by the majority of Danish politicians than they were by the Germans themselves.

A marked change in attitude towards treatment of criminals was shown in reforms of the criminal law. The old principle of punishment for punishment's sake had given way to the modern concept of rehabilitation. The death penalty, in disuse anyway, was abolished, and so was imprisonment with hard labour. Instead varying forms of imprisonment were introduced, while the suspended sentence was used in a greater number of cases. More suitable punishments for young offenders were also devised, and in general judges were given greater powers of discretion when dealing with criminals. This system has been the basis of Danish penal procedure for the past forty years.

The other major reform intended by this government, which has also been the basis for all legislation until quite recently, was the social legislation, known as the Social Reform,[5] introduced by K. K. Steincke, the Minister for Social Affairs. Both this and the penal reforms gave Denmark an aspect which even today is remarkably modern, which at the beginning of the 1930s must have been astoundingly so, and which was the result not of doctrinaire socialism but of agreement between the Social Democrats and Radicals.

The Social Democrat Party had early on begun to appreciate the virtues of moderation, and it has since retained this attitude. That it has had its rebels is quite obvious, but generally speaking, they have had the courage of their convictions and left the party, which

[5] See below, Appendix A, p. 219.

has thus for many years had the support of a very broad section of the population.

It was possible to introduce the far-reaching social reforms of the 1930s against a background of increased prosperity. For despite the economic and social difficulties of the 1920s, the overall picture was much brighter than the unrest and the unemployment figures seem to indicate. In the broader view, the difficulties had been concerned more with adapting to changed circumstances, and this had been achieved by means of widespread rationalisation both in industry and in agriculture. The drift from the farms had been offset by mechanisation, while rationalisation had served to make industry more efficient and to increase production. It also made for the creation of large firms and semi-monopolies, though this tendency was not as widespread in Denmark as in other countries. Consequent upon improved industrial efficiency, durable consumer goods made up an increasing percentage of exports, though Denmark was still predominantly a country exporting agricultural produce. However, the trend towards more industrial exports had begun and agriculture's share fell from 90 per cent to 80 per cent – mainly to Britain, which took about 60 per cent of Denmark's exports, but only provided some 13 per cent of her imports. Workers in employment earned good wages and their purchasing power was back to that of 1920. There was a feeling of affluence, despite the 15 per cent unemployment which still existed.

In general, Denmark in the 1920s had undergone the same sort of social transformation that had characterised most of Europe, the move into the modern age with its motor-cars, its radio, its aeroplanes. (In 1922 Danish Airlines opened their first regular route.) It was the age of hiking and cycling, of sport and dancing. It was also the age of popular education when, partly to counteract the nineteenth-century, Christian-patriotic influence of the Folk High Schools, the Social Democrats organised the Workers' Educational Union and attracted many pupils who studied not only general subjects, but also politics and social problems. The sex age had also dawned and the subject was discussed openly for the first time, while inhibitions began to dissolve and the divorce-rate increased. Sex replaced God : sexual freedom the rules laid down by Christian teaching. The orthodox teachings of the Church of Denmark had long been under attack – even as far back as the 1880s, says Johannes Jørgensen, it had been bad form to be a Christian if you also belonged to the intelligentsia. Now the anti-Christian, anti-clerical tendency spread to all classes, especially among the young, in whom the disillusionment caused by the World War was most profound.

The old society was dead, and the new left no room for faith. According to statistics compiled in 1921, just over 97 per cent of the population belonged to the state Church, and that claim is still made today : 'There is little reason to suppose that the proportion has appreciably changed', states the official handbook, *Denmark*. What these statistics probably mean is that 97 per cent of the population had not actually contracted out of paying church taxes. They certainly give no realistic impression of the situation in the 1920s, and even less so today. Had they done so, there would have been no need for the Social Democrats to introduce their so-called 'civil confirmation' in the 1930s. In point of fact the Department of Religious Sociology in the Institute of Ecclesiastical History, University of Copenhagen, published figures in January 1969 which seem more realistic. They indicate that the percentage of regular worshippers in Denmark as a whole has been halved over the past forty years and stands at between 2 and 7 per cent over the country as a whole as against 7 to 13 per cent in 1927. These figures are based on returns from the parishes and are probably more accurate than official statistics of church membership. It has even been suggested that they may be a little over-optimistic.

Chapter 7

1930–39

Economic Crisis

THE DIFFICULTIES WHICH DENMARK had experienced in the 1920s were largely independent of the world situation, and thus when the Wall Street crash came in October 1929, the Danes were not over-anxious about the consequences. It was expected to be a short-term crisis which would pass. But in 1930 it reached Europe, and when Britain left the gold standard in 1931, Denmark had to follow suit, despite the fact that 1930 by and large had been a year of prosperity. Some firms now went into liquidation, but this was only a beginning, and the numbers grew throughout the following years. By 1933 unemployment had reached the unprecedented level of 43·5 per cent, though during the summer of that year it fell back to 21 per cent. In this year Steincke's Social Reform came into force and the plight of the unemployed, who previously had had to exist on poor-aid when their unemployment insurance ran out, was to a great extent mitigated. The stories of the unemployed in Denmark are like those from elsewhere and tell of the hopelessness and desperation, the queuing up for the dole, and the hardship and humiliation of looking for a job. Demonstrations organised in Copenhagen were in some cases put down by the police, by methods not always gentle. Jobs were so scarce that employers attempted to take only those who would accept less than the union rate, and such terms were often accepted.

The state stepped in with plans for public works and work camps were set up for the unemployed. Ten were built in all, but they were regarded with some misgivings, as they smacked too much of forced labour camps, though they were far from being so in fact. Another way of alleviating distress was to provide free periods of residence in Folk High Schools, an experiment of some interest as it brought a completely new class of pupil to the schools. Many were not interested in learning and felt themselves in a different category from fee-paying pupils, but others resented their situation less and profited :

Askov gave them a warm welcome, and probably all found new courage, a new self-reliance, so that they were subsequently able to create a new and worthwhile existence for themselves. But it was not always easy to be an unemployed man at a high school. We hardly ever had any money at our disposal, and at Askov this was more obvious than at the Workers' High School, because many of the pupils had plenty of pocket money. For instance, I could not go home for Christmas because I had no money for the journey. But that led to my spending Christmas with the Principal and his family, and it was the best Christmas I had experienced for many years.

Thus one unemployed man remembered Askov, the biggest of the high schools.

Yet not everyone from the country districts 'had plenty of pocket money'. Agriculture suffered as much as any other part of the economy, though the difficulties created for farmers were very different from those in the towns. The hard times appeared in rural areas earlier than in the towns; by 1931 the price of corn had been halved, and this was followed by similar falls in the price of dairy produce. At one time it was said to be cheaper to use butter for lubricating machinery than to buy proper grease and oil. Farm after farm had to be auctioned : in 1930 there were 324 such auctions, and the number rose to 1,214 in 1931 and 2,043 in 1932, falling back to a mere 1,332 in 1933. It is, however, still true to say that even in 1932 total only represented about one per cent of Danish farms, so the number of farmers who actually went bankrupt was relatively small. Much higher was the number of those who only just scraped through. The fall in prices for cattle was catastrophic, to as little as 15 shillings for a medium-quality cow, while pigs fetched so little that a system of rationing production was introduced, and piglets were regularly slaughtered at birth and thrown on to the rubbish heap or burned.

In 1932–33, before we came to an agreement with England on pig supplies, I remember that when I had to sell young pigs, which I had made a speciality, I once had to sell twelve for 48 *kroner,* and I had to deliver them in Terp, about 20 kilometres away from home. I can still remember that there was a thirteenth, and I made sure of smuggling it in to get rid of it. They weighed about 40 pounds each.

This was one man's experience, and it appears to have been typical.

With the difficulties of the farmers themselves came difficulties for their suppliers, and in 1931 the government made an arrange-

ment to help those who could not pay their debts. Ten million
kroner were earmarked for aid, and the idea was that the state
should pay the creditors 20 per cent of the sum owing, provided
that the creditors were willing to give a receipt for the whole sum.
Conditions were so bad that most were only too willing to go along
with the arrangement. For their part the farmers were pleased with
the respite, but many felt that they still owed the money, and with
the arrival of better times, paid off the remainder of the original
debts.

In providing help of this kind, the government showed itself
aware of the farmers' difficulties. It knew, too, that the farmers
saw devaluation as the only real solution to their problems, a
course that would help them to export their surplus produce. Yet,
confronted by British complaints against the high rate of imports
from Denmark, it could not accede to these demands, reasonable
as they might have seemed, especially as Denmark was only taking
a very low percentage of British exports. An effort was made to
sell more British goods in the country and a British exhibition was
arranged and opened by the Prince of Wales in September 1932.
It was a success, but not sufficient to galvanise Danish importers,
and the feeling remained that more could be done. After all, with
99 per cent of Denmark's bacon exports going to Great Britain,
together with 72 per cent of her butter and 85 per cent of her eggs,
the government was loath to lose access to the British market. The
Foreign Exchange Office, created in 1932 to control all foreign
trade and issue import licences, therefore showed itself more willing
to grant licences for imports from Britain than from elsewhere.

There was widespread dissatisfaction with the foreign currency
restrictions, which to many seemed to lack cohesion. By and large
the Conservatives supported the idea of restrictions, but it was
anathema to *Venstre*. So, to clear the air, the government called
elections for November 1932 in which it increased its representation
by one, while *Venstre* lost 5 seats. The Radicals lost two, and thus
the two centre parties started to decline. The Single Tax Party
more than maintained its position, and won a second seat, probably
because of its association with the Georgist principles which had
been behind the JAK movement,[1] one of those organisations which
sought to help the hard-hit farmer and which gained widespread
popularity during the 1930s because of its opposition to the crip-
pling effects high interest rates were having on the farmers. It sought
to organise interest-free loans based on members' deposits. Originally each member was to pay 15 per cent of the loan he required;
the sum thus collected was distributed on an interest-free basis, and

[1] See above, p. 134.

as repayments were made, the principal was redistributed to those on the waiting-list.[2]

New regulations concerning import control were now agreed, coming into force for one year, the main change being that importers were guaranteed not less than 45 per cent of their imports reckoned in *kroner* from the previous year, unless unforeseen circumstances arose. The agreement brought an end to dispute and the government was then able to discuss some sort of trade agreement with Britain. During 1932 England had twice increased import duties and Danish goods were affected. First Ramsay MacDonald's National Government completely abandoned free trade principles and put a 10 per cent duty on a whole range of goods including dairy produce, but not bacon. At the same time Empire goods continued to be imported duty free. These new arrangements came into force in February and were followed by the Ottawa Agreements on Imperial Preference according to which Britain increased the duty on butter and eggs to 15 per cent, while expressing an intention to reduce bacon imports. As a consequence Denmark was asked to reduce by 20 per cent bacon shipments to Britain, virtually the only market for these exports.

Britain was, of course, in economic straits as dire as Denmark's and the imposition of duties had to be accepted as one of the admittedly unpalatable and perhaps uninspired facts of life. Yet it was a heavy blow for Denmark whose trade was obviously going to suffer. At the same time, Britain had expressed willingness to negotiate with foreign countries once the Imperial Preference Agreements came into effect and Denmark was quick to seize her chance. Within less than a month talks were in progress and an agreement was reached which, if not ideal, did at least limit the damage for the time being. Britain agreed not to increase further the duty on dairy produce and fish, and not to impose a duty on bacon. In return Denmark accepted a quota arrangement for bacon which kept exports at their 1929–31 levels; while provisions were made for minimum quantities of other Danish exports if any sort of quota arrangement should be required in the future. For her part Denmark was to give certain privileges to British exporters of industrial goods and some foodstuffs, while arrangements were 'noted' concerning other British exports, especially those of raw materials for agriculture. Denmark also agreed to buy 80 per cent of her total coal imports from Great Britain. The agreement, which was

[2] The 15 per cent rule had subsequently to be altered, but the movement continued its work – and still exists – on the basis of interest-free deposits which in turn could lead to an interest-free loan proportionate to the size of the deposit.

for three years, was probably as much as could be expected under the circumstances. It did not give the Danes absolute security, as there were numerous escape clauses, but it did mean that they now had a clearer picture of their prospects than before, and could take steps to keep production within the limits imposed on the country as a whole.

The negotiations with Britain began in December 1932 and the agreement came into effect in April 1933, but during this period Denmark was faced with what some saw as the greatest industrial crisis of her history. As a result of the general fall in prices, the employers began to demand a 20 per cent reduction in wages on the expiry of the national wage agreements in January 1933. This, they argued, would be in the workers' own interests, as it would enable the employers to keep their prices low and so to increase production. But the unions were not prepared to see any reduction and consequently the employers gave notice of a lock-out from 1 February. Despite exhortations from the government, both parties refused to try for a compromise solution, and with the prospect of a vast increase in the already widespread unemployment, the Social Democrat government decided to legislate to ban all strikes and lock-outs for a year, and to extend the previous wage agreement for the same period. Both parties to the strike were opposed to legislation, while Conservative and *Venstre* politicians were able to point out that the proposed standstill would be to the immediate advantage of the workers. The Radicals would rather have seen some form of permanent arbitration tribunal set up, but decided not to oppose the government. At this stage *Venstre* started to argue that devaluation would ease the situation, helping exports and thus improving the country's economy, and forcing up prices in a wide range of goods, thereby weakening the arguments in favour of a reduction in wages.

Now the agricultural interests joined in the debate, and both large and small farmers made demands for measures to improve their lot. They desired an alteration in the system of taxation, and some form of protection, and although in their joint declaration they stated that the 'normal buying power' of the *krone* should be maintained, it was obvious that they really wanted devaluation. This now became a main object of *Venstre* policy, whatever the cost to the negotiations with Britain.

The difficulty was for the political parties to arrive at any sort of consensus to get a bill through the *Rigsdag*. At times it appeared that no agreement was possible and fears were expressed that Denmark's entire political structure was in danger. Finally in a last effort to reach a compromise, Stauning invited a number of the leading politicians from the Social Democrat, *Venstre*, and Radical parties to his home in Kanslergade. With only short breaks for refreshment they went on for eighteen hours before producing an outline agreement in which it was possible to fill in details during further negotiations. The main give-and-take occurred between the Social Democrats and *Venstre*. In exchange for a devaluation of just over 10 per cent, leaving the rate at Kr. 22·50 to the pound sterling – a devaluation grudgingly accepted by Britain as New Zealand had just devalued by a similar amount – *Venstre* had agreed not to oppose the Social Democrat proposal to ban strikes and lock-outs for a year. Other points settled in what became known as the Kanslergade Agreement were a reduction of taxation on farms, the starting of a number of major public works – including the building of Europe's longest bridge, the *Storstrømsbro*, between Zealand and Falster – and the unimpeded progress of Steincke's Social Reform. In addition the state was to buy up a total of 150,000 head of cattle for destruction. *Venstre* was not happy about the move from free trade, but a change of heart had been forced on the party by circumstances. With the advent of a Conservative government in London there was no real alternative but to look to Denmark's immediate interests and accept state interference in agriculture. For the Social Democrats the acceptance of state interference in industrial bargaining had also been a bitter pill to swallow, and so the Kanslergade Agreement has been seen as a turning-point in the history of twentieth-century Danish politics. It was, indeed, an historic occasion : the negotiations took place on the day Hitler came to power – 30 January 1933.

Partly as a result of the agreement, and partly owing to further developments in the administration of the country, unemployment fell in 1933 to about 20 per cent, where it remained until the end of the decade, mainly because production began to look up after the lowering of bank rate to 2½ per cent and money became cheaper. It even became possible to convert earlier loans at high interest rates, which helped many private individuals fighting to stave off bankruptcy. At the same time the Foreign Exchange Office did much to stimulate industry. Primarily, it distributed foreign exchange, thus forcing Danes to buy from countries to which they exported in significant quantities – Britain especially. But it was also in a position to refuse funds for certain imports, when it was deemed reasonable for Denmark to produce such goods herself. In this way industry was persuaded to look for new products and to be self-sufficient, and so an increase in the labour force was necessary. This led to a significant reduction in the import of finished goods, accompanied by a noticeable increase in

the import of raw materials. Throughout the 1930s the Foreign
Exchange Office exerted a decisive influence on Danish economic
policy. It became necessary to have it under the control of a Foreign
Currency Council, on which, practically speaking, all branches
of Danish commerce and industry were represented. A renewed
co-operation between industry and government emerged, such as
had been seen earlier in the century, while the need to have one's
views represented encouraged the more efficient organisation of
industry into what amounted to pressure groups.

Thus the early 1930s saw the emergence of much more widespread state control of everyday life than had originally been envisaged, more perhaps than many people wanted. It had come
about because the problems facing the country were too big to be
solved by any less an agency than the state, which had to accept
a greater and greater responsibility for the wellbeing of each
sectional interest. The Social Democrats bore the chief responsibility
for carrying through this move, although it was not altogether to
their liking. Nevertheless, it was done by state control, not by
nationalisation. The state did not take over industry, but it took
upon itself to direct it in so far as the prosperity of the country
was concerned, leaving day-to-day running and ownership in
private hands. In the social field, state direction was implicit in
Steincke's Social Reform, which laid down more stringent rules
than had existed before and took away from local authorities the
rights they had previously enjoyed to decide for themselves the
amount and form of help needed. The new social legislation was
firmly based on closed co-operation between state and local authority. In conjunction with this, taxation was used to bring about a
redistribution of the country's financial resources. Taxes, indirect
and direct, were increased, accounting for some 15 per cent of
earnings.

Steincke's Social Reform, more of a rationalisation of social
legislation than complete reform, was implemented not only because of the need for extra unemployment benefits in a difficult
year, but as part of the general settlement constituting the Kanslergade Agreement. Steincke had for years worked in the social sphere
and fought hard for his measures, and because of the need to reach
agreement on as many matters as possible, he was able to keep his
bill intact, despite Conservative opposition.

The result was a thorough tidying-up of Danish social legislation,
which has been basically unaltered in principle until the present
day, though there are now moves afoot to rationalise it still further.
It introduced social service as a right rather than as an act of

charity, and was symptomatic of the increasing humanitarian ideals of modern Denmark.

The lot of the Danes was quietly but surely improving; but in Germany, humanitarian ideals were being brutally cast aside. This could not be a matter of indifference to the Danes. They were well aware of fresh German demands for the return of north Schleswig, since the Dano-German border was a direct result of the Versailles Treaty, a main target for Nazi hatred. To make matters more complicated, some unrest did exist in the region, which had suffered more from the depression than other areas. (There had been five times as many enforced auctions of farms there as elsewhere.) The German minority fastened on economic discontent to urge a return to Germany, not least as agricultural reform there seemed to offer better prospects than in Denmark. The main pressure group among Danish agriculturists, known as the LS (*Landbrugernes Sammenslutning* – Agriculturists' Association), which was later to show Nazi leanings, was active in north Schleswig and was open equally to Danes and Germans. The latter made the most of their opportunity. Hitler, for his part, insisted that they should obey his orders, and Nazi organisations were formed in north Schleswig, as indeed elsewhere in Denmark, though their activities were to some extent limited when Denmark prohibited the use of military-style uniforms anywhere in the country. This prohibition was aimed not only at Danish Nazis, but equally at other uniformed political organisations.

Anti-democratic tendencies were evident in the Denmark of the early and middle 1930s. Youth organisations attached to the major political parties were all acting in para-military style, while numerous small anti-democratic parties sprang up. The Danish National Socialist Party was formed under Frits Clausen, but although it wanted to put up candidates for the *Folketing*, it was not able to gain the necessary 10,000 signatures to take part in an election. Nevertheless, the party whipped up numerous street demonstrations, in some of which it had the support of LS and JAK. How widespread anti-democratic tendencies were in the country as a whole, it is difficult to estimate, for they had little practical effect either then or later. Certainly the Danes would have nothing to do with the anti-semitism of the Nazis and accepted the small Jewish community in Denmark as an integral part of the Danish population. Anti-semitic gibes in Danish Nazi publications probably lost the party more support than they gained.

Anti-democratic views were not, however, wholly on the Right, and indeed it has been suggested that the Nazis and neo-Nazi movements enjoyed a measure of support because of a communist threat. The Social Democrat politicians felt themselves threatened by the communists, while the unemployed were also showing signs of being receptive to the arguments of Marxist agitators. At the other end of the scale left-wing intellectuals joined in the communist chorus, the so-called drawing-room communists.

This polarisation of extreme views was a danger to the country's political system, but Stauning's government steered a careful course throughout and avoided any major splits. It was helped by the increasing number of votes polled by the Social Democrats in successive elections, which resulted in the highest Social Democratic vote ever in 1935, when the party gained over 46 per cent of the votes. This percentage has never been surpassed or even equalled since. The election meant six extra seats for the Social Democrats, and an unchanged number for the Radicals. The Conservatives lost one seat and *Venstre* ten. The Single Tax Party and communists maintained their strength at 4 seats each, while the Free People's Party – an offshoot of the LS movement – won five. With gains such as these the Social Democrats now set their sights for the first time on winning a majority in the *Landsting* in the 1936 elections. In a hard-fought campaign, the opposition painted a grim picture of what would happen if the Social Democrats were to govern without any sort of check being put on them. The party only needed to win three extra seats, and when the sounting was done, they had secured two of them. All that was left was the seat for Bornholm, and here there was a tie. The result had to be determined by drawing lots and the Social Democrats won, thus giving the party, in alliance with the Radicals, an absolute majority in both houses for the first time.

The problem of defence immediately exercised the new independent Social Democrat–Radical government. Traditionally, both parties had been in favour of more or less complete disarmament. The argument was that as Denmark would not be able, come what may, to withstand an aggressor for long, there was no real point in spending money on a defence which everyone agreed was useless. During the period of optimism in the 1920s, defence expenditure had indeed been reduced; but now, in the 1930s, when optimism had given way to pessimism, and when Germany was emerging as a powerful and warlike nation once more, Danes began to think again. The old argument of futility was, of course, still as valid or invalid as before, but the spectacles were no longer rose-tinted. As early as 1933 a leading Social Democrat politician had described Denmark as a beautiful residence which had been built by the joint efforts of the farmers and the workers, adding that 'the workers would be foolish not to secure and defend their house if thieves broke in'. This speech betokened a change in the Social Democrat attitude, and the following year Stauning himself argued that the time was not ripe for unilateral disarmament. He was supported by *Venstre* and the Conservatives, and by 1937 there was agreement between the parties that the defence budget must be increased to 45 million *kroner*.

Denmark was in a very difficult situation as far as foreign policy was concerned. The country had accepted limitations on its traditionally neutral policy by joining the League of Nations and accepting the clause on sanctions only after some hesitation. Now the Danes began to comment on the impotence of the League of Nations. In October 1933 Hitler had withdrawn from the League and flouted its principles by rearming, and subsequently by reoccupying the Rhineland – to the accompaniment of nothing more than protests from France and Great Britain. A visit to London by Stauning decided him that Britain would not be able to offer protection in the event of an invasion. After seeing the continued decline of the League during the Abyssinian crisis, Denmark, together with the other former neutral nations, reasserted her old neutrality. She had to try to protect her future as far as possible by not getting at cross-purposes with Germany.

Denmark therefore adopted what looked like an ambivalent position in European politics. Although she had a seat on the Council of the League of Nations at the time, she abstained from voting when Germany was condemned for reintroducing conscription. And later, in 1937, when there was a good deal of agitation from the other Scandinavian countries and from the opposition in Denmark for a Nordic defensive treaty, Stauning, anxiously aware of Germany's watchfulness, rejected the idea in no uncertain terms. It must be remembered that Hitler was not prepared to accept the 1920 Dano-German border as binding and Denmark had the examples of the Rhineland, Austria, and then the Sudetenland, to convince her that north Schleswig was in very much the same category, with plenty of Germans demanding to go 'heim ins Reich'. Thus when, in 1939, Germany reacted to President Roosevelt's protest about the Führer's conduct in Europe by offering non-aggression treaties to all the Scandinavian countries, Denmark was the only one to accept. There was little alternative, as Germany was on the doorstep, and a refusal would almost certainly have been regarded as an unfriendly act. Denmark had little confidence in the treaty, but felt some need for support in her attitude on north Schleswig, and Germany specifically promised not to change the frontier by force. Possible discussion on the border problem was not, however, ruled out. For her part, Sweden refused a treaty because it implied a break in her long-standing neutrality, and also, it was said, because she was afraid that such a treaty would in practice limit the freedom of the Swedish press to comment on the German situation. The Danish press was already limited in this respect. Germany had made representations about the bad press she was receiving, and the government had therefore asked editors to be careful in their treatment of German affairs. It was Denmark's hope that as a result of this very circumspect behaviour towards Germany, the country would once more be able to remain aloof in any future war which might come, and as part of this hope had managed to have written into the treaty with Germany a clause giving her the right to trade with third countries in the event of war. Legally, then, Denmark would still be able to trade with Britain if war came.

While Denmark had been concerned to secure her external position, there had been some internal recovery from the catastrophic situation at the beginning of the decade. It had come first to industry, thereby occasioning a good deal of discontent among the farming community who had sought some form of relief by organising itself and putting pressure on the government. In this the LS movement played a leading part, and helped to organise a massive demonstration of farmers in Copenhagen in 1935. A deputation waited on the king, but although he received it, he referred the members to Stauning. The government was unable to give them the help they asked for, including a further devaluation, and they tried to apply pressure by organising a dairy strike and withholding the foreign currency they earned. Their moves were not very successful, though they had the support of the opposition parties, who threatened to refuse to pass the foreign currency regulations when they came up for renewal. It was under these circumstances that the government held the 1935 elections which gave it an increased majority. 'Stauning or chaos' had been the cry, and the country chose Stauning. He became something of a father-figure in Denmark, a symbol of national unity, and it was his policy to govern the country for the good of all, not for any purely sectional interests.

Even with its new *Landsting* majority the government did not set out on a path of radical socialisation, but continued on its previous course: state control but not state ownership. And the state set out to control the unions and workers as well as the employers when necessary. Stauning aimed at close co-operation with the unions, but knew that this was possible only if the unions were prepared to look to the country's interests as well as their own. In particular an attempt was made to avoid industrial strikes by persuading the unions that differences must be settled by negotiation. The effort was largely successful, especially when it was decided that the official arbitrator could put his suggestions for compromise solutions to all the unions concerned, in the knowledge that their majority verdict would be accepted by the remainder. The system of compulsory arbitration was so well developed in the 1930s that industrial disputes on the whole were settled in a civilised, responsible manner which avoided head-on collisions between parties in dispute. And the unions did take notice of the country's economic situation, not least by withholding wage-claims when prices started to rise and by thus ensuring that unemployment did not rise with them. In fact for a time they accepted what amounted to a 7 per cent drop in living standards, though wages did begin to rise again by the end of the decade.

The end of the thirties was not a period of great reforms, though changes were made in laws concerning apprentices, while the right to one day's holiday for every month worked – in practice a fortnight's holiday a year – was made statutory. Old-age pensions were made payable at sixty, thus helping many old people out of work and persuading others to give up their jobs in favour of younger people, of whom many were still unemployed. As in Denmark local authorities derive their income from direct taxation (which had come to mean that the richer the town or district, the lower the percentage of income tax), a law was also passed which sought to distribute the tax burden more evenly amongst local authorities. The state was now trying to limit the development of a situation which had been aggravated by people moving into towns with a lower tax percentage.

The constitution also came in for scrutiny. The position now that there was a Social Democrat majority in the *Landsting*, was very different from when the *Landsting* could be relied on to act as a brake. Suggestions were made for adopting a single chamber system, but instead a new constitution was suggested in which the *Landsting* was to be chosen by direct vote, in much the same way as the *Folketing*. The suggestion was approved by the *Rigsdag* and an election held in April 1939 so that, according to the constitution, a new *Rigsdag* could vote on the same bill. The Social Democrats lost a large percentage of their votes, but the new *Rigsdag* voted for the constitutional amendment. Then the suggestion had to be put to a referendum, where it had by law to be accepted by at least 45 per cent of possible votes. It received only 44·46 per cent and was thus rejected, to the great disappointment of Stauning. The advent of war in September prevented any more constitutional

12—D · ·

moves being made and it was not until 1953 that the present constitution was finally adopted.[3]

In areas outside the immediate political arena, however, other
changes were taking place, putting Denmark in the vanguard of
European developments and at the same time showing the workings
of the social legislation which attempted to play its part in all walks
of life. The birthrate was falling and the fear was expressed that
this would have catastrophic results in the 1970s. In an effort to
stem this trend moves were made in two completely different fields.
A bill was passed in 1937 to ensure regular visits by health visitors
to mothers with small children, in an effort to cut the infant
mortality rate, then one of the highest in Europe. It also became
possible for families with three or more children to receive grants
towards the cost of housing – either loans to build or subsidised
rents.

On the other hand, in a decade when open discussion about sex
had gained impetus and when traditional moral concepts were
more and more thoroughly undermined, a move of a completely
different kind was envisaged and, to some extent, carried out.
Abortion was becoming something of a social problem and although
the existing law prescribed strict penalties for illegal abortion, more
and more cases were coming before the courts and were either dismissed or resulted in a light sentence for the offenders. Since
the law was obviously falling into disrepute, it was suggested by a
government commission that legal abortions should be granted in
cases of rape or for health reasons, and that it should be allowed
for 'social reasons' : if the birth of another child would have any
seriously detrimental effect on the financial position of the woman
concerned. Although a noticeably liberal attitude prevailed, the
suggestion of abortion for social reasons aroused a storm of protest,
and the clause was dropped before the bill was finally passed.

In making these provisions, the state also felt obliged to help in
other ways any mothers, especially unmarried ones, who were in
need. As a consequence the institutions known as Mothers' Assistance Clinics (Mødrehjælpen) were open in order to help mothers
to make the best of what in some cases was a bad job. A law was
passed giving illegitimate children the right to bear their father's
name and entitling them to inherit from him. This legislation, very
advanced for its time, was a clear indication that Denmark was
moving away from traditional social and moral concepts. The welfare state was extending its influence to people in need whatever
the cause, and trying to do away with hardship without seeking to
know or to demonstrate the rights and wrongs – a demonstration

---

3 See below, p. 192 f.

of the egalitarian principles of the government in power. This particular move was made easier by the fact that neither of the government parties made any pretence of maintaining Christian principles. They were both expressly humanist in approach and thus could easily ignore the standpoint of an earlier age, still being observed in countries with a Christian, or theoretically Christian, government.

The same egalitarian principles also prompted the government to introduce a new Education Act, the aim of which was to improve the quality of schools and to bring their standards into line. Previously a distinction had been made between those children who went through a primary school and those who went on to 'middle school'. Now, in an effort to give equal opportunities to all, the middle school was made a part of the primary school. Some middle schools led, however, to an examination, some, known as examination-free middle schools, did not. At the same time moves were made to improve school standards in country districts, sometimes by combining several small schools into one larger one serving a wide area.

Literature in the Twenties and Thirties

The thirties were a decade of social stresses and it was natural that the conflicting principles which found their expression in political and social developments should also find literary – or semi-literary – expression. Periodicals expressing the new points of view, whether political or cultural, ranged from left-wing attacks on Nazi-type politics to others with such promising titles as *Sex and Society*, containing patent prescriptions for the happy life. It was also a time of serious literature dealing with the new ideas and problems which had emerged in the 1930s.

The 1920s had produced a literature which was the natural continuation of the immediate post-war works mentioned in the last chapter, works which reflected the disillusionment of the post-war generation, even though they may have been written ten years or more after the end of the war. Tom Kristensen[4] and Jacob Paludan[5] dominated the scene, Kristensen first and foremost in his poetry, but also in novels such as *Life's Arabesque*, a fantastic piece about a revolution in Copenhagen. It is, like the Expressionist poems which Kristensen was writing, to some extent unrealistic in its portrayal, but its political import and its disillusionment are real enough. Kristensen's major novel, *Havoc*, was not published until 1930, a bitter book about men without a view of life, in which the main

[4] See above, p. 128.
[5] See above, p. 126.

figure has to destroy himself by drink in order to build himself up
again. Though published in 1930, it is still a novel of the 1920s.[6]

The same is also true of Jacob Paludan. His major work, *Jørgen
Stein*, is a novel of the immediate post-war period, but it was published in two volumes as late as 1932 and 1933 – again a part-
bewildered, part-disillusioned look at the generation. It also came
as the climax to a series of novels looking critically at modern social
developments. In other novels from the twenties, *Birds Around the
Lighthouse* (1925) and *The Ripening Fields* (1927), Paludan takes
other aspects of modern civilisation – technical progress, American-
isation, the emancipation of women – and dislikes them all. The
works of both Kristensen and Paludan have not dated as social
criticism of fifty years earlier has dated. They are full of dynamism
and treat problems which are akin to, if not the same as, those
which preoccupy many modern writers.

But as the literature symptomatic of the twenties continued to
be written in the 1930s, that typical of the thirties had begun in the
twenties. In 1928 a novel appeared in a completely different genre,
The Fisherfolk, by a young writer called Hans Kirk. Kirk was a
Marxist, and his novel, which tells of the successful efforts of a
small fishing community to settle in a new part of the country, is
a 'collective' work in which the group rather than any individual
predominates. At the same time, in showing how the group of
fisherfolk, who belong to the Evangelical Inner Mission, have a
dynamic faith which they manage to impose on the more liberal
and tolerant local inhabitants, it is a picture of the workings of a
communist cell in a non-communist society. The genre was
attempted by many other leading writers of the 1930s, some of
whom have emerged as the most important Danish novelists of
this century, though in most cases not because of their 'collective'
novels. As may be expected, however, the pervading theme in the
novels of the 1930s was the social problem, and the solution posed
was normally that of some form of socialism, whether revolutionary
or not.

Yet the traditional picture of the grey, disillusioned literature of
the 1930s is only partly true. As early as 1924 the clergyman Kaj
Munk had written his ten-act play *An Idealist*, intended to probe
the personality of Herod whom he saw as an idealist with the wrong
ideals. It was a monstrously long play, yet one of indisputable
dramatic effect. Its approach to melodrama was to recur elsewhere
in Munk's production : the dead woman brought back to life and

---

[6] In a conversation some years ago Tom Kristensen said that he was
not writing any more novels, but that if he did so, they would still be novels
of the 1920s, so deeply engrained was the age in him.

rising from her coffin or the smashing of the bust which proved Christ to be a Jew, while the discoverer walks out and marries his Jewish secretary. Munk deals with current and yet timeless problems, and deals with them from a Christian point of view. There is a certain ambivalence about him. For instance, there is just a chance that the diagnosis was wrong and that the girl was not dead, and when Professor Mensch smashes his evidence and yet marries a Jewish girl, he seems to be eating his cake and having it. Munk is ambivalent, too, in his attitude to contemporary dictatorship. Like many others, he was an admirer of Mussolini, though less so of Hitler. When the Germans invaded Denmark, however, all ambivalence disappeared and Kaj Munk stood out as an uncompromising patriot, using his pulpit to denounce the Germans, until the Gestapo in traditional style dragged him from his home one night, murdered him, and left his body in a ditch.

Among the other more colourful figures of Danish literature in the 1930s was Karen Blixen, whose *Seven Gothic Tales,* appearing under her pseudonym of Isak Dinesen, was published in the United States in 1934, the first of a series of books in which story-telling and the imagination took the place of hopeless descriptions of a hopeless reality – a brilliant exercise in escapism. More realistic, indeed intensely realistic, was her autobiographical book *Out of Africa,* published in 1937, in which the aristocratic Danish coffee-farmer produces a glowing description of contemporary Kenya accompanied by a penetrating and understanding analysis of the African mentality.

It has happened before that those writers whose work has had lasting significance have in fact been untypical of their time. This is true of the 1930s. The men who wrote, perhaps most accurately, of their own day, overlooking the deeper problems of humanity and existence beyond the struggle to keep alive, are scarcely read nowadays. Those who while in some cases being aware of the reality around them looked beyond it, still occupy a place in the national consciousness. In the 1930s such figures were Martin A. Hansen, H. C. Branner, and William Heinesen, who in the following decades were to become something different, able to rise above the immediacy of their surroundings.

The 1930s had been a time not of promise but of struggle, often without hope. By the end of the decade Denmark had begun to emerge from the economic crisis which the country had faced since 1929, and unemployment had sunk to about 9 per cent. Yet it was becoming increasingly obvious that the future held problems of a completely different dimension.

Chapter 8

1939–45

Denmark in the Second World War

WHEN WAR BROKE OUT in September 1939, there could be no doubt where the sympathies of the Danish people lay, but neither could there be any question of their acting on these sympathies. The only hope lay in remaining strictly neutral and carrying out the same tightrope act as twenty-five years previously, a hope which had been encouraged by the non-aggression pact with Germany and its express guarantee that Denmark would be able to trade with other nations provided commerce with Germany was continued. In practice, however, it was much more difficult to maintain this position, as Germany was more self-sufficient than before and therefore less interested in maintaining unbroken trade links. Germany also gave evidence of her singular disregard for treaties and arrested several Danish ships on their way to England, though when a strong protest was made, they were allowed to proceed. Subsequently Germany did nothing during the early stages of the war to prevent Denmark from trading with Britain, though this trade was not without its physical dangers, mainly because of mines off the English coast. By March 1940 6 per cent of the Danish merchant fleet had been lost.

Nor, it must be admitted, was trade with Britain particularly lucrative. While the price of foreign goods rose, and while insurance premiums on freight reached unprecedented levels, thus contributing to rising prices, Britain introduced price controls immediately on the outbreak of war and refused to increase payment for Danish goods. The fact that sterling had been falling in value made the situation more difficult for Denmark who received less for her exports than had previously been the case. For a time the *krone* was allowed to fall with sterling, but on 1 September 1939 the decision was made to tie the *krone* to the dollar instead of the pound. Thus, in relation to other currencies the *krone* was stabilised, but in relation to the pound sterling it was overvalued, and Britain was still Denmark's main customer. Accordingly, negotiations with a view to increasing the price paid for Danish exports were started and after long and difficult bargaining a rise was achieved, though at the cost of Britain's curtailing the quantity of imports – a doubtful advantage for the Danes. On the other hand, Britain acknowledged their right to continue exporting to Germany in the same ratio as hitherto, and so it looked as though Denmark's precarious position might be maintained. But whether the agreements with the two belligerent powers would in fact have enabled Denmark to steer a neutral course must remain a matter for conjecture. The agreement with Britain was signed on 2 April 1940. A week later, Denmark was under German occupation.

The real reason for the occupation seems to have been not so much a desire to take over the country as the need to secure Denmark as a stepping-stone for the occupation of Norway. Norway was of strategic importance to Germany because of her indented coast, which would provide excellent bases for the war in the Atlantic, and also because Norwegian waters were being used for the transport of Swedish iron ore from Narvik. Britain and France had plans for coping with the Norwegian situation and even mined Norwegian waters. Fearing that Britain and France might occupy parts of Norway and stop the transport of the iron ore on which Germany depended – this had been the intention until Finland had to surrender to Russia on 12 March 1940 after the winter war, thus robbing the Allies of the excuse to intervene in the North – Germany decided to move first. To begin with, the Germans acted on the assumption that only Jutland needed to be taken, but finally the decision was reached that the entire country should be occupied.

Ironically, Denmark was warned of what was about to happen. Admiral Canaris, the head of German Intelligence and a leading if shadowy figure in the anti-Hitler faction, seized the opportunity to humiliate the Führer by allowing news of the impending invasion of Scandinavia to leak to the Dutch military attaché in Berlin. By this route the news reached the Danish ambassador, who sent it straight to Copenhagen on 4 April. Although it caused a stir and was followed by a number of emergency meetings, the news was not really believed. The Danish government was aware of the country's dangerous situation, but was at the same time afraid of antagonising Germany by taking any step which might look like military preparation. Even as late as 8 April, when German ships were known to have sailed in the Baltic, and when a long column of troops was known to be moving northwards towards the Danish frontier, no mobilisation was carried out, though the armed forces were in a state of alert. The army chiefs would have liked to

mobilise, but the politicians hesitated until it was too late. At 4.00
a.m. on the morning of 9 April, the German ambassador in Copenhagen – who had known that something was brewing, but was not
fully informed – asked for a meeting with the Foreign Minister and
gave him an ultimatum. The invasion had already begun. Denmark was merely to be used as a base for German troops, but
would otherwise be left to look after her own affairs. If the German
terms were not accepted, Copenhagen would be bombed. By 6.00
a.m. the government had capitulated. There was little choice, and
the only object in prolonging resistance seemed to be to convince
the outside world that Denmark was not pro-German, but did
genuinely want to resist.

There was, for the time being, no question of Germany's taking
over the Danish government or of replacing the lawful government with one of her own choosing. Within limits, which in the
course of time became increasingly obvious, the Danes were able
to continue to run their own country, and the day after the occupation the two main opposition parties, the Conservatives and *Venstre,*
were invited to join a national administration, which they did –
though only on condition that Stauning should publicly acknowledge that it was the old ministry which was responsible for
capitulating. One of the first questions which had to be negotiated
with the occupying forces was their demand that any Dane caught
in espionage or other actions damaging to the German forces
should be subject to German jurisdiction. The Danes fought against
this demand and they were successful in their policy of evasion,
although they had to appoint a Danish 'State Advocate' to deal
with all such matters and to demonstrate that they had saboteurs
firmly under control. In this way the courts and police remained
under Danish authority for the first years of the Occupation. But
military establishments came, as a matter of course, under German
rule, and bases were built to carry out air raids against England.
The Danish army was not disbanded, although no call-up was
effected between April and November 1940. Such arms as there
were were kept in Danish hands, and the training of officers continued.

As far as possible, the Danish authorities continued as usual,
German requests for direct contact were rejected, and the arrangement was made that all contacts should be through the Ministry
for Foreign Affairs. The Danes as a whole maintained a correct
and dignified attitude, co-operating where necessary in order to
avoid a direct confrontation with the occupying power and the
inevitable taking-over of authority which would result from this.
A more or less voluntary censorship was imposed on the press and

radio, and political demonstrations were forbidden. This latter measure appeared to be a move towards appeasement, though in fact it was aimed as much at preventing the Danish Nazi Party from demonstrating as at anything else. This sort of move appeared to be based on a will to co-operate, but was in fact intended as obstruction, a typical manifestation of the non-violent opposition throughout Denmark during the Occupation.

Despite a Conservative suggestion that some sort of agreement should be negotiated to define the exact limits of sovereignty, the other parties in government refused this, arguing that it would be better to deal with each problem as it arose, rather than risk a further, legally defined limitation, which in any case could be ignored at will. The government, and in particular P. Munch, the Foreign Minister, preferred to argue each case for as long as possible, and only to give in when it became inevitable that there was no other alternative.

Meanwhile, the Danish people as a whole, although they maintained their dignified stance, felt that they had been let down badly by the politicians. There was widespread disillusionment with the way in which their chosen representatives had behaved, a feeling exploited by the Danish Nazi Party and also by the LS movement, who for different reasons wished to see the end of democratic government. Although the LS movement was not fundamentally Nazi, there were certain affinities, and the two parties began to join forces in their demands for a new start. Despite the ban on demonstrations, the Nazi Party organised one in Roskilde and an even larger one in Copenhagen, both of which were put down by the police without any intervention on the part of the occupation troops.

Nevertheless, the increasing agitation put new pressure on the government which was afraid that the Germans might make use of the opportunity to install their own puppet régime. It was not forgotten that the Danish Nazi Party had its own 'leader', Frits Clausen, though his calibre does not seem to have been such that the Germans seriously thought of letting him take over the government. Under these conditions Stauning and his Ministers decided on a government reshuffle, and it was suggested that experts should be drawn on from outside the *Rigsdag*. In particular there was a widespread desire to see the back of Munch, who was made into something of a scapegoat. Party politics were officially abandoned and a committee set up to iron out differences in outlook, and finally a composite government emerged including three non-parliamentarians, of whom Erik Scavenius, a former Foreign Minister, was by far the most important and controversial. Stauning remained Prime Minister – another example of the extent to which the Danes were allowed their head within their own country, remembering the Nazi love of Social Democrats.

Scavenius was scarcely a collaborator in the sense usually given to that word, but he was willing to go further in co-operation with the Germans than his predecessor Munch had been. What he was aiming at was to gain the confidence of the Germans by co-operating with them where possible, and thus maintaining the government in Danish hands. He foresaw that any other policy might well lead to the handing-over of power to extremists, or at the very least the forced inclusion in the government of members of the Danish Nazi Party. It was an audacious policy which almost went wrong at the outset. On coming into office he produced a document outlining the government's attitude to the occupying power, and ending with an expression of admiration for the German military victories and of Denmark's readiness to find her rightful place in the emerging new Europe. The Danes were incensed by such a declaration, but the Germans were far more impressed by this apparent change of heart than could have been foreseen. On 18 July, 1940, ten days after the formation of the new government and the publication of the document, they enquired whether Denmark would be interested in negotiating an economic link with Germany immediately rather than wait until the end of the war. Again Scavenius took the audacious course of answering in the affirmative, expecting months of delay before negotiations became a reality. Once more matters took a dangerous turn when on 30 July Germany suggested a customs and economic union, the broad principles of which could be worked out within five days or so, and the details within a couple of months. A reply was requested for the following day.

There was nothing for it but to continue upon the course adopted, and Scavenius persuaded his fellow Ministers to accept the suggestion of negotiations, which began on 5 August. It had been understood all along that Germany should have the dominant position, but what emerged as soon as the negotiations began was that this was less a question of a merger than a takeover bid. German currency was to be valid in Denmark and the Danish *krone* gradually to be phased out: Germany was to negotiate all trade agreements with foreign powers and all current Danish trade agreements were to be ended. All trade barriers between the two countries were to be removed and Danish indirect taxation and duties brought into line with those in Germany. There was also a clause giving Danish and German citizens equal rights in both countries. This was a treaty which Scavenius would never be able to get accepted, and when this was pointed out to the German

negotiator, his reply was merely that Denmark was free to refuse
to negotiate, but that terms offered at the end of the war were
likely to be less favourable. When the terms of the offer became
known in Denmark there was almost unanimous resistance, even
from the farmers, who stood to gain most from open access to the
German market. However, the situation was eased by the opposition
of German business and farming circles, who did not want the
well-organised Danish farmers to compete in Germany, and so it
became relatively easy to break off negotiations.

Although it is possible from a distance to see the point in
Scavenius' policy, it was not easy for the Danish people at the
time to see it as anything but a betrayal. The effect of this was a
reinforced Danish nationalism, some of whose forms had been seen
before : Grundtvigianism, with its special mixture of patriotism
and Christianity, took on a new significance, while patriotic songs
were sung in large numbers. Another phenomenon was *Alsang* – a
form of community singing at meetings which ran into their
thousands. Although political demonstrations were forbidden, the
regulations could hardly be stretched to people getting together
for a sing-song – even if their numbers did on one occasion reach
74,000[1]. Thus a feeling of Danishness akin to the great Romantic
patriotic upsurge in the nineteenth century made itself felt in the
country during the course of 1940, replacing the sense of despair
and disillusionment which had come immediately after 9 April.
There were no open demonstrations against the Germans, but they
were everywhere politely cold-shouldered or ignored. No one could
be in any doubt as to where the sympathies of the Danish people
lay, however ambivalent their government appeared to be. And as
a symbol of the people's feelings, the king made it his practice to
ride alone on horseback through Copenhagen every morning.

For their part, the German authorities sought to put more pressure on the Danes to co-operate, and a period began in which use
was made of what has now become known as salami tactics, during
which the Germans little by little encroached more and more on
Danish sovereignty, making use where possible of the appeasement
policy of the government. An undesirable politician, such as Christmas Møller, the outspoken leader of the Conservatives, was removed
from his post as Minister of Trade, and then gradually eased out
of political life altogether when he continued to work actively and
openly against the occupation forces. Likewise the Minister of
Justice was forced out, because he was prepared to see that justice

[1] On 1 September 1940 it was estimated that 739,000 people gathered in
groups throughout the country and all sang the same patriotic song at the
same time.

was carried out according to Danish law and custom rather than according to Nazi wishes. The Germans then demanded that a section of the Danish fleet should be handed over to them – in defiance of their earlier promises – and after some negotiations aimed at preventing the handover, it had to take place nevertheless. But the Danes removed all guns from the ships first, and they were towed out of Copenhagen to the accompaniment of flags at half-mast – by order of the king.

Various moves were made to replace the Stauning government, one by a group of non-party Danes, and one later by the Germans – though the Danish Nazi Party was in such a state of disarray that it was difficult to see how it could ever be entrusted with power. When Christmas Møller had gone, soon to be followed by Social Democrat politicians like Hans Hedtoft-Hansen (the future Prime Minister, Hans Hedtoft),[2] an attempt was made to remove Stauning himself, but it failed. Nevertheless, in return the government had to introduce legislation to curb espionage and anti-German propaganda, and also to discourage propaganda against the Danish Nazi Party. Yet a surprising aspect about the situation in Denmark was that despite the German occupation, the press was largely free to say what it liked about Danish internal affairs, and it made the most of its opportunity. Even so, moves to limit freedom both of speech and action were now made. Certain crimes were removed from the jurisdiction of ordinary courts, partly in order to prevent the occupying authorities from overriding Danish laws when the verdicts and punishments were not what they wanted.

The general public became more and more dispirited with the constant moves to appease the Germans, and began to lose confidence in their government. From their own point of view, the time had come to stop giving in to German demands. The question was how to do it, and what would be the result.

This feeling was encouraged by events in 1941. With the German invasion of Russia, the occupying forces insisted that Denmark should intern all communists. There was no question of negotiations on this issue, and however little it wished to do so, the government had to give in to the demand. Only by doing so could it ensure something approaching tolerable conditions in Denmark itself, and Ministers were aware also that if they did not do as they were told, the Germans would do it for them, and the communists would suffer a much worse fate. Yet this was by no means the last demand made after the onslaught against Russia. Originally the Germans hoped that Denmark could be persuaded to take an active part in the Russian war. The winter war against Finland

2 See below, p. 187.

had intensified Danish dislike of Russians and of communists as a whole. But Denmark stuck to her policy of neutrality and refused. As an alternative the Germans persuaded the Danes to allow the formation of a Danish Free Corps to fight on the Eastern Front. It was organised by the Danish Nazi Party, but the press and radio were given instructions to accept propaganda on its behalf, while the military authorities were told not to prevent officers or troops from joining. In fact it was basically a fiasco, and only about 1,500 joined the corps, which had to be complemented by members of the German minority in north Schleswig.

Still worse was to come, however, when later that year Germany invited Denmark to sign the Anti-Comintern Pact when it came up for renewal. By doing so Denmark would not in fact be taking on any new commitments, but the mere signature of the pact in company with Germany's allies seemed to be a step towards a full-scale alliance with the Reich. An attempt was made to decline the invitation, but the government was finally informed that a refusal would be seen as an unfriendly act, and that Germany would no longer feel bound by the earlier agreement with Denmark. Unlike other occupied countries, which were administered by the SS, Denmark was still within the sphere of the German Foreign Ministry under Ribbentrop, and wished to remain there. At the same time, Scavenius knew that Ribbentrop wished to maintain his authority over Denmark and so he was able to insist on four clauses being inserted in the pact which expressly stated that Danish adherence only obliged Denmark to take police action against communists within her own borders, and that under no circumstances was the country to be drawn into the war against Russia. With these express reservations the pact was signed.

Popular reaction was immediate, and a large demonstration was arranged in Copenhagen, in which many were arrested. But this was a clear pointer to the true sympathies of the people, who were afraid of being dragged into the war on the German side. This demonstration in itself led to nothing, except perhaps a clearer understanding abroad of the Danish attitude. It did, however, underline a stiffening resistance to the Occupation. The communists reacted immediately by going underground and setting up an illegal press, and other groups organised illegal publications under such titles as *The Free Danes* and *Free Denmark*. The circulation of these publications grew rapidly and they attacked not only Germans and Danish Nazis but also the Danish government itself for being too intent on appeasement.

At this point, on 3 May 1942, Stauning, who had been failing for some time, died and his place was taken by Vilhelm Buhl, a

politician who had been outspoken in his opposition to the Anti-
Comintern Pact. It looked as though there might be an end to
appeasement. Buhl was not nearly so ready to compromise with
the Germans as had been Stauning in his final months, but the
real trouble, when it came, was caused not through any political
clash, but because of a telegram which King Christian X sent to
Hitler. The Führer had sent a congratulatory telegram on the
king's birthday, to which Christian had replied, as had been his
custom, with a brief 'Thank you very much'. Hitler saw this as an
insult, and despite Danish protests that nothing of the sort had
been intended, made preparations to strengthen the German hand
in Denmark. The top German functionaries in Denmark were replaced by hard-liners, and the demand was made for a new government, including men closer to German ideas, under the leadership
of Scavenius. Scavenius declined the offer, but when the only other
candidate for the post who was acceptable to the Germans refused,
he was in November 1942 forced to try to form a ministry, one,
moreover, which was specifically intended to pass emergency legislation giving the government wide powers.

There was a general fear that Scavenius would form a much
more pro-German administration, but in the event there were no
Nazi sympathisers among his colleagues, who included some non-
parliamentarians but were mainly politicians. The emergency laws
were passed, but did not include the death penalty, as the Germans
wished, and a clause was inserted to the effect that the powers
lapsed on a change of government unless both houses of the *Rigsdag* renewed them after such a change. Thus there was no danger
of the laws constitutionally passing into the hands of a Nazi-based
government. The other great fear had been that Scavenius would
be forced to pass special anti-Jewish legislation, but this he promised not to do, though he told his colleagues that he would try
to avoid trouble on this issue by not promoting Jews to positions
where they would be likely to upset the Germans. The general
public had little liking for or confidence in Scavenius, but he was
prepared to go only a limited way towards pleasing the Germans.
So far Denmark had been spared the suffering of much of the rest
of Europe, and it was his hope that he would be able to continue
his policy in what were likely to be difficult months ahead : the
fortunes of war had begun to change and it might well be that
Germany would be more dangerous in defeat than in victory.

Yet the new German plenipotentiary, Werner Best, was still interested in keeping up tolerable relations with Denmark, not from
kindness, but because he saw such an attitude as being in Germany's
best interests. On the other hand, the military authorities, under

their new area commander, General Hermann von Hanneken, were for clamping down on the resistance movement, now developing in strength and efficiency. More communists were arrested, some being sent to German concentration camps, while the Germans now went on to demand that certain categories of prisoners should be handed over to them if arrested by the Danish police. The Danes again complied, though when three Danes who parachuted into Denmark from British planes were arrested and handed over, so many high-ranking police officers threatened to resign if they were executed that their lives were spared.

The great surprise in Danish political life came in 1943 when Best, to boost his co-operation policy, allowed the regular elections for the *Folketing* to take place. Local elections had already been twice postponed. The elections were allowed even though the result was a foregone conclusion, because Best wanted to have a *Rigsdag* which could pass valid laws. Moreover, it suited the Germans to show that free elections were possible in German-occupied territory. No true election campaign was allowed, and the four major parties did not compete in any normal sense, calling rather upon the electors to vote for one of the parties in the national government as a symbol of their faith in Denmark and Danish policies. The response was heartwarming: 89·5 per cent of the electorate voted, an all-time record, and of these 94 per cent voted for one or other of the coalition parties. The Danish Nazi Party received a miserable 2·1 per cent of the votes cast, the LS Party only 1·2 per cent. Neither did the communists achieve their aim of persuading people to hand in blank ballot papers: only 24,000 did so.

The election results, which broadly speaking confirmed the composition of the previous *Folketing*, were to make no difference to the cabinet, which was still to be headed by Scavenius. This fact was known from the start, and had been a condition insisted on by the German authorities.

If one of the intentions of the election had been to show that Dano-German co-operation was possible, the result was exactly the opposite of what was expected. This massive demonstration of national solidarity gave a new impetus to the resistance movement, which now became more accepted by the people as a whole and also became better equipped and organised, thanks to active help from England. It was apparent that Germany would lose the war, and Danes felt the need more and more strongly to demonstrate to the Allies that they were in no sense fellow-travellers of the Nazis. The thought of being classed as a German ally was repugnant, despite the appeasement policy of the government and however much easier life had been as a result. Consequently the resistance movement deliberately set about undermining this government policy. Everyone was aware that an active resistance could lead to a takeover by the Germans, but whatever the implications of such a step for the immediate future, it was thought preferable to the classification as a German ally. Together with a vast increase in the volume and effectiveness of sabotage, a wave of strikes hit the country, first in Esbjerg, then more violently in Odense and in other major towns.

As was to be expected, the government tried to stop the unrest, but its exhortations went unheeded, as did those of the unions and even of the king himself. This was wind in the sails of the German military authorities, who had all along wished to overrule Best's attempts at co-operation, and finally it was decided in Berlin that unless the Danes could put their own house in order, the Germans would have to do it for them. It must not be forgotten that the Danish army still existed, and further, that it was armed, and this factor was of some importance in German plans. They were afraid that there might be an invasion of Jutland, which would find them with a built-in enemy army in their midst. They made a demand that all weapons should be handed over, but this was only partly met.

Finally, on orders from Berlin, Best demanded that the Danes themselves should declare a state of emergency; that assemblies of more than five people should be prohibited; that the death penalty should be introduced for sabotage; that a curfew should be proclaimed. Moreover, Odense was to pay a million *kroner* for an attack on a German soldier. This was the moment that all had foreseen for some time, when no further appeasement was possible, and that which the resistance movement had been working for. The Danish government and the king, fully aware of the probable consequences, refused to comply, and waited for the German reaction. At the same time troops were told to offer no resistance if an attempt were made to disarm them, and a similar order was given to the navy.

The reaction was not long in coming. At 4 a.m. the following morning, 29 August 1943, the Germans introduced a state of emergency and took over full administrative powers. The plans for disarming the Danish army were put into effect, and though some resistance was made, it could not last for long. As for the navy, although orders had come from the political authorities not to resist, none had been given not to scuttle or try to slip away to Sweden. The commander-in-chief, Admiral Vedel, gave precisely these orders, and a large proportion of the fleet was either sunk or, where practicable, sailed to Swedish waters.

As on 9 April 1940, the Danes awoke on 29 August 1943 to find their conditions of life changed. All the measures demanded by the Germans a few days before were now a reality and the German forces were there to make sure they were carried out. Many prominent politicians and others thought to sympathise with the resistance were interned, though most were released within a few months. The army was likewise interned and soon demobilised. The press and radio were put under censorship of a much stricter nature than anything they had experienced before, and the censor was a German official. The period of appeasement was at an end, and what were known in Denmark as 'Norwegian conditions' seemed imminent.

Yet again, however, the worst was avoided. It was the intention of the German authorities either to have a new government appointed or to put in a purely German administration, and Best asked Niels Svenningsen, the civil service head of the Foreign Ministry, to put his proposal before the politicians. But the politicians were aware now that the time for negotiation had passed, and they finally said they were unable to form a government. The king refused to nominate a cabinet from outside the *Folketing*, as this would be contrary to the constitution. However, Svenningsen came to an arrangement with the occupying forces whereby the country was to be run by the civil service heads of department, who in fact issued instructions which had the force of law. Various of the leading judges had stated that if these instructions were contested in the courts, they would be considered legally valid. So for a period Denmark's civil service chiefs had both executive and legislative power in the country, a power which they in practice exercised in close consultation with the politicians. The main contact between the Germans and this new form of Danish administration was Svenningsen who brilliantly carried out his difficult task. Again it was a case of giving in to many of the German demands, but in some instances it was possible for the individual concerned to argue that something was outside his sphere of competence; in others the general instructions were issued by the Germans, while the working-out of details was left to the Danes. As a consequence the final draft was less inhumane than had originally been intended.

In one field, however, the German military now had a free hand. In what had for a long time been a contest between the Himmler and the Ribbentrop factions among the German authorities, the former had argued for the deportation of the Danish Jews. With the takeover on 29 August, these forces were now in the ascendant and orders were issued from Berlin that Danish Jews should be arrested and deported. Best, who knew that this was one thing the

government had always refused to countenance, and was aware
of the probable reaction of Danes if it happened, fought against
the plans, but was overruled. This same man who, as political
leader of the German occupying authorities, was a target of general
hatred, allowed his shipping attaché G. F. Duckwitz – who himself
was anti-Nazi – to leak the plans to both Danish and Swedish
politicians. It became possible to warn Danish Jews of what was
coming, and by the time the German arrests started, almost all
had disappeared. Of the approximately 7,000 Jews in Denmark,
only 472 were arrested and deported, and of these only fifty-two
died in concentration camps. The remainder were hidden by friends
and were then for the most part smuggled out of the country to
Sweden in an operation which started on an amateur basis, but
quickly became well organised.

Despite the relative failure of this action, it turned the Danish
people even more against the Germans. It gave a new impetus to
sabotage, which some sections of the public had so far viewed with
disfavour, and it gave new impetus to the development of the
resistance movement as a whole. The various groups hitherto
making up the movement were combined under what became
known as the Danish Freedom Council, which assumed, and by
the population at large was given, something approaching governmental authority. In conjunction with London the Council set
about organising an efficient underground army ready to co-operate
with any invading forces and ultimately to be under the control of
SHAEF. The Danish army, which had been interned on 29 August
and released after the anti-Jewish action, made a welcome contribution to these activities, and while the majority stayed in Denmark,
some officers went to Sweden to form a corps ready to take over
when Denmark was liberated.

This more elaborate organisation stepped up efficiency in opposing the occupying forces and acts of sabotage increased rapidly in
both number and effectiveness. They encompassed everything from
small supply dumps to major factories, and they also included the
murder of any Danes known to be betraying resistance workers to
the Germans. These informers were a great menace to the Resistance and there was no other way of dealing with them. For their
part the Germans reacted by counter-sabotage, blowing up non-
military buildings in Copenhagen such as the Students' Union and
the Conservative head office. In the end Tivoli itself was devas-
tated by fire. In retaliation for the murder of informers orders were
given to the Germans, and more particularly to their Danish supporters, to murder chosen political figures and even innocent mem-

bers of the population, Kaj Munk being the most famous of those who suffered in this way.

Such was the tension that on 25 June 1944 a curfew was introduced in Copenhagen from 8 p.m. to 5 a.m. every day, while assemblies of more than five people were once more forbidden. The reaction to this was immediate. On the following day the workers at Burmeister and Wain's shipyards stopped work at noon, in order, they said, to have eight hours of freedom before the curfew. The following day others followed suit, and the movement led to a spontaneous general strike in the capital, during which the population roamed the streets and demonstrated against the occupation forces. Martial law was introduced, and indiscriminate shooting was indulged in to cow the people; but in the end, after stopping supplies of water, gas, and electricity; cutting off the city from the outside world; and preparing to starve the Copenhageners into submission, Best was persuaded to remove his terror squads from the streets and to allow a return to normal conditions. On hearing the promise of an end to the terror, the Danes resumed work, after one of the most spectacular demonstrations of national solidarity of the war.

Aware of the attitude of the Danish people and fearing – quite rightly – that the police were working hand in glove with the resistance movement, the Germans now decided that the police must be disbanded and deported. In September they struck; but like the Jews before them, the police suddenly vanished, though not with quite such success. Some 2,000 were arrested and deported before they could go underground, while the remainder made a useful addition to the resistance forces. From September 1944 to the end of the war, Denmark was thus without a police force of any sort, though local guards were formed to try to prevent the increasing and inevitable number of crimes.

By this time it was obvious that potential power in Denmark was divided between the politicians, whose function was now severely limited, and the Freedom Council. As a result of the popular strike in Copenhagen the two factions, who had hitherto had little sympathy for each other, recognised the need to co-operate and especially to come to some arrangement about the formation of a post-liberation government. Negotiations resulted in a decision to form a government consisting of nine politicians and nine members of the resistance movement, together with representatives of the Danes who had served overseas. Under pressure from Russia it was decided that no member of the new government should have been a member of the Scavenius administration. The Prime Minister was to be Buhl. It was hoped to avoid the conflicts which had

arisen in other liberated countries, and which in some cases –
notably Greece – had resulted in civil war.

There is no need to dwell here on the violence and bloodshed of
the final months of the occupation. Suffice it to say that as the
transport of arms from Britain increased, there was a highly
organised and well-equipped partisan army in Denmark which set
about sabotaging everything of use to the Germans. The railways
suffered especially, when the Germans started transporting troops
from Norway back to Germany, but factories and stores were
severely damaged as well. Informers were liquidated in ever greater
numbers, and reprisals were made in a crescendo of violence and
brutality. The Gestapo was active and successful in arresting
leaders of the Resistance, and there was some fear that the movement might be entirely broken. These fears were, however, dis-
pelled when the three Gestapo headquarters in Jutland, Copenhagen, and Funen were bombed, and most of the archives destroyed.

Fighting on Danish territory was expected and provided for,
but in fact none came, as the German forces capitulated to the
British – though they refused to capitulate to the Danish resistance
forces. There was some sniping in Copenhagen immediately after
the capitulation, as Danish Nazi groups who felt they had nothing
to lose were rounded up. Bornholm was the only part of the country
where any serious damage was done. The German forces there
refused to surrender to the Russians, although they were prepared
to give in to the British. Consequently the Russians bombed Rønne
and Nexø, causing both casualties and considerable damage, until
the German commander was replaced by another senior officer
who then handed over to the invading forces.

In many respects the Danes suffered less both nationally and
personally from the effects of the war than did the people in other
European countries. Until August 1943 the régime was tolerable
and life could go on in many ways as normal. Thereafter things
became more insecure. The fact that the government of the country,
together with the police force, had remained in Danish hands, had
helped to alleviate what could otherwise have been an unpleasant
and dangerous situation. In the same way, food had been more
plentiful in Denmark than in other occupied countries, and the
farming industry had succeeded in maintaining a high level of
production despite the difficulty of obtaining fertiliser and fodder.
Thus, although food was rationed, it was possible to maintain a
high level of nutrition. On the other hand, industrial products
were in much shorter supply : although Germany provided a good
deal of raw material necessary for industry, it was with a view to

supplying her own war needs and the Danes had to be satisfied with what they could get.

All this, however, must not be taken as an indication of great prosperity in Denmark. There was, in fact, a great deal of money in circulation, thanks largely to special drawing rights which the Germans had in the National Bank of Denmark. At the same time Danish exports to Germany – for which a clearing account was responsible and for which the Germans often failed to pay – were far in excess of imports. As a result of the plentiful supply of money and the scarcity of goods, inflation set in, but this was brought under control by taxation and by the encouragement of saving, and also by the decision to increase the exchange rate of the *krone vis-à-vis* the mark. It has been estimated that Denmark's economic situation in 1945 had fallen back to about the same as in 1930. It had not been an entirely cheap war for the Danes.

Chapter 9

1945–70

Towards Affluence

The Immediate Post-War Problems

THE NEW GOVERNMENT under Vilhelm Buhl, who had been Prime Minister once before but forced out by the Germans, was faced with many difficult tasks when it came to power on 5 May 1945. Although not appointed in accordance with the constitution, it had the stated aim of working within the constitution and returning to full constitutional normality as soon as possible.

A return to normality meant a thorough clearing-out of the backlog of the Occupation, the punishment of war criminals, and the restoration of some sort of balance in the country's finances. The state was left with a debt of some 8,000 million *kroner* at the end of the war, and at the same time it was known that great quantities of money had been earned by more or less legal means but never declared during the Occupation. Even before the liberation, the National Bank had had new banknotes printed, and thus it was possible to introduce these and invalidate old ones as early as 23 July 1945. The process of changing currency disclosed that something in the region of 2,700 million *kroner* had never been declared to the authorities. How much more was simply destroyed it is impossible to say. There was still too much latent buying power in the country, which was desperately short of goods, and a heavy tax was placed upon fortunes earned and saved since 1939, while a high percentage had also to be deposited as a loan to the state. These taxes went a good way to pay off the debt which the state had incurred to the National Bank thanks to its guarantee for the money drawn by the Germans on their special account and never repaid. Much of this money had in fact formed the basis of the fortunes made, and so a sort of rough justice followed.

Another sort of rough justice was being done to the known collaborators and Danish Nazis from the war period. In all some 34,000 were arrested at one time or another, and some had to be punished. But laws had not been drawn up for this sort of situation, and so it was necessary to pass legislation allowing for the punishment of war criminals. Discussion in the *Folketing* took in both the principle of introducing retrospective legislation and the demands for the reintroduction of the death penalty, which had long fallen into disuse in Denmark. In the end, however, doubts were overcome, and retrospective legislation providing for the death penalty in certain cases was passed. Under these laws seventy-eight were condemned to death and forty-six actually executed.

This new legislation, passed in a short time when passions were high, was harsh in the extreme. The main law, intended for serious crimes, imposed a minimum penalty of four years imprisonment and a complete loss of civil rights, which in practice meant the complete ostracism of anyone found guilty. For lesser offences a law was subsequently passed providing for more lenient sentences, leaving to judges the decision whether to condemn guilty persons to the loss of civil rights. In the case of the first law, there was no such option available. The trouble with these laws was that, being in effect emergency legislation, they did not provide for all contingencies, and in practice judges found themselves forced to condemn a man to a harsh punishment when they did not feel that he really deserved it. In time they did in fact begin to give shorter terms of imprisonment, and the letter of the law had to be softened, while those condemned in the first outburst of zeal had their sentences reviewed and in many cases reduced. The Resistance was violently opposed to this clemency, and would have liked to see even harsher punishments, so much so that it even carried out a brief occupation of one of the prisons housing political prisoners, with the intention of itself ensuring justice.

The Resistance was dissatisfied not only with the treatment of war criminals, but in general with the return to power of politicians and policies active before the war, even though it had never formulated a political policy itself. And with the return of the politicians came a return of unemployment, though the politicians were not directly responsible for it. Whereas there had been opportunity for work during the war, there were few openings for exports so far, and trade was some time in starting. As a consequence it was obvious that unemployment must increase. Dissatisfaction with the politicians came, too, from a new trade agreement with Britain, under the terms of which the Danes were to receive much lower prices for their agricultural produce than had been paid by the Germans. The agreed minimum payment of 4·18 *kroner* per kilo was well below the price other countries were paying for Danish butter. But Britain offered an assured market for Danish produce,

and as the prices agreed were minimum ones, the prospect of an
increase seemed reasonable. It soon became clear that the liberation government could not last indefinitely, as it was a coalition of
too many divergent views, from Conservative to communist. During the summer of 1945 attempts were made to amalgamate the
communist and Social Democrat parties, but the efforts led nowhere. By the autumn conditions were such that the only way out
was an election, which was accordingly called for 30 October.

Election and New Groupings

It was probably a fateful turn of events for Danish political life
that a general election was not called immediately after the liberation, for when it did come, people were tired of the wrangling that
had inevitably followed the Occupation and were beginning to
look more to the Denmark of the future than to the occupied
Denmark of the past five years. Accordingly, although the election
resulted in a change in the balance of political power, it was a
quite unambiguous statement that Danes intended to remain on
the path they had been following before the war. There was no
rethinking of the governmental system, which some of the Resistance had been hoping for.

Nevertheless, the election brought a striking leap forward for
the communists, whose representation rose from the 3 seats of 1939
to eighteen. The reasons for this were manifold. Although the wartime government had been a coalition, it was dominated by the
Social Democrats and they duly received their share of blame for
the policies which had led to the Occupation and the state of
affairs while it lasted. This had forced many of their more left-
wing supporters into the communist camp, at the same time as the
communists had received a good deal of public sympathy for their
treatment during the Occupation, together with some reflected
glory from the Russian war effort.

With this drift to the Left taking place, middle-class Social
Democrats were leaving the party; because the party itself was
moving leftwards, perhaps trying to steal some of the communists'
thunder by putting forward a far more radical and socialist policy
than it had done under the moderate leadership of Stauning. The
confidence which the middle classes had developed in Stauning's
party was dispersed by the more openly class-based policies put
forward by the new leadership under Hans Hedtoft-Hansen. Thus
the Social Democrats lost heavily in the election, their representation going down from 66 seats to forty-eight. Moreover, the party
as a whole had lost the support of the Radicals, thanks to its more
extreme policy, which meant an end to the co-operation which

had for so long been a feature of political life. The Radicals now moved more towards *Venstre*.

The moderate votes lost to the Social Democrats went mainly to *Venstre*, which also picked up many former Conservative votes both because of Christmas Møller's unpopular trade agreement with Britain and his hard words about the profits made by farmers during the war (*Venstre* was still a party based on the farming population), and because of his refusal to work for a revision of the frontier with Germany. He wisely maintained that the frontier was fixed once and for all, but this attitude lost him much Conservative support. In fact, *Venstre* now stood as the *conservative* party, not least owing to the attitude of its leader, Knud Kristensen, who had demonstratively left the government when Scavenius was appointed Prime Minister, and yet had stood out against the extreme demands for vengeance after the Occupation. He seemed to symbolise something immutable for the Danes, and it was not unnatural that he was chosen as the new Prime Minister. When the Social Democrats refused to form a government, the choice fell upon *Venstre*, the second largest party in the new *Folketing*. The Conservatives and Radicals both refused to join, but promised their support, and so 1945, a year in which some polarisation of votes took place, saw the formation of a government which despite its name was based on moderate conservative principles.

The new *Venstre* government under Knud Kristensen was nevertheless a minority government, the first of several in the immediate post-war years, none of which in the event proved to be particularly stable. It used tacit Conservative and Radical support to embark on a policy of reconstruction. The heavy taxation it had to impose has already been mentioned, and this formed only a part of the efforts, largely successful, to improve the country's economy. With its social-liberal outlook the new government was also prepared to make a start on social reform. A new law was passed providing for state aid for building projects in an effort to ease the acute housing shortage – after years when no flats or houses had been built. This government also had to negotiate on trade with Britain in an effort to win better prices for its agricultural produce, and, when the attempts failed, it introduced a system of support for agriculture which has been further developed in subsequent years.

While the government, broadly speaking, ran into little opposition in its internal policies, it met difficulties in the external field which finally led to its downfall. The one question still, and perhaps especially at this time, sure of making Danish feelings run high, was that of Schleswig. Although the liberation government had expressly stated that it considered the Dano-German border as permanent, there were plenty of Danes who saw their opportunity to move the border south once more, and voices were raised demanding an end to German rule in Schleswig. This coincided with a rapid growth in the pro-Danish voices in south Schleswig itself, partly perhaps as a result of the disastrous years they had experienced, partly as a reaction to the resettlement there of refugees from eastern Germany who threatened completely to swamp such Danish influence as there still was. The demand for a change came most stridently from the Danish Union Party and from the Conservatives, though the Conservative leader, Christmas Møller, was the man who had originally argued for the permanence of the border, and continued to do so. The other parties were by and large in favour only of reinforcing the rights of the Danish minority in southern Schleswig. Yet Knud Kristensen, the Prime Minister, declared himself in favour of making a change. If the wave of pro-Danish sentiment in southern Schleswig was genuine – and Danish supporters won roughly half the seats in local elections and seven in the Schleswig-Holstein *Landtag* – it could scarcely be denied the right to express itself in a referendum, though, added Kristensen, this should be at some time in the future when the immediate crisis was over. The matter was debated in the press and in the *Folketing,* and finally the British government, as one of the occupying powers, asked Denmark for an outright statement on what her wishes were, giving the Danes the choice of three alternatives: of exchanging the minorities on both sides of the border; of deciding the frontier on the basis of a referendum; or of moving the border without reference to the wishes of the people. The Danish reply was that Denmark would not herself demand a frontier revision, but that the population of southern Schleswig should be given the right to decide its own future.

Despite apparent agreement on this reply within the *Folketing,* certain members, including Knud Kristensen himself, continued to argue for a frontier revision, though Kristensen maintained that he was agitating for this as a private individual, not as Prime Minister, a point which led to his downfall. By adopting this standpoint he created so much personal opposition among the parties which wholeheartedly supported the moderate line of the reply to Britain, that the Radicals – never a party with any noticeable nationalistic tendencies – put down a motion of no confidence in him, and in October 1947 that motion was carried by 80 votes to 66. It was not the best time to bring down a government basically preoccupied with post-war reconstruction, but it was the only way out once *Venstre* had rejected a demand made to it as a party by the Radicals that it should replace Kristensen. Once the motion of no confidence was passed, there was nothing for it but an election.

The Return of the Social Democrats

The paradoxical result of the election held on 28 October 1947 was a resounding victory for *Venstre* but a government formed by the Social Democrats under the leadership of Hans Hedtoft, as he now called himself. *Venstre* increased its representation by 11 seats to a total of forty-nine, but did this at the expense of the party closest to it, the Conservatives, who fell from 26 to 19 seats. This transfer of votes was a result of the Schleswig question, and *Venstre* under Kristensen seemed to represent more forcefully the wishes of those in favour of a frontier revision who had previously voted either for the Conservatives or for the small Danish Union Party, both of whom had been expected to agitate for such a revision. While there was a general redistribution of the middle-class vote in favour of *Venstre,* the Social Democrats made a comeback at the expense of the communists, going up from 48 to 57 seats, while the communists dropped from eighteen to nine and were no longer a serious threat to the Social Democrats. Of the small parties, the Radicals dropped from eleven to ten, while the Single Tax Party, campaigning against the remaining restrictions of the post-war period, went up from three to six.

As the Radicals had brought down the previous government on the Schleswig question, they could hardly be expected to support a new *Venstre* government with a similar policy, and at the same time they were wary of the Social Democrats. In the event, Hedtoft decided to form a new minority government, countenanced by the communists and supported, with reservations, by the Radicals, who effectively held the balance of power. Accordingly, the Social Democrats were forced to temper the radical programme which they had introduced in 1945 and carry out instead a moderate policy for which they could count on general support. Most important among the purely internal measures of the first Hedtoft government was a new act which enabled the state to buy larger farms and estates as they came on the market, in order to provide more land for smallholders. This was in fact the continuation and culmination of a series of laws aimed at helping smallholders, which had begun with the first Smallholdings Act in 1899.

International Developments

Of greater international significance, however, was the fact that during Hedtoft's period in office Denmark finally brought about a complete reversal of her traditional policy of neutrality. Moreover, it was done by a government led by the Social Democrats, who were traditionally in favour of neutrality and disarmament. A step away from strict neutrality had in fact already been taken when the Danish *Rigsdag* unanimously decided to join the United Nations with the setting-up of that organisation in June 1945. It will be remembered that there had been doubts and reservations when the country had joined the League of Nations, and in particular the sanctions clause had caused apprehension. This time there were no such hesitations and Denmark joined without knowing the exact and final consequences of the move. It was a step taken in the interest of peace, and subsequently Denmark joined and contributed to the various major UN agencies.

This was the time of the establishment of the International Monetary Fund and the International Bank, both of which Denmark joined as a means to industrial and financial recovery after the war. When in 1947 the Marshall Plan was launched, still more aid came to Denmark and the country seemed all set for recovery.

This period also saw the division between East and West becoming more and more painfully apparent, and although Denmark rearmed sufficiently to be able to make a modest contribution to the occupation of Germany, it was the government's intention to stay outside the two political blocs, in the hope of building bridges between them. The change in attitude came with the communist takeover in Czechoslovakia in February 1948. Here was another small country which had attempted to remain neutral and build bridges being crushed by a major power. Finland, too, was subjected to Russian pressures and there were fears that a similar fate might be in store for that country, which was considered to be closely akin to Scandinavia, if not theoretically part of it. When the Brussels Treaty was signed between Britain, France, Belgium, the Netherlands, and Luxembourg in March 1948, founding the Western European Union – in theory a defensive treaty against a resurgent Germany – Denmark was not invited to become a party to it; but the three Scandinavian countries, on the initiative of Sweden, started negotiations aimed at instituting a Scandinavian defence treaty. Although there was plenty of goodwill, it proved impossible to reach agreement owing to the widely different views of Norway and Sweden.

At the same time the WEU powers, with Canada and the United States, were negotiating to widen WEU into an Atlantic alliance, the result of which was to be the North Atlantic Treaty Organisation. It was the hope of the Scandinavians that if they succeeded in formulating a defence treaty which kept Scandinavia outside both the major blocs the USA would help them with arms. The Americans, however, informed them that this was not to be expected, and when negotiations among the Scandinavian countries broke down, Norway decided to join NATO, and was later followed by Denmark, after Sweden had indicated a lack of interest in a bilateral defence treaty with Denmark. It had been a choice between complete isolation or a renunciation of neutrality, and the government chose the latter course. In doing so it had the support of the majority of the *Folketing,* 119 members voting to join NATO as against only twenty-three assorted Radicals, communists, and Single Tax Party members opposing the motion. Denmark insisted on regarding NATO as a purely defensive organisation, and although the Danes have been prompt in making their contributions, they have consistently refused to allow the country to be used as a base for long-range rockets, which could be employed for offensive purposes, and have likewise and for the same reasons refused to allow atomic weapons to be stationed on Danish soil or to be flown over it. This latter provision applies to Greenland, and when in 1967 an American bomber with atomic bombs on board crashed there, there was considerable indignation at what appeared to be a breach of the treaty. The acceptance of this interpretation of the North Atlantic Treaty meant that in 1960 even the Radicals accepted the proposals of the other parties.

The Hedtoft government had been able to bring about a *volte-face* in traditional Danish policy, thanks largely to the tactical position it enjoyed. Economic circumstances meant that Denmark was in a prosperous way at the beginning of 1949 and this in itself gave the government a resourceful hand. Nevertheless while Denmark had come to realise the impossibility of staying aloof from the influence of the great powers any longer, so she was to realise within the year that economically, too, she was at the mercy of circumstances beyond her control. The change in the economic situation coupled with Hedtoft's attempts to cope with it brought the government down.

For the first two years after the war, Denmark had been in serious financial straits, having completely lost one of her main export markets, Germany, and experiencing difficulty in selling to the other, Britain. Because of its own economic troubles, the British government insisted on paying low prices for Danish goods, but demanded top prices for its own exports. A special credit was certainly made to Denmark, but by 1947 the Danish debt was so large that Britain had to put a stop to it. The Danes had therefore to accept more rationing than ever and the economic situation worsened, while a hard winter and a hot, dry summer in 1947, resulting in a poor harvest, did nothing to diminish the crisis. As Britain still refused to increase the price paid for Danish goods, the Danes for their part stopped all exports to Britain in September 1947, and sold instead to countries willing to pay the price they wanted. During the course of 1948, however, Britain declared herself prepared to pay more for Danish produce and the traditional relationship was re-established.

This was in itself a help to the Danish economy, but the real boost came from the Marshall Plan and the establishment of OEEC. Between 1948 and 1953 Denmark received $278 million in Marshall aid, most of it as a direct gift, so that the economy improved rapidly until September 1949 when Britain devalued the pound. Because of the close ties with Britain, Denmark was forced to follow suit, but the economy suffered. The difficulties were stressed the following year when the Korean War broke out and was followed by an increase in world, particularly dollar, prices. As a direct result of this and the general fear of another major war, Denmark agreed to spend another 400 million *kroner* on armaments and civil defence over the next two years.

Rationing had been largely abolished by this time, though import regulations were still in force. The government was pressed by *Venstre,* with its free-trade tradition, to liberalise commerce, and the pressure was increased from OEEC in December 1949. Faced with a very large trade deficit the government felt obliged to ask for powers to sharpen its trade regulations, but the *Folketing* refused to countenance such a move. For this reason a new election was called, which took place on 5 September 1950.

Internal Pressures

It will be remembered that when the new electoral law[1] was introduced it was seen in practice to favour *Venstre* and had been amended to obviate this tendency. *Venstre* still seemed to be favoured by the law, and so in 1948 the government had it amended yet again to ensure that *Venstre* only received its fair share of seats in proportion to the votes cast. The party thus seemed bound to lose 7 seats in the 1950 election. In fact it lost seventeen, dropping from 49 to 32 seats, for it had lost the support of those Conservative supporters who had voted *Venstre* in the 1947 election and who now went back to their old allegiance. The Conservatives therefore rose from 17 to 27 seats. The Social Democrats and the Radicals each gained two, ending up with 59 and 12 seats respectively. The Single Tax Party, fatefully as it turned out, doubled its representation once again and went up to 12 seats,

[1] See above, pp. 120, 136.

leaving the communists far behind with only seven. The Czecho-slovak *coup* had effectively ruined their chances of wide popular support.

Leaving the communists aside, the result was a tie – the Social Democrat–Radical group and the middle-class group getting 71 seats each; and after some negotiations, the Hedtoft government was reinstated with very little change. It was the Prime Minister's object to deal with the economic situation in a manner acceptable to all parties, and in particular he meant to implement a defence policy with the support of *Venstre* and the Conservatives, defence-minded, as always. General agreement to co-operate within the *Folketing* seemed likely. To everyone's surprise, the government fell within a week.

It fell on a technicality after an attack from an unexpected quarter. The Single Tax Party had gone to the polls on a pro-gramme calling for the abolition of all remaining wartime restric-tions and rationing. Emboldened by its doubled representation, it called for the immediate abolition of butter rationing. With an eye to the need to export as much as possible, the government refused, but was then faced with a *Venstre*–Conservative compro-mise resolution calling for the end to rationing 'as soon as possible'. The government could not accept this either and when a division was forced, it lost by one vote. Although he could well have weathered the storm, Hedtoft announced his intention to resign both for personal reasons and also because he was not getting much-needed trade union support for his austerity programme.

It was the first time for forty years that a government on being defeated had resigned without calling an election. The first ever *Venstre*–Conservative coalition succeeded it, previous *Venstre* governments having had only at most tacit Conservative support. The leader of *Venstre*, Erik Eriksen, became Prime Minister, while the Conservative leader, Ole Bjørn Kraft, became Foreign Minister.

The new government was still faced with the problem of strengthening the economy and continued the deflationary policies started by the Hedtoft government earlier in the year. There were increases in direct taxation, while a system of compulsory savings was introduced and then extended in 1951. Ministers would have liked to suspend the cost of living index, by which incomes were regulated, but the Social Democrats and Radicals were opposed to this, and the government, being in a minority, was forced to give in. On the other hand, a compromise was reached by which some of the extra taxes were excluded from the index. Despite vigorous complaints, especially from the farmers, who felt they were being singled out to carry a heavy burden, the new taxes worked, and by the second half of 1951 the economic situation had improved. By the beginning of 1953 the large deficit of previous years had been turned into a healthy surplus and Denmark was at last able to comply with the OEEC requirements for liberalisation of trade between members.

A New Constitution

Although the minority government could count on Social Democrat support for much of what it proposed to do, the Radicals were firmly opposed to the foreign policy formulated by what became known as the Atlantic Pact parties – the Conservatives, *Venstre,* and the Social Democrats. There was thus always the chance that they might seize some opportunity to bring the ministry down. With such a possibility in mind, the government let it be known that it was planning a revision of the constitution, a subject long close to Radical hearts. From the start it had declared itself prepared to accept the single-chamber principle and had also pronounced in favour of reducing the voting age to twenty-three. The communists opposed the constitution as a whole because it contained a significant clause allowing for some renunciation of sovereignty : 'Powers vested in the authorities of the Realm under this Constitution Act may, to such extent as may be provided by statute, be delegated to international authorities set up by mutual agreement with other states for the promotion of international rules of law and co-operation.' The main stumbling-block was, however, the question of voting age, and finally it was decided to put it to a referendum of all citizens over twenty-one, which was the other age proposed. Next the proposals were carried in both the *Landsting* and the *Folketing,* after which an election was necessary so that a new *Rigsdag* could also pass them. This also went without a hitch. In the referendum which followed, those in favour far outnumbered those against, but only 45·76 per cent of those qualified voted in favour, a mere 0·76 per cent above the necessary proportion. The majority approved twenty-three as the new voting age. The new constitution came into force on the traditional constitution date, 5 June, 1953.

The main innovation was the abolition of the *Landsting* and the introduction of a single-chamber parliament, the *Folketing.* In order to remove the obvious objections to a single chamber, however, provision was made for referenda to be held in certain circumstances on controversial legislation. Other provisions were made for the extension of the democratic system in Denmark, including the appointment of an *ombudsman* on the Swedish pattern. This was a special wish of the Radicals and although both the Social Democrats and the Conservatives opposed it, *Venstre* accepted the proposal, the wisdom of which has since met with general acknowledgement.

Appendixed to the Constitutional Act there was a short act providing for the possibility of female succession to the throne. Not only was this innovation logical in a country with widespread principles of equality, but it also gave expression to popular sentiment. King Frederik IX, who had succeeded Christian X on the latter's death in 1947, and his wife, Ingrid of Sweden, had three daughters, Princesses Margrethe, Benedikte, and Anne-Marie,[2] and there was a general desire to see the eldest named as her father's successor. This must be seen as a token of the affection in which the Danes hold their royal family, and perhaps also of the almost family atmosphere there is in the country. After his early difficulties occasioned by the Easter crisis in 1920, Christian X had established himself as a monarch much loved and respected, and his dignified patriotism during the war had added to his popularity. Frederik IX has maintained and even increased the popularity of the royal family by his direct interest in his country – not only metropolitan Denmark, but also Greenland and the Faroes – and by the informality of his approach. In a country where democracy is so far advanced, it has obviously been neither possible nor desirable to maintain a monarchy aloof from the people, and instead the king has chosen to be a truly democratic king. While his father lay ill, it is said that Copenhagen citizens could meet the Crown Prince, as he then was, and stop to ask him how his father was. Nowadays it is quite possible to see members of the royal family out shopping, while when Princess Margrethe (since 1967 married to a former French diplomat who has been given the title of Prince Henrik of Denmark) travels to Århus, she does so on the regular night boat from Copenhagen. Just as Frederik VI in the nineteenth century reflected the bourgeois ideals of his day, so Frederik IX seems to represent the lack of fuss and stuffiness which are so characteristic of modern Denmark.

The 1953 constitution paid special attention to Greenland, which was made an integral part of the kingdom of Denmark with the right to send two members of parliament to Copenhagen. This far-reaching change meant a start on a complete revision of Greenland's social pattern which had remained almost untouched for centuries. Danish law was to be introduced to replace the local customs, and an attempt was made to improve the material lot of the Greenlanders and also to bring the benefits of modern industrialisation.

The earlier 1953 election had been called only to pass the new

2 Married in 1964 to King Constantine II of the Hellenes.

14—D * *

constitution; the second election, based on the new electoral law, took place before the constitution could be fully implemented, on 22 September. Together with the lowering of the voting age had gone an increase in the number of *Folketing* deputies, from 149 to 179; two came from Greenland and two from the Faroes.

One of the imponderables was the number of new voters, but the overall picture of Danish politics did not change to any appreciable extent. *Venstre,* becoming perhaps less exclusively associated with agrarian interests, made some gains, while the Conservatives lost a few votes. The Social Democrats made progress, which was outweighed by Radical losses. And to balance a slight gain for the communists, the Single Tax Party lost much of its former support.

Little Change in Party Constellations

Earlier in the year the Radicals had stood by the *Venstre–* Conservative coalition in order to ensure the passage of the constitutional proposals, but they now withdrew their support. Opposed in particular to the Conservatives and their foreign and defence policies, they were prepared to support a *Venstre* government, but *Venstre's* leader, Erik Eriksen, remained faithful to his new alliance with the Conservatives. At the same time, when it became obvious that the Social Democrats intended to form a new government, the Radicals, disliking that party's loyalty to NATO and the economic policies it would have to adopt, refused to enter a coalition, promising tacit support instead and thus again effectively holding a balance of power, but without responsibility for government policy.

When the Social Democrats came to power, the economy was in reasonable shape, but unemployment was higher than the accepted norm, and the government introduced measures to stimulate production and reduce unemployment. The result was a rapid overheating of the system and a new financial crisis. *Venstre* and the Conservatives refused to support government remedies for this, and so they had to adopt a course which met the approval of the Radicals, in practice a cutting-back on defence spending. In return the Radicals were prepared to support a strongly deflationary policy. This was not sufficient, but before further moves could be made, the Prime Minister, Hans Hedtoft, died in January 1955 and was succeeded by his Foreign Minister, H. C. Hansen.

Hansen continued, as far as was possible, his predecessor's policy, but in doing so began to lose working-class support. This occurred just at the time when the regular reviews of agreements between the unions and employers were due, and these now turned out to be protracted and difficult. By March 1956 no accord had been reached and strikes were called which gradually paralysed the entire country. However, when the strikes spread to petrol- and oil-workers, the government stepped in and passed legislation forbidding the strike in the petroleum industry. A general compromise agreement was drawn up by the official mediator and accepted by the employers. Although the plan gave considerable benefits to the workers, they rejected it and continued the strike. Again the government acted and imposed the mediator's proposals on industry as a whole. The unions and workers were furious at this, feeling they had been let down by a government from which they might have expected more sympathy. The communists thereupon began to fish in troubled waters, but just as they were showing signs of progress, the Russian suppression of the Hungarian uprising turned the tide against them once more. As in 1948 after the communist takeover in Czechoslovakia, people reacted sharply to this show of force.

In the midst of these difficulties and those occasioned by the Suez crisis of 1956, the government turned its attention to some new, far-reaching social legislation. Although received by some 55 per cent of the population over the age of sixty-five, the old-age pension was essentially intended as a help to those in need, and in addition it was generally considered to be too low. Thus the Social Democrats, with the support of the other parties, apart from a few individuals and the Single Tax Party, carried through legislation providing for the replacement of the old-age pension with a 'people's pension', by which everyone over pensionable age was entitled to a minimum allowance, while much larger benefits were to be available as a right to those in need of them. The aim was now to move away from the old philosophy according to which a pension was basically a charitable act, to the view that it was the right of every citizen to maintain a reasonable standard of living.

The Triangle Government: a Time of Change

According to the constitution, an election had to be held in 1957, and by that time people were less interested in future pension benefits than in the urgent economic problems facing the country. The National Bank's foreign debts had almost doubled to 275 million *kroner* in the first five months of the year and were a welcome stick with which the Conservatives and *Venstre* could beat their political opponents, arguing that on a previous occasion[3] they had managed to re-establish a healthy economy, and now was the time to do it again. It was a good argument and they certainly won some votes on it. But with 75 seats in all they did not win an

[3] See above, p. 191.

absolute majority. Social Democrat strength now stood at seventy – a loss of 4 seats. The Radicals kept their representation at fourteen, while the Single Tax Party made a comeback and increased from 3 to 9 seats. The communists stood at six.

A completely new political situation had now developed, as the Radicals no longer held a balance of power. They were not sufficient to ensure a Social Democrat majority alone, nor were they prepared to support a *Venstre*–Conservative coalition. The Single Tax Party had made considerable gains, but its support would not be sufficient to ensure a strong minority *Venstre*–Conservative government. The crisis was unprecedented and despite recent antipathies between the Single Tax Party and both the Radicals and Social Democrats, the outcome of negotiations was a coalition government based on these three parties, with H. C. Hansen as Prime Minister. It became known as the 'Triangle Government'.

There were protests from *Venstre* and the Conservatives at its formation, but there was little they could do to prevent what was, for the first time in many years, a majority government, provided the three partners could agree. They did agree, largely because of Hansen's sensitive and tactful leadership. Their first task was still to deal with the financial situation and they were able to introduce stern measures without looking over their shoulders at the other parties. Moreover, they followed a far-sighted policy. Unpopular though it was, the government introduced a scheme for enforced savings, which took some 400 million *kroner* out of circulation. This was coupled with investment incentives for industry which were to have considerable effect. The opposition parties argued in favour of import deposits as being a more effective means of reducing expenditure, but they had no success. These new measures to save the economy were accompanied by a fall in world prices, so that industry was helped from two directions, and this change saw the start of a period of hitherto unknown prosperity in Denmark.

It fell to the Triangle Government to lead Denmark at a time when Europe was dividing into different economic units. The gradual movement towards Nordic co-operation which had begun before 1939 and was fostered by events during the war, had led to the formation in 1952 of the Nordic Council. (This is in no way a supra-governmental organisation, but a conference of members of parliament from Denmark, Iceland, Norway, and Sweden, who meet at regular intervals in the member countries. In 1955 Finland had been admitted to the Council.) Specifically excluded from making suggestions relevant either to foreign or defence policy, the Council had many useful ideas for co-ordinating internal legislation

in the Scandinavian countries, and in 1954 its proposals had led
to the formation of a common labour market in Scandinavia.
Passport restrictions were removed, first for Scandinavian citizens
and subsequently for all others, while more recently Scandinavian
citizens have been given access to social benefits in each other's
countries. As has already been seen,[4] negotiations in 1948 aimed at
forming a defence union in Scandinavia came to nothing, but the
success of the movement towards Nordic co-operation in other
fields had led to the emergence of the idea of a Nordic common
market – an idea which has re-emerged during 1969 and shows
every sign now of being realised.

However, events elsewhere in Europe overtook these plans for
Nordic co-operation in the mid-1950s, when the EEC was being
discussed. As she exported a large percentage of her agricultural
produce to EEC countries, Denmark was faced with an uncertain
future. So difficult and delicate was the situation that when Britain
and Sweden took the initiative to form EFTA, Denmark was at
first somewhat reserved, fearing that an economic war might result,
with damaging consequences, whatever the outcome might be for
others. On receiving assurances from the other countries that this
was in no way the intention behind EFTA proposals, Denmark
decided to take part in the negotiations. When the treaty was
finally signed in 1960, the only opposition came from the communists, though *Venstre,* in the main more eager to enter the
Common Market, refrained from voting. One of the immediate
results of the move towards EFTA was the end to negotiations for
a Nordic Common Market, as Britain was not prepared to countenance a bloc within the free trade area in which tariffs would be
reduced at a different rate from elsewhere. Now that tariffs have
been abolished, there is, of course, no further objection to an
economic union within EFTA.

Once the coalition government had made up its mind on joining
EFTA, it was able to proceed without difficulty. It was the strongest
government for many years, and thanks to this position of strength
and to a rapid improvement in Denmark's economic position, it
was also able to propose and carry out a number of important
social and educational reforms. The change in the economic climate
after 1957 was partly, but not entirely, the achievement of this
government. The fact that after 1957 the country considered it
respectable to seek and take up foreign loans was a point very
much in its favour. An immediate improvement in the balance of
payments was the result, for hitherto Denmark had used a good
deal of the money she had earned to pay off long-standing debts.

4 See above, p. 188.

At the same time foreign capital began to flow into Denmark, especially from the major American oil companies. Such a financial influx provided the means for capital investment in Danish industry. The sudden industrial boom furnished jobs for the sizeable force of unemployed, 10·2 per cent in 1957. Yet, as most of the early deflationary measures were still in force, internal buying power was for a time kept down, and most of the initial increase in production went to exports. For a number of years, then, there was a period of unprecedented wealth in Denmark, until in 1961 the economy became strained, and a fresh deflation was necessary.

Meanwhile, however, the government's social and educational reforms had been introduced. First, new building laws were passed. So far the state had been prepared to provide loans for buildings of certain categories, especially for flats, which were in short supply. Now a number of loan-giving institutions were set up and the state withdrew from this sector of the economy. Rents, which had been fixed since 1939, were partly freed, though the new and greater profits were in some measure recouped by the state through increased property taxes. The general effect of these new building laws was a building boom, related, of course, to the now buoyant economy.

The educational reforms affected the schools system, so far based on seven years' instruction with selection for grammar schools at the age of eleven or twelve. Those not selected for grammar-school education went on for a further two years in a secondary school but were to some extent stigmatised as failures. The new legislation of 1958 provided for universal comprehensive education for seven years – in practice up to the age of fourteen – after which a pupil was free to leave school, to continue for a further two years on a voluntary basis, or to take a three-year course leading to the middle-school examination or, if desired, an extended academic course ending with the Student Examination, the equivalent of the British General Certificate of Education Advanced Level examination. As the title suggests, the student examination gives automatic access to one of three Danish universities.[5]

With improved schooling thus available better opportunities for those who had previously been denied a full schooling and those who desired to further their technical knowledge were demanded, and these demands were met. Funds have also been provided for those in need. The education explosion resulting from these reforms has lately begun to create its own difficulties. A student examination automatically entitles its holder to a university place and the demand far exceeds the number of places available. To help cope with

5 See below, p. 199.

this situation, a third university was opened in Odense in 1966 to ease the load of the universities of Copenhagen and Århus, while plans are now afoot to open what in practice will be a fourth university at Roskilde. The problem has been aggravated by the traditional flexibility of Danish university education; an absence of fixed timetables has meant that seven years spent at university was the norm and ten years by no means unusual. This system has clearly become unworkable, partly for reasons of limited space and partly because the demand for scholarships and grants is so much more widespread. Although the practice of student loans is current in Denmark, it is obviously impracticable to provide students with money over an indefinite period. New syllabuses are now being introduced which will shorten the length of study and be more suited to present-day realities. How far the reforms will go, and how the new graduates will fare, remains to be seen. So far the Danish graduate has not had such freedom to choose a career as the American or British graduate, and in most cases his course has been aimed at a specific future. A student of English or Danish would almost inevitably end up with a teaching career of some kind – and would probably be vastly overqualified in some fields. Now, with the streamlining of the courses, this overqualification should be obviated. To compensate for what is in fact going to be a rather lower qualification, a new second degree is to be introduced, a licentiate, which will be akin to the American or British Ph.D.

Social services provided the Triangle Government's third sphere of reform. Although the changes did not all happen at one time, those started by this government and continued by its successor have been referred to as the Second Social Reform. The people's pension was really the beginning. Financial aid for the disabled carried the new ideas still further. Disablement benefits were increased in 1965 and those eligible received more than a people's pension – obviously on the assumption that people injured in road or factory accidents often had greater financial responsibilities than the aged and thus needed more help. Widows' pensions were also increased and brought into line with the general trend. These laws, taken together, have given practically every Dane freedom from fear of poverty or hardship, whatever sudden change may take place in his circumstances.[6]

A Return to Austerity

The government parties could not be blamed for their high hopes when the next election to the *Folketing* came round in November

[6] A more detailed description of Danish social legislation past and present will be found in Appendix A, p. 219.

1960. The result, however, was a shock for everybody concerned. Of the three government parties only the Social Democrats did well, increasing their representation from 70 to 76 seats. The Radicals lost ground, going down from 14 to 11 seats, while the Single Tax Party was completely eliminated. Outside government there was an almost equal confusion, with *Venstre* losing ground and the Conservatives increasing their representation, while the Independents, the party founded by the old *Venstre* leader Knud Kristensen[7] and opposed to all forms of compromise with socialism, finally managed to get into the *Folketing* with 6 seats. At the other end of the scale the communists lost all their seats, but they were replaced by a new left-wing group, the Socialist People's Party, under Aksel Larsen, the former communist leader. An obvious polarisation had once more taken place in Danish politics, the three centre parties, *Venstre*, Single Tax, and Radical, having fared worst. The inevitable post-mortems seemed to show certain logical patterns in this apparently confused situation, some of them stemming from internal strife within the parties, and some from the policy of the previous government.

The Radicals, it was decided, had lost a good deal of support because, though by tradition pacifist, they had agreed with the other parties in the *Folketing* on a new defence law earlier in 1960. They had accepted a military budget of 1,053 million *kroner* (rather less than the 1,400 million asked for by the NATO Commander-in-Chief, General Norstad), and this figure was in future to be tied to the cost of living – to avoid new and difficult negotiations brought on by inflation. On the other hand, they had successfully opposed suggestions that the country should be armed with atomic weapons and could reasonably claim that they had gone some way to standing by their principles. Nevertheless, it must be admitted that much of the party's support came from confirmed pacifists, who now looked elsewhere – to Aksel Larsen's Socialist People's Party. Larsen had been an able and respected leader of the Communist Party, and the Hungarian Revolution had not dented his loyalty. Yet, he gradually came to work for a communist policy which would be less dependent on Moscow and more in tune with Danish life, something akin to Titoism. In 1958 the party stalwarts expelled him and asked him to give up his seat in the *Folketing*. This he refused to do, and on being assured of wide support among his former comrades, he formed his new party which duly ran in the election. He refused to budge from his strictly socialist principles and thus brought a number of Social Democrats and communists into his fold. As he was also a strict

7 See above, p. 186.

pacifist, he attracted the votes of sympathisers who would never have voted communist. Thus a new left-wing party emerged which for a time posed a new problem for the Social Democrats, who had been able more or less to ignore the communists.

Venstre had also had its troubles. Together with the Conservatives it had agreed on a joint election programme and also on a joint approach to tax relief. *Venstre's* financial spokesman, Thorkild Kristensen, who reacted strongly to a programme with which he did not agree and which had been concocted in his absence, resigned from the party and stayed for the rest of the *Folketing* session as an independent *Venstre* member. In contrast to Aksel Larsen, he did not seek to form a new party, and he retired from active politics at the next election in November 1960. His action had, however, started a *Venstre* split from which the Conservatives and, presumably, the Independents, were able to profit. The explanation of the Single Tax disaster seemed to be that the party had relied heavily on the votes of defectors from other parties, who now reacted against its contribution to the previous government. It was assumed that the People's Socialists won many of their votes.

Whatever the reasons for this fascinating change in the composition of the *Folketing*, it was plain that fresh negotiations on the formation of a new government would have to start. They did not prove difficult, but again resulted in a break with tradition which so far has not been of far-reaching importance. The Social Democrats and Radicals were together one vote short of an overall majority, and this they found in the person of one of the two Greenland members, Mikael Gam. It had been customary that the non-Danish members, the Faroese, Greenlanders, and Schleswigers, should keep out of internal Danish politics, but now the precedent of taking a direct part had been created, and Mikael Gam became Minister for Greenlandic Affairs.

The new government, headed by the Social Democrat Viggo Kampmann, who had succeeded Hansen, ran straight into trouble. During a period of boom and full employment, wages and salaries had tended to rise faster than had been allowed for in the regular round of national salary negotiations. Thus, when a new round came early in 1961, serious complications quickly set in and the unions demanded large increases. A strike in the steel industry was soon settled, but a transport strike became protracted and was only called off when the government legislated to make acceptance of a compromise solution obligatory. An agricultural strike followed, organised by the farmers, who had been unable to keep pace with the general wage rises and wished to draw attention to their difficulties over the past few years. Even though a system of subsidies had been introduced in 1958, they now demanded more to enable them to pay further increases. When sufficient was not forthcoming, they refused to make deliveries. An agreement was finally reached which gave the farmers their increased subsidy and the farmworkers the rise they so badly needed. The government was less fortunate when a postal strike was called because an offer of a 14 per cent increase was not accepted by the postal-workers, who as civil servants were in any case forbidden to strike.

On a different front the government was faced with a momentous decision. Britain announced in the summer of 1961 the decision to apply for membership of the EEC. Denmark decided to follow suit, and lodged an application, which was withdrawn after the French veto of the British application.

The question of whether or not to apply for membership of the EEC was thoroughly debated both in and out of the *Folketing*. Account was taken of far more than the mere economic aspects of membership, not least of the possible effect on relations with the rest of Scandinavia. In putting forward this question, speakers and writers made plain how much stronger the sense of a Scandinavian personality had grown in recent decades. There was a feeling of Nordic culture and a fear that this might in some vague and indistinct way be threatened if Denmark entered the Common Market. The need for Nordic unity in any future expanded Common Market was clearly expressed by Franz Wendt, the General Secretary of the Nordic Council and himself a Dane : 'Only if the Nordic countries act in unity as far as possible can they defend their material and spiritual interests and play their part in implanting in the European community the ideals and the social concept which we in the North feel should be spread wide.'

A different view of the need for Nordic solidarity was put in a book issued by the Danish Foreign Ministry in 1962 (*Danmark og Det europæiske økonomiske Fællesskab*), in which it was pointed out that while the OEEC had been a great help, from the Danish point of view it was a weakness that its provisions had not covered agriculture. Nor had GATT resulted in reducing tariffs – only in preventing increases. This in itself underlined the importance of Nordic co-operation. To continue this trend from a 1969 standpoint it is of course possible to observe that agriculture was also expressly left out of the EFTA provisions, again to the disappointment of Denmark; but the intention of creating a Nordic common market is that it should include agricultural produce – though in practice difficulties have already been encountered in working out an arrangement. Despite the rapid growth of Danish industry since the war, Denmark remains and will remain a major agricultural producer and exporter, and until she belongs to some free trade association which provides for free trade in agricultural produce, she cannot possibly be entirely happy. Joining the Common Market together with Britain would have solved this problem – though with a similar agricultural financing policy to Britain, Denmark was obviously going to have difficulties in adapting herself to the EEC structure. Without Britain, Denmark as a member of the EEC would see barriers going up between herself and her other major agricultural trading partner, and there was also the danger that agricultural produce might become of less importance as the southern European countries themselves increased production. Even so, an Agricultural Council report published in February 1969 still estimated that membership of the EEC would mean an annual 2,500 million *kroner* gain for Danish agriculture.

The problems raised for Denmark by the establishment of the EEC and EFTA have obviously been very serious. The avoidance of a lasting split in Europe and the achievement of suitable terms with the EEC while herself belonging to EFTA became a major aim of Danish foreign policy early in the 1960s. From 1963 to 1966 this policy was under the control of Per Hækkerup, one of the most outstanding Danish Foreign Ministers of the present century, who won international respect during his period in office (1962–66). His successor, Jens Otto Krag, again followed Britain with a second application to the EEC in 1967, and, like that of Britain, the Danish application still stands.

Membership of the EEC would automatically have brought rises in the price of food, and as Denmark would have had to raise tariffs on the imports of raw materials from third countries, imports which would still be needed, some industrial prices would also have risen, despite the opening-up of a larger European market. As wages in Denmark are tied to the cost of living, it might seem that the effect of these price rises on the Danes could have been minimised by rising wages and salaries. There was, however, some apprehension as to what effect such rises would ultimately have on prices. Wages in Denmark were already higher than in the EEC countries, and fears were expressed that the automatic price–wage spiral might result in Denmark's pricing herself out of the market. On balance, the feeling was that while the short term might bring problems, membership of the EEC together with Britain would bring benefits in the long run.

Wages and salaries had in fact risen over the whole country by some 12–15 per cent during 1961, and pensions by 9 per cent, while production went up by a mere 7 per cent; such a dangerous inflationary tendency had to be countered. The usual tax increases

on petrol and liquor were not enough, and so the government
decided to introduce a purchase tax of 5 per cent. Two of its
members, however, objected on principle, and the government
had to come to an understanding with *Venstre* and the Conservatives to carry through the proposed legislation. To achieve this
some of the original proposals had to be whittled down. Ministers
were persuaded to put the purchase tax on wholesale, not retail,
prices, and they also had to promise not to use the increased income
for government expenditure, but to ensure a treasury surplus.
Thereafter the surplus was to be brought down to a balance by a
reduction in direct taxation as from 1963. Although the government
did not consider that the situation justified them, it had to bow
to these conditions and was in fact forced to introduce a further
measure of compulsory savings to compensate for them.

These measures came as a part of comprehensive legislation
introduced early in 1963, quite obviously the work of the government, but supported by a recommendation from a new organ which
it had set up in the second half of 1962. An advisory body made up
of representatives of the most important sections of the Danish
economy had long been considered overdue in some quarters. The
result was the creation of the Economic Council, consisting of representatives of the unions and employers' organisations, the banks,
commerce, and agriculture, as well as three professors of economics.
The aim was to have enlightened discussions on any problem
directly related to the economy. The Council had only advisory
powers, but it had the right to initiate the discussion of any question instead of waiting for subjects to be referred to it. In December
1962 the Council recommended that all negotiations about incomes
for 1963 should be conducted at the same time and a general
solution worked out. This 'general solution' was in fact an incomes
policy aimed at ensuring that wage, salary, and profit rises should
be kept within limits dictated by the national economy. *Venstre* and
the Conservatives voiced opposition, but the government forced
it through the *Folketing*, and it ensured a major stabilisation of
the economy in 1963. Apart from the compulsory savings clause,
the 'general solution' allowed for limited rises for the lowest-paid
workers in 1963, accompanied by some improvements in pensions
and social benefits. Larger increases were promised for 1964. Prices
and profits were also regulated by law. Employers were thus successfully dissuaded from giving larger increases in 1963 than those
allowed for by the law, as they would have to absorb the cost
themselves and knew perfectly well that they would have to grant
more the following year. The state had entered the field of salary
and price negotiations with a vengeance. Conservative–*Venstre*

opposition was silenced by the threat of an election. The People's Socialists could not be expected to agree.

The general solution not only offered the prospects of fresh increases the following year, but also promised legislation to introduce supplementary pensions for workers. All employees were to pay a proportion of their income to a private pension fund which was to be independent of the state. Not everyone in the country was to be included in the new act to begin with, but it was extended to cover civil servants in 1965, and the idea then was to extend it further to include self-employed persons. This, too, provided not only greater security, but took a good deal of money out of circulation.

Although the government had thus managed to carry the *Folketing* with it through some fairly controversial legislation, it failed to gain necessary support for a number of bills on land reform. There were ten altogether; four were passed by the *Folketing* with Conservative and *Venstre* opposition. These were aimed at preventing the sale of land to foreigners – of special significance if Denmark were to join the EEC – and also introduced some limitations on the rights of Danish citizens when selling land : in some cases the local authorities were to have first option on larger estates, while measures were introduced to secure land for smallholders whose plots were based on the original smallholder legislation[8] and thus too small for modern conditions and ideas. *Venstre* and the Conservatives were vehemently opposed to these apparent encroachments on individual rights, and when they failed to prevent the passage of the bill, they invoked the clause in the 1953 constitution by which the opposition of one-third of the members of the *Folketing* could lead to a referendum on controversial legislation. In the ensuing referendum the four bills were rejected by large majorities, and the government was forced to drop its plans. There was some doubt about whether the government would now feel obliged to resign, as it was obviously out of line with public opinion. On the other hand, there were fears of setting a precedent, by which any future government would be forced to resign on losing a referendum even if it had in fact carried the *Folketing* with it. This was a possibility scarcely foreseen when the constitution was drawn up and in the event the government did not resign. Some of the dropped proposals were no longer so pressing with the withdrawal of the application to join the EEC in January 1963.

Return to Social Democrat Minority Government

Because of the negative result of the referendum, there was an

8 See above, p. 95.

added interest in the statutory general election in 1964, but in some ways the result was a confirmation of what had gone before, despite the additional unknown factor of the increasing number of voters since the reduction of the voting age to twenty-one in 1961. There was little change in the parties' representation, with the Social Democrats keeping their strength at seventy-six. The Radicals, however, lost one seat and refused to join the government. There was in any case no longer an overall majority, and when no other viable coalition was found, the Social Democrats, now led by Jens Otto Krag, decided to form a minority government.

The new government had to steer a middle course and, as before with minority governments, chose to legislate in such a way that one or other of the main parties would support a specific bill. With Radical support (if ever it were proffered) insufficient and co-operation with the People's Socialists out of the question some sort of *rapprochement* with *Venstre* seemed to be called for, made easier by the inclusion in that party of some members who could be termed left-wing and who wished to see some form of co-operation. A tendency to draw closer together was marked in 1964 after the British Labour government broke the EFTA agreement and imposed a 15 per cent duty on EFTA goods. Denmark was hard hit by this, and the Social Democrats, who so far had been adamant in demanding that Denmark should not enter the EEC without Britain, began to have second thoughts. *Venstre* stipulated no conditions for joining.

However, dissensions within *Venstre*, leading to the resignation of its two leading left-wing members, put an end to the honeymoon, and there were rumours first of a union between the bulk of *Venstre* and the Conservatives, and then of negotiations to find common ground with the Radicals.

Despite party dissensions this particular session of the *Folketing* led to new housing legislation which has been of importance in the continual battle to end the housing shortage. New houses and flats to rent had been rising constantly in price for years, while the rents of the older flats, some of them very large indeed, had remained stationary. In an attempt to ease the situation for the occupants of new buildings, an agreement was reached in the *Folketing* gradually to raise the rents of the older houses. One proportion of these increases was to go to the owners, another to maintenance, and a third, larger, proportion to the financing of new buildings in an attempt to keep down costs in an inflationary situation. Although a piece of legislation with attractions for the opposition parties, it provoked bitter feelings among Social Democrat supporters. Consequently, in the Copenhagen local elections of 1966, the governing Social Democrats suffered a severe defeat, the People's Socialists making gains at their expense. The obvious swing against an unpopular minority government persuaded Krag to call an election in November 1966, well before the end of the statutory term. The result was one foreseen – and feared – by many : the emergence of the Socialist People's Party as a candidate for government coalition.

Left-Wing Co-operation

The other, and perhaps the main, reason for the unexpected election was the difficulties the government had encountered in its efforts to reform the taxation system. The purchase tax on wholesale prices had turned out to be insufficient, and the main question at issue was how to increase it without hitting trade too badly. Putting it on the retail price of goods was a possibility, but this suggestion was not seriously considered for long, and instead the idea of a value added tax gained ground. The general consensus was that this tax should be at 10 per cent, though *Venstre* would have liked to see a higher tax percentage coupled with a reduction in direct taxation. In general the parties could not agree on the exact terms of the value added tax. The government's intention was to couple it with the introduction of the pay-as-you-earn system of direct taxation, which won increasing support from the electorate. With direct taxation as high as it was, there was increasing resentment at the large tax accounts which had to be paid ten months in the year. It was thus largely because of the inability to agree on the value added tax that the government decided to call an election on the issue of taxation at source, which was thought to be a vote-catcher.

But the attempt misfired and the electorate seemed more concerned with the effects of the unpopular legislation just passed than with the hope of things to come : the Social Democrats fell from 76 to 69 seats; the People's Socialists, who reaped the main benefit of dissatisfaction with the Social Democrats, doubled their representation to 20 seats; *Venstre* fell from 38 to 35 seats; and the Conservatives from thirty-six to thirty-four. The Liberal Centre Party, formed by the two former left-wing members of *Venstre*, won 4 seats, and the Radicals went up from ten to thirteen. All this seemed to indicate some reaction against previous polarisation, but it had the result of putting the two socialist parties together in a commanding position. And as the Social Democrats this time had avoided committing themselves to a policy of non-co-operation with the People's Socialists, a coalition of the two parties seemed the obvious solution.

When it came to the point, however, the People's Socialists refused the bait, largely because of opposition from some members
to the Social Democrat foreign policy. Accordingly, yet another
minority government was formed, which went ahead with plans
for tax reform. Here it found support for its views from the People's
Socialists, whose votes assisted the passage of bills. A value added
tax of 10 per cent was to commence in July 1967 and from 1 January 1969 the system of taxation at source was to be introduced.
In fact this date has since been postponed to 1 January 1970 owing
to the administrative difficulties involved.

In practice the People's Socialists held a position comparable to
that of the Radicals in previous years, a balance of power without
the responsibility of government. They were not interested in pro-
voking a fresh election, and so they supported the Social Democrats
in their financial policy, whereas they had previously opposed it,
and they showed signs of a compromise attitude on the Common
Market. But even now signs of a split began to emerge within the
party, some of its members wishing to limit the area of co-operation
with the Social Democrats, against Aksel Larsen's wishes.

Hilmar Baunsgaard, Prime Minister since 1968, has argued that
this period of co-operation between Social Democrats and People's
Socialists marked a change in Danish political tradition, in that
the government was for the first time subjected to direct and intense influence from the extreme Left. The Social Democrat government was effectively hamstrung by its allies, who were uncompromising in their demands for socialist legislation. It is not, therefore, surprising that the tacit coalition came to an early close. The
subsequent decision to call an election in 1968 was supported by
six of the twenty Socialist People's Party members of the *Folketing*,
and this brought the disunity within the party to a head. On 16
and 17 December 1967 a conference of the twenty members took
place and the six dissidents decided to leave the party and form
their own left-wing party to be known as the Socialist Left. These
six members had the previous day voted against a government
decision to suspend payment of a cost of living-based wage, salary,
and pension increase in order to stem the rising tide of inflation,
while the remainder of the party had voted for the motion. The
left-wing members felt that the Socialist People's Party as a whole
was in danger of becoming a mere appendix to the Social Democrats, in contra-distinction to many others outside the two parties
who felt that the People's Socialists were in danger of becoming
the tail that wagged the dog.

About half the People's Socialist deputies now left the party and
joined the Socialist Left, a split reflected throughout Denmark, even

down to local committee level. The exact significance for Danish political life of this split is not yet clear, but it could be the most significant split within a party since the Radicals broke away from the parent *Venstre* in 1905. Other internal party quarrels leading to attempts to form new parties – such as Danish Union and the Independents – have merely led to the brief appearance of a new group which has played little part in national life. The present dissension gives rise to the feeling that the consequences might be more far-reaching.

The People's Reaction

However that may be, the Social Democrats in the 1968 election paid the price for their flirtation with the left wing. They lost appreciably, falling from 69 seats to sixty-two. The following list shows a comparison of the election results in 1966 and 1968 :

	1966	1968
Social Democrat	69	62
Radical	13	27
Conservative	34	37
Venstre	35	34
People's Socialists	20	11
Liberal Centre	4	0
Socialist Left	—	4

In 1968 participation was the largest since the war – 89·3 per cent; and the second largest ever (it reached 89·5 per cent during the Occupation). The socialist majority disappeared and *Venstre* lost its place as the second party to the Conservatives, a result foreshadowed by previous developments. The Radicals, on the other hand, despite earlier Conservative protestations that they were no longer a party to be reckoned with, made an impressive comeback, presumably having gained a lot of the disgruntled votes previously given to the Social Democrats and People's Socialists. Whatever else this election could be said to show, it was a resounding repudiation of left-wing policies. A non-socialist government was now feasible and the outcome was a new three-party coalition, this time between the Radicals, Conservatives, and *Venstre*, under the premiership of the Radical Hilmar Baunsgaard. This government had the largest majority of any government since 1935, the three parties together commanding 98 seats of the 179 in the *Folketing*. Even the Stauning government in 1935, with its clear *Folketing* majority, had to fight a *Landsting* dominated by the opposition parties.

15—D • •

The new government inherited the question of balance of payments, in Denmark a perennial problem.

The 1967 deficit was the largest in Denmark's history, and had been seriously affected by the 7·9 per cent devaluation which followed on Britain's 14·3 per cent in November, a devaluation estimated to have cost Danish agriculture something in the region of 282 million *kroner* a year. This in itself was a sign of the difficulties inherited by the government, and to it can be added the rising unemployment figures, a very high interest rate, and, almost inevitably under these circumstances, many bankruptcies. The system of linking wages and salaries to the cost of living was having a spiral effect, and it was expected that wage levels would probably rise by about 13 per cent in 1969 to a level considerably above those of Denmark's competitors.

It thus became the ministry's aim to save money wherever possible and to hold consultations with industrial and trading interests to contain inflation. The ultimate target was to prepare a new economic advance, which the government felt to be well within the country's ability. On the other hand, despite the attractions of the EEC for one of the coalition parties, and despite some disillusionment with Britain's attitude to EFTA after the imposition of the 15 per cent surcharge on imports,[9] there were no plans for a change in foreign policy, except that the government was interested in consolidating the Nordic alliance – a desire which has been instrumental in opening negotiations on a possible Nordic common market, to be known as Nordek. In a broader field the hope was to work for a breaking-down of trade barriers within Europe, possibly by means of an enlarged common market including the EEC and such EFTA countries as wished to join it. Negotiations were to begin with Germany on Danish agricultural exports, which had been badly hit by EEC tariffs. In addition it was the government's intention to bring in educational reforms, including the introduction of a compulsory eight years at school, with a possible extension to nine and ten years. New social legislation was announced, and the government plans to widen support for the arts. Greenland and the Faroes were to be further developed and aided. (From 1 January 1968 the Faroes, at their own request, were to be included in EFTA.) The civil service was to be reformed, and the voting age lowered.[10] It was doubtless a further sign of the desire for increased Nordic co-operation in a completely different sphere

[9] See above, p. 206.
[10] A referendum held in 1969 rejected the proporsed age of eighteen, and in November 1969 it was announced that a new referendum is to be held on a proposal that the age should be fixed at twenty.

that Denmark in 1968 ordered a squadron of Swedish Draken fighters for the air force and took an option on a second – the first time that a NATO country had bought its fighters outside the NATO area itself.

In immediate action to stop the economy getting out of control the disconto rate was raised from 6½ per cent to 7½ per cent, and on 15 February 1968 a move was made to stop price increases. Firms were compelled to report projected increases to the Monopoly Control, and they were not, except in certain circumstances, allowed to implement such plans without permission. Likewise professional fees for services were pegged. The regulations remained in force until 1 November 1968. Wages were not affected, though when the two-yearly round of wage negotiations came up in February 1969, they were difficult and protracted, and looked at one time like leading to a general strike. In the event, the only strike was one of twenty-four hours' duration on the railways in protest against a new wage structure for civil servants. Farmworkers also struck, but the strike was ended by legislation.

The negotiations carried out by the government to reach agreement with the two sides of industry on stabilising the economy were without result, and consequently it had to act alone, introducing a fifteen-point plan of which the most important features were: the control of prices; savings of some 600 million *kroner* on civil and military expenditure; rises in internal prices for agricultural products to be postponed until after an agreement between the government and agriculture on an improved financial situation for agriculture; the introduction of fixed prices and times for public works; value added tax to be increased from 10 per cent to 12½ per cent; disconto rate to be gradually reduced (done by ½ per cent on 19 March); foreign investment to be encouraged. The energy with which the government set about tackling its problems is well-illustrated. In May 1968 the Finance Minister sent out a circular dealing with the 1969–70 budget and with budget prospects for the following three years. The aim was still to reduce expenditure and all Ministries were to report with suggestions for doing this by the end of August.

Despite the stringency of the legislative programme, new moves have been made towards reform. New land laws are to be introduced aimed at procuring more land for building, while new regulations controlling areas of natural beauty have been introduced. In the social sphere efforts are being made to improve the people's pension scheme and to link pensions not only to the rise in the cost of living but also to the general rise in the country's economy. On a more practical level work is proceeding on reducing the number of local authorities and county councils. The number of local authorities will be reduced to about 300, as against 1,108 in 1966, while the number of *Amter* will from 1 April 1970 be thirteen instead of the present twenty-five. The aim is to introduce new boundaries throughout the country before the next local elections in 1970. The delicate matter of distribution of powers between the state and the local authorities has yet to be thrashed out, but it is government policy to leave as much power as possible in the hands of the local authorities, though the county councils may have fewer responsibilities than at present.

The new government, relatively strong as it is, has not found it easy to deal with the economic situation. The disconto rate has had to be raised again to a record 9 per cent, but unemployment, in March 1969 relatively high at 6·8 per cent, had fallen to 2·6 per cent by November. The coalition, composed of two parties traditionally in favour of a high state of military preparedness and one in favour of disarmament, has also to plan its attitude to NATO for 1970, the year in which the treaty comes up for renewal. After a promise to reduce the period of conscription from fourteen to twelve months, Ministers have also expressed willingness to accelerate financial contributions to NATO as well as to increase the military contribution. The Social Democrats are afraid that the latter commitment might be made at the expense of the former, and the government is searching for the basis of an agreed policy between the ruling parties and the Social Democrat opposition. The invasion of Czechoslovakia in August 1968 has acted as a spur to Danish intentions in the defence field : having once been caught unprepared there is a great reluctance to take any risks, and yet with this goes the difficulty of paying for the defence needed in the mid-twentieth century.

Present-day Standards

Denmark stands now as a country with one of the highest standards of living in Europe, although she is at the same time rapidly becoming one of the most expensive. Whether N. F. S. Grundtvig would approve of the Denmark of today – he wanted a country in which 'few have too much and fewer too little' – may perhaps be a debatable point – Grundtvig had surely never envisaged such prosperity as has been achieved; but the second half of his dictum has certainly become a reality. There *are* still slums in Denmark, in certain areas of Vesterbro in Copenhagen for instance, but the country's wealth has been distributed equally to an amazing extent. Thanks to grants towards housing costs for those in – merely relative – need, and thanks also to long-term mortgages (despite the fact that the terms will be reduced), it has been possible to make high-quality housing available to most of the population. In high-density areas this has been done by the provision of houses on plots, the minimum sizes of which are carefully regulated so as to avoid overcrowding of individually good houses, which is often seen in Britain.

An outstanding example of the careful planning which goes into high-density building is to be found in what is known as the Gjellerup Plan. This is a scheme for what almost amounts to a small, privately built town on the outskirts of Århus, which is being erected on the area previously occupied by three farms bought by a co-operative building association in 1961–62. The total area is 1,160,000 square metres, and when finished the scheme will consist of 1,776 apartments and provide homes for 10,000 people. Traffic and pedestrians will be completely separated, so much so that the entrance to the flats will be from a seven-metre-wide terrace on which children will be able to play in complete safety, as motor-cars will be kept at a lower level in the immediate vicinity of the flats. Yet plenty of provision is to be made for cars, each flat being provided with garage or parking-space for two. Moreover, there will be extensive facilities for sport in the scheme, including tennis courts, pitches for ball games, a swimming bath, and even a slope for tobogganing. A shopping centre is obviously to be built in, and so are crèches and nursery schools as well as junior schools and a centre for further education.

The flats themselves will vary in size from three large plus two small rooms, to one-room flats with their own bathroom, and the aim is to provide apartments larger than the average. The need for versatility in design is catered for by moveable walls (said to be thoroughly sound-insulated) between the rooms in some of the flats, so that families can arrange the sizes to suit their individual taste. All the larger flats have two bathrooms and a workroom, and they are equipped with automatic washing-machines and drying cupboards, together with large refrigerators and electric cookers. In addition they are provided with a separate storeroom about 10 square metres in area, with facilities for storing bicycles and perambulators. Instead of dustbins, the whole area is provided with a vacuum system which carries rubbish to a central incinerator.

The cost of these flats varies from a deposit of 8,800 *kroner* and a monthly rent of 1,215 *kroner* for the largest type to a deposit of 2,900 *kroner* and a monthly rent of 375 *kroner* for the smallest. Facilities are available for borrowing the deposits, which are to cover repairs to the flats on removal and are otherwise returnable, while the monthly rent includes the cost of central heating, hot water, and electricity. The rather high cost of the flats is, however, offset by modern social legislation which provides for subsidies to families who wish to live in them and cannot afford to do so.

Together with the high standard of living has gone a manifestation of good taste – taste in buildings, in furnishing, in dress, and in art. It is difficult to distinguish between a sense of beauty and a sense of good taste, and in doing so one moves from the sphere of objective fact to subjective judgement. However, if good taste could be defined as a predominantly materialistic sense of what is pleasing, a sense of form and colour without any profounder connotations, then it is to be found all over Denmark. In a Copenhagen newspaper article in March 1969 the Irish journalist Maureen Mullan, after eighteen months in Copenhagen, talked of her attraction towards the Danes and of an equal dislike for the materialism which she found in Denmark, a materialism which, she argued, is accompanied by restlessness and dissatisfaction. It is a state of affairs often observed in Denmark, though whether it is an altogether valid point may well be doubted. Not all Danes are dissatisfied or restless : in fact a general air of contentment, not to say complacency, is to be found in many who take a kind of patriotic pride in the achievements of their small country. Many of the younger generation tend, however, to react against the inevitable self-satisfaction of a people who have accomplished so much, though what they have to offer in its place is a different matter. A country which is prepared to offer one per cent of its national income for help to underdeveloped countries is not without a social conscience. Indeed, the Danish international social conscience is becoming as firmly established as has been its internal social conscience for many years.

Together with the materialism which is an indisputable part of the Danish modern character goes a passionate belief in the freedom and equality of the individual. It is tempting to see this as an integral part of the Danish character going back to the Viking Age when Rollo's men on the Seine proclaimed that they were all equal. Tempting, though probably wrong, despite the various attempts of the peasantry to throw off the yoke of the aristocracy in the Middle Ages, and despite the tolerance of the Danes even after the Reformation. Today tolerance has become almost a doctrine of modern Denmark. Society has long tolerated and accepted the unmarried mother, not only officially and theoretically, but also in practice. Homosexuality has long been accepted, if not exactly welcomed, and attempts have been made to replace the word homosexual, and all its overtones, with a modern invention, 'homophile' – clinical and devoid of character. Racialism is now a concept alien to Danes, though it has not always been – and in any case there is no real racial problem in the country. Evil tongues would also point out that not all Danes treat Greenlanders as their equals. Liberty in the field of sexual morals is also well established, and the divorce rate is high. Divorce, however, does not necessarily mean a definite break between the partners of a marriage and family get-togethers are not at all unusual.[11] Little wonder that the Socialist People's Party in 1968 suggested what it called a 'family at large', which was to be a legalised form of polygamy : as many wives and husbands and their offspring living together as may desire to do so, the relationship being recognised for taxation purposes. Yet it is doubtful whether the Danes, and especially the younger generation, are more promiscuous than other nationalities : they have in the past perhaps been less inclined to gloss over things, and they have been and still are inclined to rationalise on their morality more than others. At the same time it should be remembered that not all Danish legislation is as liberal as that elsewhere, and that, to take a subject uppermost in people's minds today, their abortion laws are at present stricter than in Britain. Whether these will remain so, is another matter.

Denmark has taken the lead, however, in the liberalisation of the laws on pornography. Despite the protests of many who were ashamed of what was being proposed, the former Social Democrat government removed all restrictions on the printed word, and overnight Copenhagen became an international centre for pornography, with bookshops specialising in it. Indeed, at the German border at Krusaa, a singular bookshop has been opened for this type of literature, and it is said that they are doing a roaring trade, while the traditional sale of dairy produce has fallen. According to press reports the German customs authorities have finally been forced to turn a blind eye to the pornographic literature being brought through. Whether this latter is a criticism of the Danes for exporting it or of others for buying it, the fact remains that pornography has now become a significant Danish export. Now the Baunsgaard government, more conservative and therefore more unexpectedly, has removed restrictions on pictures from 1 July 1969 and has thus given rise to a new boom. Again protests and even demonstrations have been arranged, but the government has not been prepared to relent. That many Danes, especially Danes abroad, are ashamed at the reputation their country is acquiring abroad seems to be of little significance, and when Per Hækkerup wrote to the

[11] It is not unknown for perfectly respectable and respected Danes to parade around with their present wife on one arm and their former one on the other, and boast that they have two wives for the evening.

press protesting against the damage being done to the Danish image, he made little impression. It is all in the name of freedom.

Post-War Literature

Danish literature over the past thirty years has faithfully mirrored the social and economic changes that have taken place. It has perhaps also told something of the unconscious attitudes to them. The immediate result of the occupation of Denmark was, not unnaturally, the disappearance of certain established authors because of their communist sympathies. Hans Kirk,[12] whose social novels had continued to appear until the end of the 1930s, was an obvious example, and although he continued to write, even while interned, there were obvious limitations on him. Even when books by Kirk reappeared, they were no longer the direct social novels that he had written earlier, but rather studies in dictatorship, as in *The Slave*, in which such action as there is takes place on board a Spanish galleon returning from South America, a microcosm giving scope for political discussion and the illustration of brutality by those in power, or *The Son of Wrath*, a communist interpretation of the life of Christ, showing him to be the leader of the common people in revolt against oppression.

The character of dictatorship had exercised people's minds long before the war, Kaj Munk for example, and he had been paralleled by Hans Christian Branner, whose early novel *Toys* from 1936 had also analysed the workings of a dictatorial régime by portraying the way in which a firm of toy manufacturers builds itself up, thrives on terror, and finally collapses. Unlike Kirk, Branner was able to write throughout the war, but obviously he kept away from themes which were too dangerous, examining rather human motivation and loneliness against the background of the war. In his novel of the Occupation, *No One Knows the Night* (1955), these themes dominate in a book which tells directly of the resistance movement in Denmark. Branner is characterised on the one hand by his humanity and on the other by his Freudian approach to personality which at its best can result in penetrating analyses by means of a stream of consciousness technique worthy of James Joyce, but at its worst can be clumsy and primitive.

Both these writers were liberal or radical in their approach to life, and both kept themselves very close to the materialistic interpretation of life. So, too, in some ways, does William Heinesen, whose novel *Noatun* (English title: *Niels Peter*) from the 1930s was in the collective tradition, but whose problems in the years since the Occupation go beyond a mere mechanical, chemical view of life.

12 See above, p. 164.

A Marxist in theory, though not a dogmatic one in his written work, Heinesen again uses the microcosm approach, making the Faroe Islands the centre of his universe. His novel *The Black Sauce-pan* is one of the few outstanding Danish war novels to come from the Second World War, but it deals with the occupation of the Faroes by British troops, not the German occupation of Denmark. Yet a close analysis of this novel shows that the war is only the outer shell of the novel which in reality is more concerned with human relationships and with human goodness being undermined by the forces of evil, be they Christian-sectarian or sexually per-verse. Heinesen is concerned with Life. He is a man who may almost be said to have a religious sense of awe for life, and who logically progresses to an examination of the juxtaposition of life and death, a theme which dominates in his best novel, *The Lost Musicians* and his longest and latest, *Fair Hope*, both of which also allow of a Marxist social interpretation on the surface.

In his cult of life and his search for a tenable interpretation of life, Heinesen is typical of many writers of the wartime and post-war eras. Although theoretically a Marxist, he goes beyond Marx-ism. Martin A. Hansen,[13] on the other hand, began as a Marxist in the 1930s, but, after his first two books, turned his back on that doctrine and spent the rest of his life looking at personality and seeing it against the traditional culture of his country. Thus his most profound novel, *The Liar* (which has been translated into English), is a study of human motivation, showing how the teacher on a small island (again a microcosm) gradually becomes aware of and receptive to the island's ancient culture and in so doing gradually commits himself to the life of the island instead of cut-ting himself off from it. In some ways it is a very Danish book, but unlike so many Danish novels it requires no knowledge of Den-mark to be appreciated, and being a representation of a microcosm, its perspectives are vast and profound. A subjective judgement might well class this as the best Danish novel of the century and place it among the best dozen or so in Europe as a whole.

To some extent its thought is abstract, but a more concrete subject had been the foundation of a rather earlier picaresque novel called *Lucky Christoffer*, telling the story of the wanderings of a would-be knight errant at the time of the Reformation, and allow-ing plenty of scope for the discussion of views of life. In its por-trayal of an age when views of life were in direct conflict, an obvious parallel could be drawn with the present day, and thus the novel becomes a book on the search for a view of life. Martin A. Hansen stands as a man who was seeking, and in this he is a

[13] See above, p. 165.

Danish parallel to the internationally better known Swedish author Pär Lagerkvist. His death at the age of forty-three robbed Denmark of one of its outstanding writers of the century.

The literature of the 1930s had been predominantly a literature of prose, grey depictions of an unembellished reality, and as such it had certain affinities with the Naturalist literature of the 1870s and 1880s – of which it was a direct descendant. And as the 1890s had seen a lyric reaction to this, so the 1940s and 1950s saw a new upsurge of lyric poetry in Denmark. It was an introspective poetry, a poetry of search, just as Martin A. Hansen's work had been a search, and something of a school arose around the periodical *Heretica* – symbolising not that the poets were heretics in any religious sense, but that they rejected the orthodox view of life, the 'establishment'.

Again like the poets of the 1890s, these poets differed widely in their positive views and inclinations : some were agnostic, some Christian. At bottom this poetry could be said to be a rejection of the rationalist approach to life in all its forms, social and political, scientific and psychological. It introduced a new irrationality which has left its mark on Danish literature right up to the present day.

The literature of the 1960s is likewise concerned with man in society, and is likewise a search, perhaps a more desperate search than before, in the face of an apparent failure. Poetic forms have been stretched to the limit, and experiments made with *lyrique concrète* and other extreme forms. There is an anti-art, anti-lyrical movement among the young, some of whom are artists and poets in their own right without knowing where they want to go with their art. Even an anti-opera has been written. Literature, and with it painting and music, seems to be in a state of flux in Denmark at the moment : the artists seem to be looking for somewhere to go, in what is still their reaction against the establishment. Yet the establishment representing, when all is said and done, material wellbeing, and those reacting against it themselves not looking beyond the bounds of materialism, it is difficult for them to channel their efforts beyond anarchism or some ill-defined desire for revolution for revolution's sake. Perhaps there is complacency in modern Denmark – it would be difficult to achieve so much without a trace of it appearing; but the search for something radically better than the existing society must be a long one.

Appendix A

Social Legislation

THE GRUNDTVIGIAN IDEAL of Denmark as a country where 'few have too much and fewer too little' has found its modern expression in the social legislation of which Denmark has been very proud since the 1930s. Although there is at present some discussion as how best to co-ordinate and group under one administration the authorities at present in charge of various aspects of social legislation, one of the most interesting features of the system to date has been its lack of centralisation, despite a degree of state control in it all.

This lack of a central administration, which distinguishes the prestn Danish system from many others, is due ultimately to its historical development. Social help started relatively early in Denmark – provision for public aid to those in need was made in the constitution of 1849 – and as improvements and additions have been made, the state has tended to help individual organisations rather than organise the help itself. In addition to maintaining some control with each source of social aid, the state has tended to subvent them all to a greater or lesser extent, the remainder of the financial burden being either on the local authorities or whatever other body runs the scheme.

Thus the Poor Law of 1891, one of the earliest pieces of legislation in this sphere, laid down more detailed rules for poor-aid than had been done before. The administration, however, was left in the hands of the local authorities, who, moreover, had to bear most of the cost. They could also decide whether to give help in cash or kind, and also the amount of aid to be given in each individual case. This principle, which has subsequently been abandoned, gave rise to considerable abuse, as the local authorities were often more interested in keeping down costs than in helping the poor. As has been seen in the historical account of the relevant period,[1] the local authorities were run in the main by farmers who were themselves the major taxpayers and thus had a personal interest in keeping local authority expenditure to a minimum. Another less humane

[1] See above, pp. 94 f.

aspect in the legislation was the fact that accepting poor-aid meant
in most cases losing legal rights, a clause which in theory was maintained until 1961, though in practice it fell into disuse as different
forms of aid were made available. Poor-aid legislation was, however, supplemented by 'aid funds' which had been established in
1856 with the object of helping people in temporary difficulties
without the loss of civil rights occasioned by poor-aid proper. This
system of temporary aid was more firmly established in 1907 when
each local authority was compelled to have its own 'aid fund'.

The year 1891 saw also the passing of another important piece
of social legislation in the Law on Support in Old Age. This primitive form of old-age pension worked in much the same way, and
was administered by the same people as the law on poor-aid, but
acceptance of old-age relief did not carry the same legal consequences. Its aim was in fact precisely to help old people who
were in need but had managed to steer clear of poor-aid, and
although it was obviously of some benefit, the option of local
authorities concerning the amount and type of aid granted was at
that particular time and in those particular circumstances a significant weakness.

While both these early pieces of legislation had been based on
the taxation principle, the first Law on Health Insurance Societies
was based on the insurance principle, on the idea of help to self-
help. Health insurance societies had sprung up on a local basis
before this, partly inspired by the co-operative ideals of the time.
The object of the 1892 law was to encourage the formation of
further societies and to lay down rules for their being run on a
voluntary basis, but with state aid for those conforming to state
requirements. Again, subsequent developments have taken place
on the basis of this principle, although membership in one form or
another has become compulsory.

Further developments of the insurance principle were contained
in laws passed up to 1921. In 1898 came the Law on Accident
Insurance, making employers responsible for accidents suffered by
employees during working hours. This was followed in 1907 by the
Law on Recognised Unemployment Insurance Societies, providing
for state subvention for voluntary insurance. In 1921 came the Law
on Disablement Insurance, providing for pensions in the case of
complete disablement for contributing members of recognised health
insurance societies.

Thus, by the early 1920s, there was a good deal of social legislation on the Danish statute book, though the humanity which had
given rise to it was to some extent impaired by the way in which

it could be administered. It was a social system in embryo, but it needed attention before it could hope to be anything like completely satisfactory. A first step towards reform was taken in 1922, when the Law on Old Age Pensions came into force, replacing the old law of 1891. Local option was abolished, and instead the new law introduced new and comprehensive rules on old-age pensions. The move towards uniformity had begun.

It was not, however, until 1 October 1933 that complete uniformity was achieved in what became known as the Social Reform,[2] the most complex piece of legislation in Denmark to date, the achievement of the Minister of Social Affairs of the time, K. K. Steincke. The Social Reform entailed the repeal of all existing social laws and their replacement by four new acts :

1. General Insurance Act – i.e. sickness insurance, disablement insurance, and old-age insurance.
2. Unemployment Insurance Act.
3. Accident Insurance Act.
4. Public Care Act.

While the first three of these acts, as their titles imply, were based on the insurance principle, the fourth has no such foundation and is ultimately financed by taxation. Meanwhile, the real significance of the laws was not merely co-ordination of rules, but the fact that help in all its forms was now a right and no longer an act of charity. And such help as was granted was aimed at maintaining a dignified standard of living, not merely at the provision of bare necessities, as had hitherto been the case. The object of the legislation, and of subsequent acts, has in fact gone beyond this in the desire to prevent cases of hardship from arising – for instance, closely allied to legislation aimed at alleviating distress has gone legislation the object of which has been to maintain full employment and thus provide security against poverty. There has been state aid for building and efforts have been made to ensure good health by stringent laws on hygiene in the food industry. The ultimate result was the demand for social security for all during the Second World War, a demand which, it must be stated, has very largely been met. Indeed the social view is expressed in the constitution of 1953, § 75 :

(1) In order to advance the public interest, efforts should be made to ensure work for every able-bodied citizen on terms that will secure his existence.

(2) Any person unable to support himself or his dependants shall,

2 See above, p. 156.

where no other person is responsible for his or their maintenance, be entitled to receive public assistance, provided that he shall comply with the obligations imposed by Statute in such respect.

Consequently there are laws concerning the occupation of disabled people, especially for those permanently incapable of normal employment, while in 1956 laws were passed providing help for the rehabilitation of the disabled. In 1960 a further law was passed aiming at state aid for removal expenses and travel for those moving home in order to take up employment. At the same time the law providing for care for the disabled has been extended to include the chronic sick, sufferers from tuberculosis, polio, rheumatism and cancer, and has also provided for improved benefits for unmarried mothers and widows with children. Also in 1956 legislation was introduced providing for a people's pension based on earnings, to replace the former old-age pension.

Although the Social Reform of 1933 has provided the basis for social legislation until the 1960s, the four laws have been broken down into various more specialised acts :

Widow's Pension Act, 1959
Rehabilitation Act and Public Health Insurance Act, 1960
Public Assistance Act, 1961
Children and Youth Assistance Act, 1964
Disability Pensions Act, 1965
People's Pension Act, 1965
Invalid and People's Pensioners Assistance Act, 1968

Insurance schemes under these acts are either organised or at least controlled by the state, and are sometimes given state subvention. This is the case with health insurance, which covers the entire population, and to which employers make a contribution of 11 øre per work hour and the employees $5\frac{1}{2}$ øre, giving an hourly contribution of approximately twopence (2 cents) in all. In theory unemployment and sickness insurance is voluntary, but all must make a minimum contribution, as passive members of health insurance societies, while most trade unions, which in practice administer unemployment benefits, insist that their members should pay unemployment insurance contributions. While health and unemployment schemes are in effect state financed, invalid and people's pensions are run by the local authorities but paid for by the state. The insurance principle does not enter into this and every Danish citizen is entitled to one of these pensions if and as the need arises, though each wage-earner must make a contribution of 3 per cent of his taxable income. The scheme is run by the state and local authorities in conjunction.

All payments under the insurance and pension laws are fixed and are tied to the cost of living, and all are over what on Danish standards is a minimum subsistence level. Payments under the public assistance and rehabilitation laws are regulated according to need, but their aim is to help those affected to maintain, within reasonable limits, the standard of living to which they are accustomed. It is, however, a principle that payments are only made under the public assistance law if help cannot be given under any of the other social acts – i.e. through a pension, aid to rehabilitation, or insurance. When public assistance is granted, it goes to a maximum the basic amount of payments under a people's pension.

It is obviously not possible in a brief review of social legislation to look at all the complexities and all the benefits, but a closer look at two or three of the more important aspects will enable readers to compare benefits in Denmark with those in their countries.

First, then, health insurance. This is organised by means of state-recognised health insurance societies. Each *kommune* (local authority) will have one except in the case of Copenhagen, where there is one to each district. Though every citizen has to be covered by health insurance in one form or another, there are various categories of membership. The most important distinction is that between A members and B members, the A members being those whose income is below a level determined each year by the state, and corresponding to a full year's income for a skilled worker, and the B members being those whose incomes are above that level. B members pay rather more for the benefits they receive. In either case membership can be active, i.e. making full contributions and enjoying full benefits, or passive, making minimum contributions and receiving no immediate benefits. On applying to become full members people become entitled to benefits after a waiting period normally of six months – but ten in the case of a confinement. Everyone must be covered by a minimum contribution except in the case of those above the income level who choose to pay to what are known as Continuation Insurance Societies, in effect private insurance schemes. In practice it is also compulsory for wage-earners to be full members of the membership class to which their incomes assign them. There is also a special category known as 'abeyance members', confined to certain classes of people : national servicemen, pensioners in homes, convicts.

As the health insurance societies work in conjunction with the tax authorities, these latter supply every year a list of people whose incomes are above the 'health insurance limit', and so the progression from A to B members becomes automatic and compulsory; on the other hand, B members whose incomes fall can remain B members if they wish. A members receive the following considerable benefits :

1. Free medical treatment (from a general practitioner who can only be changed once a year).
2. Specialist treatment.
3. Hospital treatment.
4. Three-quarters of the cost of essential medicine prescribed, if it is on a list approved by the state.
5. At least half the cost of preventive dental treatment.
6. Free home nurse.
7. Free midwife.
8. Help towards funeral expenses.
9. Daily payment in case of sickness.

A members can also demand free transport to hospital etc., but this is paid for by the local authorities.

B members have the right to :

1. Free hospital treatment.
2. Help towards medicine and dental treatment.
3. Home nurse.
4. Help towards funeral expenses.
5. Daily payment in case of sickness – as for A members. Also the *refund* in part of fees paid to doctors and in connection with a confinement.

The health insurance association might, but is not obliged to, help with less necessary medicine and pay for further dental treatment, and also help to pay for spectacles.

A members must go to a doctor on one of the panel of health insurance doctors, with whom there is an agreement on charges. B members can go to any doctor, though there are provisions for dealing with any abuse.

For hospital treatment the health insurance society pays only half the sum charged to those paying for themselves, i.e. 5–8 *kroner* per day. This is obviously far less than the cost of hospitalisation, and the remainder of the hospital's income comes from the authorities running it, normally the local authorities with state subsidies. The health insurance societies themselves are financed partly by members' contributions, and partly by state subsidies. Some support was once obtained from local authorities. The daily payment in case of sickness is financed by contributions from employers, employees, and the state.

Another field which is of immediate interest to the non-Dane and especially for purposes of comparison, is that of pensions. While the health insurance scheme has its obvious weakness and complications – as well as its good points – the pension schemes in Denmark are by any standard singularly good. The people's pension, introduced in 1956 and intended to be functioning fully by 1970, is designed to give a full pension to all, not merely the pittance which old age pensions so often are. The pension is paid to all over the age of sixty-seven irrespective of income. Others eligible include people aged between sixty and sixty-seven who are in bad health, unmarried women between sixty-two and sixty-seven, and married women of that age whose husbands receive an invalid's pension.

The intention is that from 1 April 1970 there will be what is known as a general people's pension, a full-rate pension for everyone. Meanwhile the pensions are at different rates, everyone being entitled to the minimum irrespective of income earned or unearned. From 1 January 1970 the full rates will be 7,512 *kroner* per year for single people plus a supplement of 1,740 *kroner* for those without any other source of income. For married couples the rates will be 11,316 *kroner* basic pension plus 3,480 *kroner* supplementation. In addition there is a further supplement payable for people over eighty years old.

Taxation is the ultimate source of these pensions, the state paying the full expenses. The individual's contribution to this consists of a levy of 3 per cent of his or her taxable income (after deductions of various kinds), though contributions are not claimed under 10 *kroner* a year.

Disablement or invalid pensions are paid from the ages of fifteen to sixty-seven, when they are replaced by the people's pension. There are three scales of payment, clearly regulated according to the degree of disability; and at all events the payment of a disability pension is subject to the condition that rehabilitation measures are not likely substantially to improve the earning capacity of the applicant. The intention is clearly to help him to maintain his customary standard of living (within limits), rather than have the worry and humiliation of seeing his standards fall through no fault of his own. The aim is to maintain people's dignity, by ensuring their standards as a right, not as a charity. The stigma of receiving help has been removed by the legislation, and it seems also to have been removed these days from the public consciousness.

16—D • •

Pensions are, however, not the only way in which older people are helped in Denmark. Special flats are built for those living on people's pensions, the intention being to construct suitable flats of good quality which are available at special rates.

The losses on these flats are covered by the local authorities, who contribute two-thirds of the amount, and the state, which supplies the remainder. There are, of course, not sufficient of these flats to meet the country's needs, and so people living on people's pensions are eligible for subsidies which will reduce their rent in ordinary flats to that in a flat built for people's pensioners, or, if living in more expensive accommodation, subsidies which will reduce their rents considerably. It is possible to find cases where rents of over 1,000 *kroner* per month are reduced to under 500.

The danger that the construction of old people's flats might lead to old people's ghettoes is one of which planners are aware, although some towns have built special blocks for old people. However, the state has the right to require the inclusion of a certain number of old people's flats in any building which receives a state grant. The prime object is in fact to keep old people within the community as a whole, to take care of their special needs, but to ensure that they do not come to feel as a class apart, segregated from the active, younger members of society.

For those who cannot any longer fend for themselves, provision is made for old people's homes and care homes for those on people's pensions or invalid pensions. It is the responsibility of the local authorities to provide these homes, either separately or in conjunction when it is a question of a small authority. Alternatively, local authorities can make arrangements to have access to homes in other districts, or to private homes, of which there is a fair supply. This is the theory, but it must be admitted that in practice there are not sufficient places to go round, and waiting-lists are long in some places, however many attempts are made to overcome this difficulty.

Widows' pensions are closely related to the two categories just dealt with and are the same as income-regulated pensions for single people at the normal rate. They are paid to widows over fifty-five, and over forty-five if they have two or more children under eighteen. Widows under forty-five can be given special help for thirteen weeks (in special cases six months) after the death of their husband. Over forty-five they will receive this special help for six months. The aim is to help them over a difficult time and to assist them in stabilising their homes. This help will cover money for housekeeping, clothes, fixed expenses such as rent, light, fuel, insurance, etc., and possibly also hire purchase. Assistance will sometimes be given in the running of a small business if it looks as though the widow sooner or later will be able to carry it on. Help will also be given to certain categories of widow to enable them to undergo training of various sorts, though not normally for courses of long duration for which it is possible to pay through study loans or scholarships.

Child allowances, which used to be paid in the form of deductions from tax, have with the introduction of the pay as you earn system in January 1970 been transferred to the social services. The basic allowance is 936 *kroner* per year per child, the amount being tied to the cost of living index. There is adequate provision for extra allowances for children with only one parent to support them and for the children of people receiving disablement pensions, etc.

This is only a selection of facts on pensions and allowances, social benefits in general, but it must emerge from these figures that they are good. Standards are high and a genuine attempt is made to deal with the entire question on a generous and humane basis, on the assumption that if a person has made his contribution to the country's economy, then the country owes it to him to see to his comfort and security in old age or bad times. The cost in terms of taxation must necessarily be high, but there is a general feeling that the taxpayers are getting something for their money. This last remark has been known to elicit the somewhat cynical response 'especially if they do not have any'; but all in all people are content with the way the social services work and they are content to pay for them.

Despite the present integrated status of Greenland and the Faroe Islands, the social legislation of Denmark proper does not apply to them. The Faroes have had something approaching the Danish system since 1960, and now Greenland has also been given her own 'social reform'.

The Faroe Islands

ALTHOUGH THERE ARE EARLIER ACCOUNTS of journeys to islands north of Scotland, which must be the Faroe Islands, the earliest use of the name by which they are known today is in a manuscript of *c.* 1225, where they are called Færeyiar. This name, meaning Sheep Islands, is almost certainly a reference to the mildness of the climate, which allows sheep to graze out throughout the year, and it has presumably also led to the Faroese national symbol – a ram. The islands seem to have been inhabited from about A.D. 700 by Celtic monks, and a certain Dicuil tells how they were driven out by Vikings around the year 800. The Vikings then proceeded to colonise the islands, either direct from Norway or indirectly from the Scottish islands – in the view of some scholars, a few traces of Gaelic words in the Faroese language seem to indicate this latter course. On the other hand, the Saga of the Faroe Islanders – historically as unreliable as most other sagas – tells how the colonisation of the Faroes was carried out from Norway in order to escape from Harald the Fair-haired, an assertion in agreement with Snorre. The Saga also tells how the Faroes became Christian in 1000, at the same time as Iceland, and how, after a period of complete independence, they acknowledged, probably in 1035, King Magnus the Good of Norway as their king, thus becoming in effect a province of Norway though being held in respect by the inhabitants of Norway proper.

However, an account from 1273 indicates that there was a period of decline after coming under Norwegian rule, for now the Norwegian king promised to send at least two ships a year to the Faroes. It looks as though the Faroese, originally seafarers themselves, were no longer sailors, possibly indirectly because of the lack of trees on the islands with which ships could be built. Trade with the Faroes now became more or less a Norwegian monopoly, and the changed status of the islands is also shown by the fact that Norwegian law was extended to include them. Before 1300 the old Faroese *Lagting,* which had so far enjoyed a legislative function, had its role reduced to that of administering the Norwegian law. Norway's appropriation of the Faroes is also indicated by the fact that the Hanseatic states were in theory stopped from trading there in 1294, a privilege not restored until 1361. With the union between Norway and Denmark in 1380, the Faroes came under Danish rule together with all other Norwegian possessions, and were governed as a province of Norway.

Exactly what the legal status of the Faroes was during the early part of Danish rule is not certain, but there are indications in the reigns of Christian III and Christian IV that they were not considered as an integral part of Norway. The first completely unambiguous evidence of this, however, is the fact that Frederik III on becoming king in 1649 sent a deputation to receive the homage of the Faroe Islanders as distinct from the Norwegians. It seems that the islands, rather like Iceland, were considered as provinces within the kingdom, but not as part of the kingdom itself. Certainly by the seventeenth century the old connection with Norway had no longer any significance. The administration, hitherto based on Bergen, was moved to Copenhagen and the only real sign left of the Norwegian connection was the fact that the legal system continued to be based on Norwegian law.

From 1602 there had been a trade monopoly in Iceland in the hands of the Icelandic Company and in 1619 the Faroe Islands were included in this. It was not to begin with a state monopoly, but was leased to various people, perhaps the most notable and notorious being Christoffer Gabel. Gabel received the islands in fief in 1655 and was furthermore given a trade monopoly in 1662 which was to last for his lifetime and that of his son Frederik, in fact until 1708. The Gabels used their monopoly for their own ends, not for the good of the population, and the period of their governorship is generally considered to be one of the blackest periods in the history of the Faroes, one which has, incidentally, furnished the subject for one of the finest novels in modern Danish, *Fair Hope,* by the most outstanding of all Faroese novelists, William Heinesen. Upon the death of Frederik Gabel, the monopoly reverted to the state, which operated it far more for the benefit of the Faroes themselves, more in the spirit of the monopoly operating in Greenland. This state of affairs lasted until 1856 and was aimed at providing the islanders with their needs rather than at making a profit from the trade. None the less, it was in some ways a doubtful benefit, not least because of the refusal until 1836 to allow trading anywhere in the Faroes but Tórshavn, and was doubtless largely contributory to the backwardness of the Faroese people and economy in subsequent years.

Like Greenland, the Faroe Islands should in theory have gone to Sweden along with Norway proper in the Kiel Peace Treaty of 1814. That this did not happen was partly because the Swedish negotiator was not sure of his historical facts, but also partly because Sweden was not interested in acquiring distant provinces, only in unifying the Scandinavian peninsula. Thus any remaining sense of unity between the Faroes and Norway was removed, and the islands passed purely into Danish control, although Christian V's Norwegian law continued to operate there. Moreover, certain complications arose later in the century as Norway never acknowledged the provisions of the Kiel Treaty and could thus lay claim to her old territories. Now the process of closer incorporation into Denmark continued, and the Faroese parliament, the *Lagting,* probably the oldest parliamentary institution in Europe, was abolished in 1816. Henceforth the Faroes were to be considered as a Danish *Amt* (county).

This move, coming at an economically unfortunate time soon after the Danish state bankruptcy, was perhaps symptomatic of the Danish attitude towards the Faroes in the nineteenth century. The Danes failed to recognise the individuality of the Faroe islanders, who temperamentally were more akin to the Icelanders than to the Danes. Like them they had preserved their ancient culture in a purer form than those Scandinavian countries closer to the continent of Europe, while their language was also akin to Icelandic and far removed from Danish. Yet at the beginning of the nineteenth century this was lost on the Danes, who considered the Faroes as a colony or at best a province. Danish civil servants were overbearing towards the Faroese and refused to consort with them. The Faroese language was not officially recognised, though Danish never became the language of the Faroese themselves, as to some extent had happened in the kingdom of Norway. Poverty was rife in the islands, partly as a result of the financial state of Denmark herself and her consequent inability to provide help for the Faroes. In addition the ancient custom of dividing up a farm between all one's offspring had led to gradual impoverishment of many families. Conditions deteriorated so much that from 1777 to 1856 only those who could afford to maintain a family were allowed to marry. In an attempt to alleviate distress, experiments were made to introduce deep-sea fishing into the Faroes, but they were an immediate failure. By 1840 it was being suggested that the trade monopoly should be abolished in an attempt to revitalise the Faroese people, but the *Rigsdag* decided in 1844 to continue it. It was felt that to end it might bring more hardship to the population, but what was not realised was that free trade would have spurred the people on to achieve more for themselves instead of relying on artificial trading conditions.

In that same year, 1844, an appeal from the Faroes to the Roskilde Assembly, in which they were represented, requested an improvement in educational facilities. There were in fact no schools in the islands, and instruction was given in the home by itinerant teachers. The result of this appeal was a new proclamation on schools in the Faroes on 28 May 1845. This provided for the establishment of schools in the islands, but there was little support for the project in the Faroes themselves. The schools were thought of as being Danish schools, not least because the language of tuition was to be Danish, and in addition the population showed little willingness to contribute taxes necessary to pay for the schools. This was perhaps not surprising, considering the economic state of the islands, and the situation was aggravated by the unwillingness of parents to send their children to school. They wanted them to work instead. A new act was therefore passed in 1854, leaving parents to provide for their children's education as they thought fit.

A further example of the Danish lack of understanding for the Faroes came in 1850, when the June constitution was extended to include the Faroes, although the Faroese people were not themselves consulted on this. They were now entitled to elect one member to the *Folketing* and one to the *Landsting*, although their numbers were only about half that required to qualify for such representation. However, the people did not see this as generosity, but, becoming increasingly conscious of the depressed state of the Faroes and seeing a national awakening as the only solution, they elected a Faroese as their representative in both chambers in place of the Danish candidates who also stood. This was in itself a defeat for the Danish administration, made worse by the fact that although the *Landsting* member, Hendrik Wejhe, was a fairly conservative figure, the new member of the *Folketing*, Niels Winther, was a radical and outspoken Faroese patriot who immediately began to work for a status for the Faroes comparable with that of Iceland. For while the Faroes had been formally incorporated into the Danish kingdom, Iceland had successfully opposed a closer union. Winther aimed at an increased amount of self-government in the Faroes, and in order to achieve this, he had two immediate objectives – the reconstitution of the Faroese *Lagting*, with similar powers to those of the Icelandic *Althing*, and the end of the Danish trade monopoly.

The first of the objectives was quickly achieved, and the *Lagting* was reconstituted in 1852, though it was a purely consultative organ without the powers which Winther had sought. In fact it was more akin to a Danish county council than to the *Althing*, and the Danish *Amtmand* (Sheriff) and *Provst* (Dean) – the main representatives of the state and Church in the islands – were *ex-officio* members. This *Amtmand* subsequently made himself so unpopular that he had to be removed. The abolition of the trade monopoly took longer, but that, too, was achieved by 1 January 1856 after a unanimous vote by the *Lagting*. There was a feeling that a turning-point had been reached in Faroese life, and that without a trade monopoly the standard of living could be improved until it equalled that in the Orkneys and Shetland, two groups of islands with a Norse background and conditions of life roughly comparable with the Faroes.

Free trade did in fact quickly bring about an improvement in the Faroese economy, for whereas the monopoly had encouraged the wrong industries, under different trading conditions the people ventured into different and more appropriate fields. The increasing export of fish now became the basis of the Faroese economy and has since come to account for some 90 per cent of the Faroese national product. The first trawler was bought at the end of the nineteenth century and others followed, although it was not until 1934 that the first steam trawler was acquired. As late as 1939, when the Faroes owned ten deep-sea trawlers, they still used some fishing boats which were fifty years old and more. Even with improved equipment they were still liable to difficulties, either because of the refusal of permission to fish within Greenlandic territorial waters or because of the loss of the Spanish market for dried fish during the Spanish Civil War. Nevertheless, despite what was still a hard life, and despite social legislation still far behind that of Denmark proper (there was no unemployment benefit in the Faroes), the economy was soon capable of supporting a larger population. Instead of living on smaller and smaller plots of land, the people were now able to engage in profitable employment. Consequently, even with an increase in population from 8,922 to 15,230 in 1901 and 24,000 in 1930, the economy was able to provide for the people, and the Faroes did not experience the effects of mass emigration which were known elsewhere, not least in Iceland.

After the abolition of the trade monopoly, attention was turned to education, which was still suffering from the unpopularity of the previous school legislation. In 1861 a secondary school was opened in Tórshavn, and three teachers were found capable of running it. The next step was the opening in Tórshavn in 1870 of a training college to provide the teachers necessary for a real expansion of education. However, the first real improvement came in 1872 when Denmark decided to support local efforts at establishing schools. The language of instruction was still in theory to be Danish, but in practice much of the teaching was done in Faroese, and this was made official in 1938. The main obstacle to a more rapid increase was still, for a time, the Faroese unwillingness to pay the necessary taxes. Finally, because of the Grundtvigian interest in the Faroes as a source of genuine Nordic culture, a Folk High School was opened in 1899, but had little immediate effect until it moved to Tórshavn itself in 1909.

Meanwhile, despite improving standards, the national consciousness, originating in the nineteenth century, grew steadily, and, to some extent inspired by the granting of independence to Norway in 1905, an Independence Party was formed under the leadership of Jóannes Patursson in 1906. At first it made slow progress, and by 1914 the Union Party, formed in opposition to it and with the aim of being as closely tied to Denmark as possible, had the support of some two-thirds of the *Lagting*. However, the Independence Party gained the support of youth, and by 1918 it had a majority in the *Lagting*. The *Lagting* itself was reformed in 1923 and given more powers. From then onwards all its members were elected, and the appointed members who had previously been a feature were removed. It could now elect its own chairman and the *Amtmand* could take part in its deliberations, but could no longer vote. The Dean of the Faroes lost his seat altogether. The *Lagting* was now also empowered to choose its own representatives in the *Landsting* in Copenhagen. Although the Faroes remained a county, their special position became more apparent. Many Danish laws were no longer valid in the islands, and laws originating in Denmark but concerning the Faroes alone should if possible be passed by the *Lagting* before coming into force. Acts concerning Denmark as well as the Faroes should also if possible be passed by the *Lagting* before coming into force in the Faroes. In its turn the *Lagting* was empowered to make its own proposals for legislation.

Although the Danes thus gave increasing powers of internal government to the Faroes, they opposed any attempt on the part of the Faroese to express themselves as an individual nation. They had acquiesced in the use of a Faroese flag designed in 1919, but when it was officially flown at the Icelandic *Althing* celebrations in 1930, a protest was made, and it was lowered. However, the Faroese had their revenge the same year during their annual celebrations on St Olaf's day, 29 July. The *Dannebrog* was cut down by nationalists to the chagrin of the Danish *Amtmand*, who walked out of the ceremony in protest. The flag was a point of irritation until the Second World War, when it was allowed by British authorities in order to distinguish Faroese ships from those of occupied Denmark, and thus gained international recognition to which the Danes themselves have subsequently subscribed.

In a way the British occupation of the Faroes furthered the ultimate cause of Faroese nationalism, for the internal administration of the islands was now left almost exclusively in the hands of the Faroese themselves. Regulations for administering the Faroes without the aid of the Danish authorities were passed in 1940 less than a month after the British occupation, and the *Amtmand,* after issuing a formal protest to the British forces, took over the powers of the Copenhagen government. Although their stay was formally an occupation, relations were good between the British forces and the Faroese population, who in fact found a great economic advantage in the situation. They traded in fish with the British, even buying up fish in Iceland to sell in the British Isles, and lost many lives in this way, while for their part the British saw to it that sufficient provisions reached the Faroes. Under these conditions a second nationalist party, the People's Party, demanded independence and in 1943 could command a near majority in the *Lagting.* Britain refused the demand, arguing that this was a matter to be settled with the Danish authorities when the opportunity arose. However, the Flag was recognised and the Faroes issued their own banknotes.

After the war there was no inclination to return to the *status quo ante* and the temporary arrangements were allowed to continue until such time as some arrangement should be made with Denmark. The Danes themselves expressed a desire to maintain their association with the Faroes, but agreed to independence if this was the desire of the people. At the *Lagting* elections immediately following this declaration, parties in favour of continuing the union were elected. Plans were made for a referendum on the independence question and the results were generally confusing: 33 per cent voted for independence; 32 per cent for union; while the remainder either abstained or spoiled their papers. When a member of one of the two ruling parties changed sides on this issue, there was a majority of one for independence, which was proclaimed immediately. The opposition parties protested and the Copenhagen government refused to grant independence on such a narrow and inconclusive majority. Instead, the *Lagting* was dissolved and in the subsequent election there was a clear majority for maintaining the union with Denmark.

Nevertheless, there was an obvious desire for complete internal self-government, and this was granted in March 1948. It had the support of a majority of the *Lagting,* though the People's Party

opposed it as a misfortune for all concerned. The new act stated
that the Faroes were a self-governing community within the kingdom of Denmark, entitled to send two representatives to the *Folketing* and one to the *Landsting*. This was changed to two representatives in the *Folketing* after the 1953 change of constitution. The
Lagting was given legislative powers in all matters concerning the
Faroes alone, and whereas previously Faroese legislation should
preferably be debated and passed by the *Lagting* before coming
into force, now it was stated that it *must* go through the *Lagting*
first. Moreover, the Faroes were now made into an independent
customs area in which all duties and taxes were to be decided by
the local government. The Faroese flag was also recognised and
the Faroese language was given equality of status with Danish.

A community which has been so depressed as the Faroes could
scarcely be expected to make any outstanding contribution to
world culture, but in the field of literature the nationalist movement did give rise to a new and purely Faroese literature in the
nineteenth and twentieth centuries. Only two writers have, however, achieved a reputation outside their homeland, and ironically
enough both of them have used Danish as their medium.

First there was Jørgen-Frantz Jacobsen (1900–38) whose early
death from tuberculosis prevented his writing more than one historical novel entitled *Barbara* – available in English translation.
Then came his friend William Heinesen, also born in 1900, un-
doubtedly the most important novelist writing in Danish today, a
man who combines writing of life in a tiny community with the
treatment of vast themes: good versus evil; life and death; time
and eternity. Although on the surface writing of life in the Faroes,
he is in fact creating a new mythology illustrating ancient themes.

Furthermore, the Faroes make one outstanding but very different
contribution to culture, in that they are the only part of the world
where the medieval chain dance is still performed as a part of
everyday life. The ancient ballads – a significant part of the Scandinavian ballad heritage – are still sung, and the dances performed
much as they have been for centuries. The dancers form a chain
by linking hands and the dance is led by one man who sings the
verses of the – often very long – ballads, while the remaining
dancers sing the refrains. The monotonous rhythm of the dance is
enlivened by the mime and expression of the dancers, of whom it
has been said that they do not merely recite the stories of the
ballads but actually experience them, really live them. The dance
is gradually losing its position in favour of modern dances – so
called – but it is nevertheless still a living force in the islands and
a symbol of the continuity of their old Nordic culture.

Appendix C

Greenland

AROUND THE YEAR 960 Erik the Red, having accompanied his father into exile from Norway, again fell foul of society and was outlawed for three years from Iceland. He had heard rumours of a land to the west, and so he set out to find it, arriving on the east coast of Greenland. In search of a more hospitable shore, he followed the coast southwards and then westwards, where he found a fertile area around what is now called Julianehaab and settled for a time in what became known to later Viking settlers as the East Settlement. The following year he travelled further north and found the West Settlement, now Godthaab.

Iceland itself was overcrowded at this period, and on his return it was not difficult for Erik the Red to entice more settlers to Greenland – hence his rather optimistic name for the new land – and at one time there were some 3,000 Norse settlers, occupying about 200 farms in the East Settlement and a hundred in the West Settlement. So many people were there that Erik the Red's son Leif (who subsequently sailed to America) was able to bring a priest from Norway in 999, while a bishop was appointed by King Sigurd the Crusader in 1126. With their Norwegian antecedents the Greenland Norsemen must obviously have felt it natural to receive their clergy from that country, although they did not acknowledge Norwegian jurisdiction. It was in fact 1270 before they did homage to the King of Norway and recognised him as their lord and master.

This action was largely the result of a decline in trade between Greenland and Europe. The narwhale tusks on which this had been based had lost their attraction for the Europeans, and consequently the trade gradually stagnated. By acknowledging the suzerainty of Norway and giving Norway a trade monopoly, the Norsemen hoped to improve their lot. The time coincided with a move southwards by the Eskimos, who had hitherto had little or no contact with the Norsemen. As they came into contact with them, they learned a good deal from them, but there are plentiful signs of war as well as of peaceful co-operation. In the middle of the fourteenth century the West Settlement was wiped out by Eskimos, and in 1379 an attack was made on the East Settlement.

Although Norway did make attempts to accept her responsibility and relieve the Norsemen of Greenland, she was in decline at this time and could offer little assistance. Finally contact died out and by about 1500 the Norsemen were left to their own devices. In 1540 some Danish sailors landed and found a Norseman lying dead on the ground. It is tempting to think that he was the last survivor of the Norse settlers, the last of a community which archaeological excavations and grave finds have shown to have suffered from malnutrition, disease, and debilities caused by constant intermarriage. Nevertheless, a thesis published in Copenhagen in 1969 examines blood samples of the Greenland Eskimos and discovers similarities between the blood of Eskimos in one region and that of the Icelanders, while Eskimos from another region show similarities with some Norwegians. This seems to open up the rather less romantic possibility that some at least of the Norsemen were assimilated into the Eskimo population.

Despite the lack of communication, the Norse settlers were not entirely forgotten, and in 1721 the Norwegian-born Hans Egede decided to go there as a missionary and preach the Lutheran faith to the survivors (remembering that contact had been lost before the Reformation). He had persuaded the authorities in Copenhagen to help him on his expedition and they had agreed on condition that his mission should be linked with a resumption of trade between Denmark and Greenland. He found only Eskimos.

However, he decided to stay and preach to them, and from a spiritual point of view his mission was a success. It was less so from a commercial standpoint, as the Greenlanders showed a propensity for preferring to trade with the Dutch, despite the fact that the Bergen Company, which had been formed to trade with Greenland, was given a theoretical monopoly in 1723. Between 1719 and 1728, 748 Dutch ships are reported to have called at Greenland, bringing back 1,250 whales and making a profit of 1·35 million guilders. Yet by 1729 the Bergen Company was in such financial straits that the state had to take it over and move its administration from Bergen to Copenhagen. There was still no improvement, and by 1731 King Christian VI was threatening to drop the whole scheme. An attempt to colonise Greenland by deporting convicts there in 1727 had also been a failure, and had almost cost Egede his life.

In 1749 the Greenland Trading Company was given back to private enterprise in the period of mercantilism, but by 1774 it was in state hands again, this time under the name of Royal

Greenland Trading Company. Trade did in fact improve at this time and the Danes had a stroke of luck in 1777 when twenty-five Dutch and German trading vessels were wrecked on the ice. Competition was less keen after this.

A further boost was given to trade with Greenland in the mid-nineteenth century by C. F. Tietgen, who during his stay in England had come across a new metal called aluminium, which could be made from cryolite. Cryolite was known to be in plentiful supply in Greenland, and Tietgen managed to have a ship equipped to bring home a cargo of it. Despite initial doubts as to the feasibility of the plan, it was a success.

Meanwhile the increased volume of trade between Greenland and the outer world brought about profound changes in her pattern of life. So far the Greenlanders had enjoyed a natural economy based on seal-hunting. The seal provided them with practically speaking all their needs – food, clothing, and the skins needed for their kajaks. Now, with the ships coming every summer from Denmark carrying cargoes of goods the Greenlanders had not known before, such as sugar and coffee, these luxury wares became coveted, accounting for almost half of Greenland's imports, and the Greenland population was prepared to barter far too much of its own produce for them, with the ironical result that hardship set in. The people had bartered so many skins that they lacked the warm clothes they needed for the winter. The dangers inherent in this were appreciated by the Danes and the Greenland trade monopoly was maintained very largely with a view to protecting the Greenlanders from themselves. It is easy to be sceptical about the maintenance of a monopoly for centuries and about keeping foreigners out of a colony of the size of Greenland, but the motives of the Danes in this instance have been genuinely humanitarian. They saw it as their duty, even as early as the eighteenth century, to preserve the Greenlandic civilisation, and it was for this reason that the trade monopoly was maintained there even when it was dropped in Iceland. This attitude still obtains, and earlier this century the Danes paid prices for Greenland fish which were above world prices, and even increased their prices gradually while world prices were falling. And this seems to have been done without pressure from the Greenlanders themselves.

It was decided at an early stage that despite the success of the paternalistic policy in Greenland, something should be done to bring the population to greater maturity and to give it at least some responsibility for running its own affairs. At a time of some social progress at home, H. J. Rink suggested in 1856 the setting-up of a management committee in each settlement consisting of both Danish and Greenland representatives. The aim of these councils should be to help in cases of social need, to exercise certain legal powers and also the power to obtain loans for building and for the general improvement of amenities. The experiment was introduced in south Greenland in 1857 and was so successful that it was later extended to the north.

Greenland, however, was entering a period of stagnation and even of decline. The increase in wealth and the changed economy resulted in an increasing population. Numerically this increase was small – from 7,500 in 1834 to 9,900 in 1855 – but in terms of percentage it was large. Moreover, it was accompanied by a decline in the number of seals caught, owing to the activities of European sealers off Newfoundland. Rink, who was director of the Greenland Trade organisation from 1871 to 1882, had to cope with more and more formidable problems on this count and also with a diminishing interest in Greenland on the part of the Danes themselves. It was not until after the turn of the century that Danish interest in Greenland revived. This revival found its expression through the activities of various members of a new organisation called the Danish Atlantic Islands, formed in 1901 to encourage concern for the various islands Denmark owned in the Atlantic, from the West Indies to Greenland. It consisted of people with varying interests, but typically enough, those concerned with Greenland were overridingly humanitarian in their aims.

Efforts to encourage Greenlanders to strive for greater participation in their own affairs were made despite some opposition from the Greenland Trade organisation and its desire to keep to paternalism. Politicians adopted a sympathetic attitude and in 1908 a law on Greenlandic government was passed, introducing local councils and also a national council elected by the people and invested with considerable authority on internal matters. The Danish *Rigsdag,* of course, kept the final say through its Greenland Administration, originally a department in the Home Ministry and subsequently of the Ministry of State. The Greenlanders for their part were now better equipped to look after themselves, better educated, thanks to nineteenth-century educational policy and the founding of training colleges, and also because greater numbers had given up their traditional sealing and taken up a trade.

Seals were becoming more and more scarce, but this scarcity coincided with an increase in Greenlandic mean temperatures. In 1917 large quantities of cod appeared in Greenlandic waters and there was a gradual switch from sealing to fishing. The Danish government realised that the switch was vital and was prepared

to give financial aid for the purchase of the new boats and equipment needed. Depots were built to treat and salt the fish, which
were still sold through Greenland Trade and at prices decided by
it – though, as has been remarked, normally above world prices.
Because of the revival of trade, the Greenlanders themselves could
now import greater quantities of European food, and thereby completely altered their feeding habits. Further changes were brought
about with temperatures increasing sufficiently to allow sheep to
graze. Sheep-farming became a practical proposition – as it had
been in the time of Erik the Red – and in 1914 a sheep station was
opened in Julianehaab to provide farmers with credit and to buy
back their sheep for slaughter. Again Greenland Trade bought up
the carcases at inflated prices. Obviously the loss had to be made
good by some means or other, and this was done by the export of
Greenland cryolite.

The year 1925 saw a new law on Greenlandic administration,
aimed at fostering co-operation between the Greenlanders and the
Danes, and giving, among other things, local rights to Danish civil
servants who had been resident in Greenland for a minimum of
two years. The two national councils were now allowed certain
judicial rights, though their decisions had to be accepted by the
two sheriffs (landsfogeder), who thus had a veto, or by the Minister
in Copenhagen. It was laid down that the councils should meet
at least once a year. In the same year, but independently of the
new act, it was decided to start continuation courses for the best
pupils from Greenlandic schools. There was still no higher education as such and those considered to be worthy of it were sent to
colleges in Copenhagen.

In 1926 a new Education Act was passed giving Greenland
broadly speaking the same school laws as existed in Denmark
proper, though they proved difficult to enforce. Instruction was
given in both Greenlandic and Danish, though it was not until
about 1930 that Danish became firmly established and well taught.
There was no question of forcing a completely foreign language on
the Greenlanders. They themselves wanted to learn Danish, which
gave them their first direct opportunity of benefiting from European
culture.

Danish jurisdiction over Greenland was almost universally
accepted. Norway, however, to whom Greenland once belonged,
still refrained from acknowledging Denmark's right to the entire
island. It should be remembered that Denmark had acquired
Greenland together with Norway, with the formation of the original
Union in 1380, and that when Norway was taken from Denmark
in 1814, many Norwegians felt that Greenland should not have

been dealt with separately. Thus Norwegian interest remained and Norway maintained her right to fish off the coast of east Greenland. In 1931 a group of Norwegian fishermen landed in east Greenland and occupied it in the name of King Haakon VII. They gained the support of the Norwegian government and it was only by going to the International Court of Justice at the Hague that Denmark reasserted her rights there. The verdict was gracefully accepted by Norway and since then Danish sovereignty has been acknowledged by all.

During the Second World War the question of sovereignty again arose in a different form. Because of the strategic importance of Greenland in a possible German attack on Canada or the United States, it was thought likely that either of these countries might occupy the territory, not least because the island was still nominally under the control of occupied Denmark. The Danish ambassador in Washington, Henrik Kauffmann, took it upon himself to draft a treaty with the United States allowing American bases in Greenland so long as there was thought to be a danger to America from enemy action. The two Greenland sheriffs agreed to the treaty and also decided not to recognise the government in Copenhagen, but to govern Greenland themselves as long as the Occupation lasted. A Greenland Commission was set up in the United States to take care of Greenland trade now that connections with Denmark were severed. The government in Copenhagen naturally protested about this and dismissed Kauffmann, but he was acknowledged as being the true representative of Denmark in the USA, and maintained this position throughout the war. In 1945 the agreement he had signed was then accepted by the liberation government.

In 1953, when Denmark adopted a new constitution, certain clauses affected Greenland profoundly. Her colonial status was abolished and she was incorporated into Denmark proper, with representation by two members of the *Folketing*. Provision was also made for a Parliamentary Greenland Commission consisting of eight Danish and two Greenland representatives.

Prior to this, in 1950, the two west Greenland district councils had been merged into a single National Council elected by direct ballot by all Greenlanders over twenty-three. This new Council was headed by a Governor, the *Landshøvding*. Local councils were also reorganised and given greater powers in local affairs and social legislation. Church and education, which had been one so far, were separated, and education has since been administered by a Board of Education consisting of the Governor, the Dean of Greenland, and the Director of Education. The health service was extended to cope with modern conditions and provision was made for free medical treatment. State trading was maintained. In 1951 a Greenland Justice Act was passed bringing legal practice in Greenland into line with that in Denmark. The Greenlanders had hitherto enjoyed their own judicial organisation, much praised by Hans Egede in the eighteenth century, and there were those who deprecated that a system which had stood the Greenlanders in good stead should be replaced by a system based on entirely different principles; yet conditions had altered, and it is possible that the time had come for a change.

As a result of all these reforms and a more modern pattern of life, Greenland's population increased at about four times the rate of Denmark proper. This has happened not only because of an increased birthrate but also through a rapid decline in mortality rates. By 1960 the population had reached 30,000 – ten years before it had been expected to reach that size.

There are plans for large-scale investment in Greenland during the 1970s – some 4,000 million *kroner* has been mentioned as the figure to be invested before 1970.

A front-page article in *Berlingske Aftenavis* on 29 November 1969 claims that there is almost certainly a sizeable oilfield in northern Greenland and that it is now possible to extract and transport the oil. Elsewhere, in the Disco Bay on the west coast, copper, nickel, and zinc have been discovered in workable quantities.

All in all Denmark has probably put more into Greenland than she has derived from it. Whether the situation will alter remains to be seen, but there is no denying that Denmark has shouldered the burden of modernising a large, rambling and, until recently, primitive economy and has put the standard of living as far as possible on a European level.

Appendix D

The Danish West Indies

As ONE OF THE RESULTS of the expansionist and mercantile policies of the seventeenth century, a Danish West Indies Company was set up in 1671 with the aim of colonising St Thomas and possibly other islands. The island was placed under the Danish flag in May 1672, when a ship carrying a motley assortment of men, including adventurers and convicts, landed there. But these men were scarcely suited to the life necessary to start building up a viable colony, and so slave labour was introduced, slaves being imported from Guinea, where the East Indies Company had a fort.

Few Danes were attracted to the island and although the white population stood at 148 by 1688, only seventeen of these were Danes, the remainder being predominantly Dutch. There were by now some ninety plantations on the island, but the project ran at a loss – as did many other national projects at the time – and the islands were accordingly removed from the Company's sphere of influence and placed under the Crown by Frederik V in 1754. The Company's trade monopoly was ended and trade was opened up instead to all Danish citizens. The resultant commercial boost led to an increase in the number of slaves, while Copenhagen benefited from the exports of tobacco in the seventeenth century and sugar in the eighteenth. In the nineteenth century cotton was to become the main export.

This trade growth brought with it a considerable rise in the island's population, and between 1673 and 1692 the white population rose from ninety-eight to 399, while the slaves went up from about a hundred to 555. As the entire island came under cultivation the demand for labour became so great that the slave population was ten times as large as the white population. It tells much of the attitude of the farmers that the cultivation of St Thomas reached its climax in 1725, after which production declined as the soil was worked out. Rather than try to use fertilisers, the settlers moved from St Thomas to St John, which had been occupied in 1717. By 1733 there were 109 plantations on the latter island, providing work for over a thousand slaves. Conditions became so bad that in 1733 a slave rebellion broke out, in the course of which

243

about 25 per cent of the white population was killed. To compensate those who suffered losses in the rebellion, settlers were now able to buy cheap land in plenty on the island of St Croix, which Denmark bought from France in the same year. Within a short space of time, St Croix became the most important of the Danish West Indian islands, and the Governor moved his residence to the town of Frederiksstad. From the settlers' point of view this set the seal on colonial life in the West Indies and the large plantations gave rise to an ever increasing number of slaves.

The settlers themselves showed little consideration for their slaves and they maintained a strict code of discipline. Punishments for wrongdoing were severe and any slave raising his hand to a white man was liable to instant execution. This was at the time of the enlightened liberal rule in Denmark itself at the end of the eighteenth century, and by way of contrast to the brutality of the settlers, it must be emphasised that the Danish government acted with a new understanding for human dignity. Denmark became in fact the first country to abolish the slave trade, doing so by a law passed in 1792. As with other contemporary laws – for instance that abolishing *stavnsbaand* – a period of time was to elapse before the law came into effect, and in this case the date was to be 1803. Paradoxically enough the state then provided the settlers with loans so that they could build up their stock of slaves before the trade was stopped. Nevertheless, the government looked on the slave population with humanity, so much so that it was reproached at the time for being more sympathetic to the slaves in the West Indies than towards its own smallholders and day labourers.

In the nineteenth century new moves were made to improve the lot of the slaves. A law of 1803 gave Negroes the right to receive instruction in Christianity and encouraged legal marriage between slaves. Hitherto some 50 per cent of all their children had been illegitimate and it was felt that these new moves would increase their self-respect and dignity. Earlier, private initiatives had investigated this side of the slaves' existence. As early as 1732 Moravian missionaries had gone to St Thomas, but they had not – perhaps not unnaturally – received much sympathy or understanding from the white population. The Moravians were followed by Lutheran missionaries and others, and so great became Lutheran interest in the islands that 1777 saw an order prohibiting Negroes from becoming Roman Catholics.

The next real effort to improve slave conditions came in the middle of the nineteenth century when Governor von Scholten (1835–38) made efforts on their behalf. He issued a new regulation concerning the punishment of slaves and limiting the number of hours they might work. He was also behind the implementation in 1839 of new laws on slave education – an attempt to prepare them for their freedom. It was then the intention to grant freedom to the slaves in 1860, but a revolt on St Croix in 1848 speeded up liberty for the negro population. In 1877 compulsory schooling for all was introduced, not a popular move at the time, but resulting in a new sense of negro responsibility. It was now possible, both in theory and in practice, for Negroes to reach high office and negro officials were often to be found with white settlers under them.

So far the West Indies had been a trade asset to Denmark, not least during the wars between England and France, when they were a transport centre. They were occupied by the British in 1801 and from 1807 to 1815, but after their return to Denmark the good times returned, because of the South American struggles for liberation. They were a centre from which supplies of all kinds, including arms and ammunition, could be bought, and they flourished accordingly. The standard of living for the settlers was high, and modern, almost luxurious, colonial-style buildings were erected, including three theatres.

However, the depression in the middle of the nineteenth century brought an end to all this, and the change was made even more painful for the settlers by the end of slave labour. Many plantations simply could not be run at a profit without this source of cheap labour, and the soil on a fair number was exhausted. Subsequent lower productivity and higher costs came just at the time when West Indian sugar was finding a serious rival in the new beet sugar produced in Denmark itself. This was the reason for the change from sugar production to cotton-growing. (By now St Croix is itself an importer of sugar.) A further blow to the islands' economy was the advent of the steamship. These new large ships had a far larger range than the old sailing ships, which needed to put into port to restock, and so the Danish West Indies lost another regular source of income.

Nevertheless, the Danes were hoping that the Panama Canal and improved harbour facilities might bring back trade to the port of Charlotte Amalie on St Thomas, but this hope did not materialise. Once an elegant colonial port, by the end of the nineteenth century it had become no more than a bunkering station. Disappointed in their hopes, the Danes decided in 1917 to negotiate the sale of the islands to the Americans, who had been expressing an interest in them since the middle of the nineteenth century. On 31 March 1917 they became American property. The sale price was $25 million.

Rulers of Denmark

Gorm the Old, *d. c.* 940
Harald I Bluetooth, *c.* 940–*c.* 985
Svend I Forkbeard, *c.* 985–1014
Harald II Svendsen, 1014–18
Knud I, 1018–35
Hardeknud, 1035–42
Magnus the Good, 1042–47
Svend II Estridsen, 1047–74
Harald III Hen, 1074–80
Knud II the Holy, 1080–86
Oluf I the Hungry, 1086–95
Erik I the Kind-Hearted, 1095–1103
Niels, 1104–34
Erik II, 1134–37
Erik III the Lamb, 1137–46
[Oluf II Haraldsen, 1140–43]
Svend III Grathe, Knud III, Magnussen (rival claimants), 1146–57

VALDEMAR DYNASTY

Valdemar I the Great, 1154–57–82
Knud IV Valdemarsen, 1182–1202
Valdemar II the Victorious, 1202–41
Erik IV Ploughpenny, 1241–50
Abel, 1250–52
Christoffer I, 1252–59
Erik V, 1259–86
Erik VI, 1286–1319
Christoffer II, 1320–26, 1330–32

Valdemar III, 1326–30 (joint ruler)
[Interregnum 1332–40]
Valdemar IV, 1340–75
Oluf III, 1376–87
Margrethe, 1387–1412
Erik VII of Pomerania, 1412–39
Christoffer III of Bavaria, 1439–48

HOUSE OF OLDENBURG

Christian I, 1448–81
Hans, 1481–1513
Christian II, 1513–23
Frederik I, 1523–33
Christian III, 1534–59
Frederik II, 1559–88
Christian IV, 1588–1648
Frederik III, 1648–70
Christian V, 1670–99
Frederik IV, 1699–1730
Christian VI, 1730–46
Frederik V, 1746–66
Christian VII, 1766–1808
Frederik VI, 1808–39
Christian VIII, 1839–48
Frederik VII, 1848–63

HOUSE OF GLÜCKSBORG

Christian IX, 1863–1906
Frederik VIII, 1906–12
Christian X, 1912–47
Frederik IX, 1947–

Bibliography

John Danstrup og Hal Koch (eds.) : *Danmarks Historie,* i–xiv,
   Copenhagen, 1962–66.
Aage Friis, Axel Linvald og M. Mackeprang (eds.) : *Schultz Dan-
   markshistorie,* i–vi, Copenhagen, 1941–43.
John Danstrup : *Danmarks Historia,* i–ii, Malmö, 1946.

F. Aagaard : *J. C. Christensen,* Copenhagen, 1941.
Hans Christian Andersen : *The Fairy Tale of my Life,* Copenhagen,
   New York, London, 1955.
H. Westergård Andersen : *Dansk politik i går og i dag,* Copenhagen,
   1967.
R. Andersen : *Danmark i Trediverne,* i–ii, Copenhagen, 1968.
Klaus Berntsen : *Erindringer,* i–iii, Copenhagen, 1923–25.
Johannes Brøndsted : *The Vikings,* Harmondsworth, 1960.
Danmark og Det europæiske økonomiske Fællesskab, Danish Foreign
   Ministry, Copenhagen, 1962.
Denmark, publ. by Royal Danish Ministry of Foreign Affairs,
   Copenhagen, 1961.
Danmarks statistiske Årbog.
Povl Engelstoft og Frantz Wilhelm Wendt : *Haandbog i Danmarks
   politiske Historie fra Freden i Kiel til Vore Dage,* Copen-
   hagen, 1934.
L. P. Fabricius : Danmarks Kirkehistorie, Vol. 1, Copenhagen,
   1934–35.
Færørne, i–ii, publ. by Dansk Færøisk Samfund, Copenhagen, 1958
P. G. Foote : *On the Saga of the Faroe Islanders,* London, 1965.
K. Hansen : *Det danske Landbrugs Historie,* Copenhagen, 1934–45
Stephen Hurwitz : *The Ombudsman,* Copenhagen, 1968.
Kristian Hvidt : *Venstre og forsvarssagen 1870–1901,* Århus, 1960.
Orla Jensen : *Sociallovgivning,* Århus, 1962.
Orla Jensen, Carl Vigild, Arne Sørensen : *Studievejledning i den
   sociale lovgivning,* Århus, 1964.
W. Glyn Jones : 'The end of a system', *The Norseman,* 1956, Vol.
   14, pp. 230–38.

W. Glyn Jones : 'Paulus Helie and the Danish Reformation', *The Month*, 1965, CCX, No. 1176, pp. 160–70.

Harald Jørgensen : *Studier over det offentlige fattigvæsen i Danmark i det 19. Aarhundrede*, Copenhagen, 1940.

Tage Kaarsted og Ole Samuelsen : *Kilder til Danmarks politiske historie 1920–1939*, Copenhagen, 1967.

Ib Koch-Olsen : *Danmarks Kulturhistorie*, I–II, Copenhagen, 1968.

Erling Kristiansen et al. : *Danmark og de Seks*, Copenhagen, 1962.

T. Larsen : *En Gennembrudstid*, Copenhagen, 1918–34.

Vilhelm Lorenzen : *Studier i Danske Herregaardsarkitetur*, Copenhagen, 1921.

Kenneth E. Miller : *Government and Politics in Denmark*, Boston, Mass., 1968.

P. M. Mitchell : *History of Danish Literature*, Copenhagen, 1957.

Nordisk Kontakt

Adam Oehlenschläger : *Erindringer*, Copenhagen, 1850.

Henning Ravnholt : *The Danish Cooperative Movement*, Copenhagen, 1950.

Roar Skovmand : *De folkelige bevægelser i Danmark*, Copenhagen, 1951.

Fridlev Skrubbeltrang : *The Danish Folk High Schools*, Copenhagen, 1952.

Fridley Skrubbeltrang : *Der står en ny tids bonde*, Copenhagen, 1948.

Axel Steensberg (ed.) : *Dagligliv i Danmark*, Copenhagen, 1963.

B. Nüchel Thomsen & Brinley Thomas : *Anglo-Danish Trade 1661–1963*, Århus, 1966.

H. G. Topsøe-Jensen : *Scandinavian Literature*, London, 1929.

J. P. Trap : *Danmark*, I–XII, Copenhagen, 1968.

Kjeld Winding : *Danmarks Historie*, Copenhagen, 1958.

Index

[For convenience if not consistency the Danish letter å is treated as a, æ as ae and ø as o]

Kjær, Magnus, 98
Knud II, the Holy, King, 21
Knud IV Valdemarsen, King, 22
Knudsen, Jakob, 104
Kold, Christen, 69
Kongens Nytorv, 37
Korean War, 190
Kraft, Ole Bjørn, 191
Krag, Jens Otto, 203, 206 f.
Kreditforeninger, see Credit Societies
Kristensen, Knud, 185–7, 200
Kristensen, Thorkild, 201
Kristensen, Tom, 128 f., 163 f.
Krogh, Christian, 105
Krøyer, Peter Severin, 105

Labour government (British), 206
Lagerkvist, Pär, 218
Lagting, 228, 230–34
land reform, 205, 211
Landsting, 52, 73, 75, 79, 85–7, 107 f., 112–14, 120, 125, 144, 158, 160 f., 192, 209, 230, 233, 235
Langeland straits mined, 116
Larsen, Axel, 200 f., 208
Lauenburg, 44 f., 50 f., 54–6
League of Nations, 132, 139 f., 159, 188
Left, *see Venstre*
Left Reform Party, 86 f., 110 f.
legal reform, 121
Lehmann, Orla, 48, 51, 63
Leif (Eriksson), 236
Liberal Centre Party, 207, 209
Liberal Democrats, *see Venstre*
liberalisation of trade laws, 88, 91
Lind, Jenny, 64
local authorities, 94 f., 110, 156, 161, 212, 219
lock-outs, 89, 136, 145, 154 f.
London, 128, 155, 159, 178
London conference (1864), 56
London Protocol (1850), 53
London, Treaty of, 54
London University, 69
Lornsen, Uwe, 46
Louis the Pious, Emperor, 20
Louis XIV, King of France, 17, 35
L.S. movement, 157 f., 160, 169, 175
Lübeck, 23, 27 f., 30
Lund, 21
Lur mark, 97
Lutherans (at Reformation), 29
Luxembourg, 188; Grand Duke of, 44

MacDonald, Ramsay, 153
Madsen-Mygdal, Thomas, 145
Mainz, 20
Malling, Peder, 61
Margrethe, Crown Princess, 193

Margrethe, Queen, 18, 25 f.
Marshall Plan, 188, 190
martial law (1944), 179
Marx, Karl, 77, 100
Mecklenburg, 23
Methodists, 70
Metropolitan School, 61
Metternich, Clemens Wenzel Nemopuk Lothar von, 46
Miklagard, *see* Byzantium
Mill, John Stuart, 100
Moderate Left, 81 f., 85–7, 99, 106, 110 f.
Modern Breakthrough, 78, 100–4, 129, 218
Møller, Christmas, 146, 171 f., 185 f.
Møller, Poul Martin, 67
Monopoly Control, 211
Monrad, Ditlev Gothard, 56
moral concepts, 148, 162, 214 f.
Moravians, 70, 244
Moscow, 38
Mothers' Assistance Clinics, 162
Mullan, Maureen, 214
Munch, Peter, 122, 169 f.
Munk, Kaj, 164, 178, 216
Mussolini, Benito, 165
Mynster, Jacob Peter, 60 f., 70

Napoleon Bonaparte, 42, 43
Narvik, 167
National Bank, 57, 117, 144, 181 f., 195
National Liberals, 51 f., 55, 72 f., 75 f., 78, 131
NATO, 188 f., 192, 194, 200, 211 f.
Naturalism, *see* Modern Breakthrough
Neergaard, Niels, 111, 132, 139
Netherlands, King of the (William I), 44
neutrality, 86, 114, 116, 120, 140, 159, 166, 172, 188 f.
Newfoundland, 239
New Zealand, 155
Nexø, 180
Nexø, Martin Andersen, 90, 105, 127
Nielsen, Carl, 93, 128
non-aggression treaty with Germany, 159
Nordek, 202, 210
Nordic common market, *see* Nordek
Nordic co-operation, 197, 202, 210
Nordic defence treaties proposed, 159, 188
Nordic Seven Years War, 32
Normandy, 18
Nørreport, 62
Norse literature, 18
Norstad, General Lauris, 200

Printed in Great Britain by The Garden City Press Limited
Letchworth, Hertfordshire

Date Due

MAY 4 1983			